The

ENGLISH NOVEL

in

TRANSITION

The

ENGLISH NOVEL

in

TRANSITION

1885-1940

By

WILLIAM C. FRIERSON

Norman

University of Oklahoma Press

1942

To
K.J.F.

CHAPTERS & PAGES

ACKNOWLEDGMENTS

I cordially thank Richmond C. Beatty, of Vanderbilt, for criticism of the manuscript and L. Cazamian, of Paris, and G. Rudler, of Oxford, for encouragement of my early efforts. Thanks are likewise due G. H. Gerould, of Princeton, for provocative comments and to the following libraries for the use of their facilities: The Bodleian, the Widener, the Bibliothèque Nationale, the Vanderbilt University Library, and the Amelia Gorgas Library of the University of Alabama. Further indebtedness is acknowledged to *PMLA,* the *Sewanee Review,* and the *French Quarterly* for permission to use articles which they originally published, and to the following authors, periodicals, publishers, and individuals who have permitted me to quote passages included in this volume: J. B. Priestley, Joseph Warren Beach, H. G. Wells, "George Egerton" (Mrs. Golding Bright), W. Somerset Maugham, Holbrook Jackson, R. H. Sherard, J. Middleton Murry, Amy Cruse, Frank Swinnerton, Walter Myers, Helen Thomas Follett and Wilson Follett, Stefan Zweig, J. D. Beresford, Gilbert Cannan, Compton Mackenzie, Edgell Rickword, E. M. Forster, Aldous Huxley, Philip Henderson, R. S. Lovett and Helen S. Hughes, Grant C. Knight, Agnes C. Hansen, A. C. Ward, Norman Douglas, H. M. Tomlinson, Rose Macaulay, Beverley Nichols, Clemence Dane, Douglas Goldring, Hugh Walpole, Margaret Storm Jameson, Richard Aldington, Liam O'Flaherty, John Cowper Powys, Walter Greenwood, Elizabeth Bowen, the *Journal of English and Germanic Philology, PMLA,* the *Contemporary Review,* the *Fortnightly Review,* the *Living Age, Life and Letters Today,* the *Nation,* the *New Statesman and Nation,* the *National Review,* the *Nineteenth Century,* the *Quarterly Review,* the *Spectator,* the *Saturday Review of Literature,* the

Acknowledgments

editors of *The Yale Review* (copyright, Yale University Press), Doubleday, Doran & Co., Random House, Houghton Mifflin Co., Charles Scribner's Sons, Henry Holt and Co., Longmans Green & Co., Ltd., Thomas Nelson & Sons, Ltd., Hodder and Stoughton, Ltd., Little, Brown & Co., Methuen and Co., Ltd., Chatto and Windus, Greenberg, Alfred A. Knopf, D. Appleton and Co., Hutchinson and Co., Ltd., and Mr. B. M. Huebsch. And thanks to Jane for an index and for much other help.

WILLIAM C. FRIERSON

University, Alabama

St. Valentine's Day, 1942

INTRODUCTION

THE phenomenon of literary expression during the last fifty years has been the development of the novel, the extension of its range, the variety of its appeal, and the constant modifications of its form. Yet the historians of the novel have done little by way of limiting and defining successive and contemporaneous changes in spirit and technique. Movements are neglected, as well as vital matters of causality, influence, and relationship.

The transition of the English novel was effected as the result of two upheavals. The first was produced by the impact of French naturalism. As the translations of French naturalistic works, beginning in 1883, fell upon an amazed and horrified England, the excitement of controversy divided critics into hostile camps. Until 1890 criticism was largely unfavorable to naturalism because of its materialism, its determinism, its disregard for decorum, and its brutality; but in 1890 and the years immediately following, the insistence of naturalism upon fact-finding had won many supporters. These turned upon the conventional English novel, "a refuge for distressed needle-women," and ridiculed it with a vengeance. By 1893 the naturalistic aims were approved and by 1896 Zola himself seems to have been accepted.

The change in the trend of critical opinion was, no doubt, partly influenced by the reticent yet relentless novels of George Moore and George Gissing, for Moore had written naturalistic novels which omitted brutality of language and Gissing had written decorous novels giving a naturalistic vision of society in its lower orders. Henry James, also influenced by the Paris group, had popularized the naturalistic principle of logicality and veracity. Furthermore, beginning in 1893 and continuing through 1898, eighteen volumes of *nouvelles* written by disciples of Maupassant attested that a new philosophy in fiction was becoming manifest.

It is difficult, and perhaps needless, to define periods in fiction-writing and to give precise dates to general tendencies. A considerable amount of overlapping occurs. The Victorian "matter-of-fact romance" continued to be written during the eighteen-nineties, the regional novel was making headway, and during the last five years of the century the historical novel assumed a position of unparalleled importance, which was to continue to, say, 1905. Yet as we view developments with the perspective of forty-odd years, we note as most significant the fact that Maugham, Morrison, Whiteing, and Gissing were undermining the authority of Dickens as the interpreter of poor folk, that the novel of marital incompatibility, springing from Scandinavian drama and French naturalism, vied with the historical romance for first place in the public's attention, and that a number of sporadic novels with naturalistic leanings testified to a revival of social consciousness. Furthermore, if we consider the inspiration of important writers of the early twentieth century, we find that it springs from French naturalism and the modified naturalism of their English disciples. The line from Zola to Gissing to Wells to Onions, Beresford, Cannan, May Sinclair, Cronin, Hanley, and Greenwood is sufficiently clear. The line from the "Paris group" to Henry James to Katherine Mansfield and Dorothy Richardson and Virginia Woolf and Frank Swinnerton and Ford Madox Ford and Elizabeth Bowen, and others, is not hard to see. Maugham began his career with a naturalistic novel and his best work is dominated by the naturalistic consciousness. Joyce published first a group of naturalistic short stories. Galsworthy avowedly had for masters Maupassant and Turgenev. Arnold Bennett began to work "under the sweet influence of 'Flaubert et Cie.' " Conrad modeled his sentences on those of Flaubert and, with Ford Madox Ford, modified the formulas of Henry James. The list grows tedious.

So naturalism focused attention upon the possibilities of the novel for expressing a critical view of the institutions of society, of codes of conduct, and unsatisfactory ways of living. Naturalism, even a rather decorous naturalism, however, was not altogether successful in England because it necessitated that the novelist be impersonal, or at least objective. The naturalistic novelist must hold aloof from his characters, and England did not see the necessity. But she welcomed the social probing which had freed her own novel from bondage. Naturalism called attention to the evils of restraint and taboo, and it revealed the world of everyday affairs as being of marvelous interest if viewed in the critical spirit and treated with honesty. It established the artistic importance of a logical sequence of events, even while it revealed to its partisans the limits of a dogmatic determinism.

I turn to the second phase of the transition. J. Middleton Murry stated that around 1910 Dostoievski and Tolstoi had "exploded" the English novel by revealing the novel's enormous potentialities. "The novelists of the West had been concerned with some private conception of 'art' while the Russians had been saying tremendous things." Thereafter the attention of Englishmen turned to the value of the thing said, rather than the way of saying it.

Mr. Murry is a propagandist for the Russians and no doubt overstresses his point. The explosion of which he speaks was the result of a general undermining of the objective or impersonal novel. Wells had attracted sympathetic attention by insisting, through precept and example, that the novelist must necessarily give his vision of life and should make no bones about it. Samuel Butler had written a thinly veiled autobiography with as much honest intensity as any Russian could offer. And a second French influence, this time the spiritual life history, *Jean Christophe,* extended the English conception of the novel and reaffirmed the reaction against naturalism which the later George Moore had felt under the influence of Huysmans.

Thus there came into being a subjective "novel of ideas" and a new type of spiritual biography which was closely akin to autobiography. The whole social framework was critically examined and a new vitality given to fiction by the expression of unconventional social, moral, and religious ideas. The search, begun during the nineties, for a new ethic became intensified. Then came the war.

In the postwar world the life-novel was dead. It had served a useful end in destroying patterns of novel-writing—Victorian patterns, naturalistic patterns, dramatic patterns. It had established the right of the novelist to integrate experience, to communicate personal conceptions and philosophic states of soul, to search for the meaning of existence. But the postwar world was cynical of integration and philosophy. The seriousness of the life-novel was out of keeping with a sophistical generation.

To the war-generation the truths of science were the only acceptable truths, and science had little human wisdom to give. It was bent upon asking factual questions, not upon solving ethical enigmas. So the war consciousness expressed itself in a protest at absurdities. It begot a spirit of confident agnosticism, known as sophistication, which on the one hand delighted in a frank paganism and, on the other, ridiculed the accumulated wisdom of the ages. Novelists betook themselves to private worlds where the characters acted with a logic of their own. Stream of consciousness, an offshoot of naturalistic probing, became the vehicle of certain experimentalists and in the work of Joyce assumed a naturalistic frankness. Psychoanalysis found expression in the work of Lawrence and in isolated novels of other writers. The general result was that censorship of language and ideas was finally abolished, technique altered in a variety of ways, and the last restraints upon the English novel cast aside.

We might conclude, then, that the transition was completed by 1930. Restrictions had, at least temporarily, ceased to exist and the novelist might write in a wide variety of modes, or with little consideration for any accepted mode at all. Somewhere between 1926 and 1929 new urges, new experiments, were ended and writers harked back to the various ideas and forms that prevailed during, and before, the transition.

This study would be incomplete without a full consideration of developments during the thirties. We are interested in observing the continuance of recently established modes, the persistence of influences, the new ramifications of the critical spirit, as well as the adaptation and fusing of techniques. Interpretations of a score of the latest English writers are given in some detail since comment on their work is not readily obtainable elsewhere.

The word "transition" should occasion no difficulty. The fact that change took place is obvious. Even a person like Mr. J. B. Priestley, who does not favor change greatly, is willing to admit that something vital occurred:

> If we compare the mass of intelligent fiction of the last twenty years with the bulk of nineteenth-century fiction, we notice a marked difference in the attitudes of the two sets of novelists. Briefly, it is this. The older novelists wanted to tell a story, to describe an action, to let us know what happened to Tom and Mabel; they began a definite narrative in the first chapter and rounded it off in the last; they were anxious to be as lifelike as possible, but they were determined to impose some particular pattern of events upon life, shaping it decisively to suit the purposes of their particular art. But many of the novelists of to-day do not approach fiction in this way at all. For the story, the ordered action, they substitute what has been called the "slice of life." They do not try to tell us what happened to Tom and Mabel, but how life appeared to Tom and Mabel for a season. "I suppose what I am trying to render is nothing more or less than Life—as one man has found it. I want to tell—*myself,* and my impressions of the thing as a whole, to say things I have come to feel intensely of the laws, traditions, usages, and ideas we call society, and how we poor individuals get driven and lured and stranded among these windy, perplexing shoals and channels." This is from H. G. Wells, and it is a fair statement of his aims.[1]

[1] *The English Novel* (London, Thomas Nelson & Sons, Ltd., 1935), 124–25.

But Mr. Priestley's hasty summary bridges too wide a gap. Important and exciting things happened between nineteenth-century fiction and that "of the last twenty years." Moreover the fiction of "the last twenty years" (1907–27) has been by no means static. During these years the English novel became autobiographical before it became "ventriloquial"—with the illumination of widely contrasted views of life, thanks to Norman Douglas. The English novel became the novel of protagonists—more or less after the Russian fashion—and tremendous things were said. But this takes us only to the late twenties. What next?

What came next was the war-novel, which had been delayed until men could bear to think of the war again. This was the final advent, the culmination of realistic urges. Not until the late twenties were the war-lacerated tissues healed. Then facts were faced. And once faced, they were forgotten. . . Forgotten? No. Merely buried, encased. Men had "fed upon death which feeds on men" and death, despair, was dead—"there's no more dying then."

Thus was a transition completed. What followed was relaxation. Authors played with the techniques, and the emotions, of a preceding decade. They toyed with sentiment, reaching with trembling fingers back into the traditional past. They sported with emotion, half conscious of its claims. Occasionally with new-found liberty they lashed out at the social structure. The speculations and probings of a renaissance were ended. Active spirits might use the spoils.

The

ENGLISH NOVEL

in

TRANSITION

❧ I ❧

SOME REMARKS ON
REPRESENTATIVE LATE VICTORIANS

THE Victorian novel was a brand of fiction and, now that my youth has passed, I think I can speak about it with equanimity. I can even see that the man was over-wrought who described it as "a mawkish phantom of hectic virginity, moonlight, violet-scent and dew-drops." Such a remark can apply to only half the Victorian novels. But I find nothing to combat the remark of Thomas Seccombe that the Victorian novel contained "moral thesis, plot, under-plot, set characters, descriptive machinery, Herculean proportions, and the rest of the cumbrous and grandiose paraphernalia of *Chuzzlewit*, *Pendennis*, and *Middlemarch*."[1] Seccombe, indeed, might have said much more.

He might have said, for one thing, that the Victorian novel was Tory—omitting Dickens, of course. By "Tory" I mean socially conservative, but I mean more than this. I mean that the dear and proper gradations of society are treated with respect and mostly with admiration; that the institutions of the realm are accepted as altogether fitting; that pride of race and imperialism occasionally obtrude but are always latently present. We could go further and say that a feudal criterion of worth prevails, tending to equate inherent worth with the gradations of a highly stratified society. Here the exceptions prove the rule.

Again Seccombe might have said that God was in His Heaven and, if all was not right with the world, it certainly

---

[1] Introductory Survey to Gissing's *House of Cobwebs* (London, A. Constable, 1906), viii.

wasn't God's fault. In fact, God was definitely interested in His more well-intentioned creatures, particularly the poorer ones; and even when disaster prevailed, the mortal result was not necessarily the end.

And, of course, we must not forget Victorian Womanhood.

In the realm of ideas there was the preoccupation with spiritual values and free will, and a tendency to look on the sunny side of doubt as well as of life. Some novelists, of course, and often with considerable interest and charm, commented on events and personages, but this was hardly necessary. The hero-villain, fair maiden arrangement made the author's views perfectly clear. Few important characters were permitted any mixture of Good and Bad qualities.

A strange and important fact draws our attention. By far the greater number of these novels were originally printed in three volumes. Trollope traced the practice back at least as far as the late novels of Dickens, Thackeray, and Mrs. Gaskell. Vizetelly and Company claim to have struck the first blow toward slaying the three-volume novel in 1880, for it was in that year that, upon the advice of George Moore, they abandoned the three-volume standard and issued their new novels in one volume only. The three-volume standard continued well into the nineties, however. Nine of the thirteen novels which Hardy wrote before 1892 were written in three volumes, as were ten of the thirteen Gissing published before 1894.

Just why was this?

Someone has suggested that it was because a novel must have a beginning, a middle, and an end. More serious is George Moore's explanation that a clever business deal of the circulating libraries was responsible. These guaranteed to buy four hundred copies of any three-volume work and pay the current price of seven shillings six pence per volume—an amount prohibitive to the general reader. Publishers wanted the safe guarantee.

The decorum of the Victorian novel is thus better explained. Publishers did not want to chance the disapproval of Mr. Mudie, chief operator of circulating libraries. Obviously

4

the three-volume standard encouraged a leisurely account—and padding. Trollope finds that another difficulty was invited by the author's eagerness to send each volume, when completed, "red-hot to the press," and thus to forfeit the opportunity for revision. "The rustic driving his pigs to market," as Trollope quaintly puts it, "cannot always make them travel by the exact path he had intended for them. When some young lady at the end of the story cannot be made quite perfect in her conduct, that vivid description of angelic purity with which you laid the first lines of her portrait should be toned down."[2]

In 1896 Kipling celebrated in nautical terminology the passing of the "Three-Decker," explaining in a subcaption, "The three-volume novel is extinct":

Full thirty feet she towered from waterline to rail.
It took a watch to steer her, and a week to shorten sail;
But, spite all modern notions, I found her first and best—
The only certain packet to the Islands of the Blest.

Fair held our breeze behind us—'twas warm with lovers' prayers;
We'd stolen wills for ballast and a crew of missing heirs;
They shipped as Able Bastards till the Wicked Nurse confessed,
And they worked the old three-decker to the Islands of the Blest.

* * * * *

We asked no social questions—we pumped no hidden shame—
We never talked obstetrics when the little stranger came;
We left the Lord in Heaven, we left the fiends in Hell,
We weren't exactly Yussufs, but—Zuleika didn't tell!

No moral doubt assailed us, so when the port we neared,
The villain got his flogging at the gangway, and we cheered.
'Twas fiddles on the foc'sle—'twas garlands on the mast,
For everyone got married, and I went ashore at last.

I left 'em all in couples akissing on the decks.
I left the lovers loving and the parents signing checks.
In endless English comfort by country-folk caressed,
I left the old three-decker at the Islands of the Blest....

[2] *Autobiography of Anthony Trollope* (New York, Harper & Bros., 1883), 126.

The generalizations made by Kipling may with some indulgence be accepted. Yet our concern with trends in the novel demands a more precise and factual treatment. Late Victorian fiction must be essentially the fiction of its most representative novelists. Suppose we choose as typical of the years 1865–80 Anthony Trollope, Charles Reade, and George Eliot. An exposition of their approach and general performance will be of some benefit in laying the groundwork for future comparisons.

These writers are called "realists"—that is, people who deal with the *matter* of life but not necessarily with its *manner*. We are told that the popularity of Dickens continued through this period just as it did during his lifetime. The local and domestic scene was established as the proper sphere of the novelist. Romantic and sentimental realism continued to find favor, and little criticism, other than that of George Eliot, was directed against the long-established rules of attraction and intrigue.

Saintsbury supports us in choosing Trollope: "It is probably not too much to say that of the *average* novel of the third quarter of the century . . . Anthony Trollope is about as good a representative as can be found."[3] Trollope's books are, as Nathaniel Hawthorne once said, "just as English as a beefsteak."[4] He published forty-six novels, the greater part of them in three volumes, besides four books of stories, between the years 1847 and 1883. His financial success is worth mentioning. He records that for his writings up to 1879 he realized a profit of 68,939 pounds, 17 shillings, and 6 pence. And this sum does not include the proceeds from fourteen novels subsequently published.[5]

Trollope is his own best interpreter. "A novel," he says, "should give a picture of common life enlivened by humor and sweetened by pathos. To make this picture worthy of attention the canvas should be crowded with real portraits,

---

[3] George Saintsbury, *The English Novel* (New York, E. P. Dutton & Co., 1913), 252.
[4] Quoted in *Autobiography of Anthony Trollope*, 132.
[5] *Ibid.*, 326.

not of individuals known to the author, but of created personages impregnated with traits of character that are known. To my mind the plot is but the vehicle of all this."[6]

He is somewhat careless about his plots. "When I sit down to write a novel," he says, "I do not always know, and I do not very much care, how it will end."[7] Once he got himself into a jam: "Taking it as a whole *The Last Chronicle of Barset* is the best novel I have written. I was never quite satisfied with the development of the plot, which consisted of the loss of a check, of a charge against a clergyman for stealing it, and of absolute uncertainty on the part of the clergyman as to the manner in which the check had found its way into his hands. I cannot quite make myself believe that such a man as Mr. Crawley would have forgotten how he got it; nor would the generous friend who was anxious to supply his wants have supplied them by tendering the check of a third person. Such a fault I acknowledge—acknowledging at the same time that I have never been capable of constructing with complete success the intricacies of a plot that required to be unravelled."[8]

The author is quite frank in stating that he wrote novels to make money. After the favorable reception of his first works he reached the point where the success or failure of his books did not concern him greatly for, he says, "if I wrote a novel, I could certainly sell it." Accordingly he determined to write three novels every two years. Even this, he decided, was not sufficiently ambitious, so he proceeded to outline a plan for writing three novels a year.[9]

"Three hours a day," he says, "will produce as much as a man ought to write. ... It had at this time [1867] become my custom—and it still is my custom [1878], though of late I have become a little lenient to myself—to write with my watch before me and to require of myself 250 words every quarter of an hour. I have found that 250 words have been forthcoming as regularly as the watch went. This division of time allowed me to produce over ten pages of an ordinary

6 *Ibid.,* 114–15.   7 *Ibid.,* 231.   8 *Ibid.,* 247–48.   9 *Ibid.,* 245–47.

novel volume a day, and if kept up would have given as its result three novels of three volumes each in the year.

"I have never written three volumes in a year; but by following the plan above described I have written more than as much as three novels; and by adhering to it over a number of years I have been enabled to have always on hand ... for some time back now—one or two, or even three, unpublished novels at my desk beside me."[10]

People suspected that Trollope drew his characters from observation, but his procedure, he tells us, was otherwise. He mentions that he had often been congratulated on the realistic portrayal of the archdeacon in *The Warden;* but, he says, he had not even spoken to an archdeacon, and he adds that the creation was "the simple result of an effort of my moral consciousness."[11]

Trollope wished to give offense to none who read his novels. He wished to include nothing that would cause embarrassment to a girl who read the story to her father. Nor was he averse to moral preachments through example. "The novelist, if he have a conscience," he writes, "must preach his sermons with the same purpose as the clergyman, and must have his own system of ethics."[12]

Such is Trollope's explanation of his own work. Like him, Charles Reade and George Eliot were voluminous writers. They also pictured the local scene; they domesticated the novel, and they were deferential to the proprieties.

Trollope's subject matter pleased the complacent, incurious, and self-respecting Tories of Victorian England. They saw themselves and their country friends portrayed faithfully and sympathetically by an author who was generally uncritical of social institutions. Trollope showed the restraints, the kindnesses, the silent, unobtrusive courage of the people he lived among. We may find him tame and wearisome because we do not have the settled peace which he and his people enjoyed. Our wider concerns make us feel that the concerns of his "highest class of society" are trivial.

[10] *Ibid.*   [11] *Ibid.,* 84.   [12] *Ibid.,* 200.

Whatever we may think of these matters, we cannot help admiring the consistency of Trollope's characters with the world he describes. His personages are easily distinguished from those of such a writer as Charles Reade. Trollope's criticism of Reade's writing is, therefore, to be expected. "There is no novelist of the present day," writes Trollope, "who has so much puzzled me by his eccentricities, impracticabilities, and capabilities as Charles Reade. . . . So good a heart and so wrong a head no novelist ever before combined."[13]

Contemporary criticism agrees with Trollope. The fifty-odd volumes which Reade published have, with the exception of *The Cloister and the Hearth*, a historical novel, been virtually forgotten. *Charles Reade*

Perhaps Reade might have done better as a writer of romances of the older sort. But the reading public showed a preference for the local scene. So Reade, with a dime-novel temperament, enlivened the local scene with "dramatic moments." In order to bring these about it was necessary for him to force quarrels among his characters as well as to create a splendid array of incorrigible villains.

Reade lacked the easy grace of writing which Trollope possessed. The speech employed by his characters is the high-flown jargon of the stage. He gave little thought to construction and sometimes pursued at great length the fortunes of a minor character.

What assures Reade of a permanent place in literary history is that he was a forerunner of Zola in the matter of documentation. Years before the Goncourts had coined the "human document" expression, Reade had compiled large volumes of newspaper clippings and personal accounts, as well as collected notes from personal observation, on which to base his exposures of life in prisons and asylums. In preparing for delineations of life among sheep raisers, gold miners, and fishermen he read books of travel and collected accounts from those familiar with the intimate detail of the life of such people. Strangely enough, Zola was working in the French pub-

[13] *Ibid.,* 228, 230.

9

lishing firm of Hachette at the very time that Hachette was getting out translations of Reade's novels. Zola's debt is quite obvious.

I mention Reade's documentation at the risk of spoiling my picture of the late Victorian novel. Actually the picture is in no wise spoiled. Reade is much closer to Dickens than to Zola and the other documentors. Reade used his material on prisons and asylums in order to write lachrymose stories of superhuman cruelty. And facts about the vast expanses of Australia were used as colorful scenic background.

Reade possesses every vice which either Seccombe or Kipling attributed to the Victorian novel. He is a slave to plot formulas depending upon coincidences and extraordinary happenings. But his tendency to sentimentalize and idealize the commonplace is so pronounced that our endeavors to treat him with justice are discouraged. Of one of his heroines he tells us, "Modesty, intelligence, and, above all, enthusiasm shone through her and out of her, and made of her an airy, fiery, household joy. Briefly, an incarnate sunbeam."

Now George Eliot would never have written about an incarnate sunbeam. As a matter of fact she showed a certain amount of originality in not enthroning virginity and innocence. She sentimentalized and idealized the commonplace, and she poured her heart into all well-intentioned creatures.

I once talked with a French writer who approved of George Eliot. Asked the reason he was undecided for some time, "I'll tell you," he said at length. "We've been fed up over here on the other side of life. I like her pastoral simplicity. I like to think there are places where people are kindly and gentle to one another. I want the peace that she describes."

George Eliot liked the quiet charm of simple life and avowedly sought to create "rural paintings of the Dutch School." She began as a portrayer in the humanitarian spirit of the local and domestic scene. We know, of course, that many of her "studies" were merely illustrations of the ethical axiom that every act has its eternal consequences. But aside from purpose, she was essentially interested in portrayal of the calm, quiet life that she had known. She discovered, as she said, a source of inexhaustible interest in that careful presentation of a monotonous domestic existence which was the lot of most of her fellow creatures, rather than a life of richness or poverty, of tragic suffering or high-sounding strife. "At least eighty out of a hundred of our male, adult fellow-Britons returned in the last census," she writes in *Amos Barton*, "are neither extraordinarily silly nor extraordinarily wicked nor extraordinarily wise; their eyes are neither dead nor liquid with sentiment nor sparkling with suppressed witticisms; they have probably had no hair-breadth escapes or thrilling adventures; their brains are certainly not pregnant with genius, and their passions have not manifested themselves at all after the manner of a volcano. ... Yet these commonplace people—many of them—bear a conscience and have felt the sublime prompting to do the painful right; they have their unspoken sorrows and their sacred joys; their hearts have gone out towards their first-born and they have mourned over the irreclaimable dead."[14]

The sympathetic portrayal of ordinary creatures was not a quality peculiar alone to George Eliot's works, although it may serve to distinguish her in the eyes of a continental reader. It was rather a tendency in the treatment of realistic themes from the times of Smollett, and it had been hardened into a convention by Dickens. It was dependent upon "a fellow-feeling that makes us wondrous kind." "A deep and tender sympathy," said a writer for the *Quarterly Review* in 1890, "was felt with all poor friendly creatures, with the outcast, the weak, the vexed and the persecuted, with little children and with the very dogs and ravens."

Some speak of George Eliot's works as reflecting the philosophical ideas which were beginning to be current in her day. It will not do to stress this point, however, since her novels, as Wilbur Cross points out, show ways of thinking less in accordance with the teachings of Comte than with those of Wordsworth and Thomas à Kempis, both of whom taught renunciation as a command; while she readily admits

[14] Chapter V.

transcendentalism in what she says about the inner and the better self.[15] Her novels are, indeed, novels of purpose. That purpose was to show the dignity and sanctity of life, that "what a man soeth, that shall he also reap," that the cup of service "is bitter to the lips, but within the crystal goblet there lies a fragrance which makes all life below it seem dross forever."

More generally we might say that George Eliot was for the most part sympathetic with the religious interests of her characters and that she accepted the institutions of society like a good Spencerian. Furthermore she is as reticent about sex as the rest of the late Victorians.

Her technique is rather typically Victorian. She does not ask herself, "How does man act?" Rather she asks, "How might or *should* man act?" She strove in a measure against "literary" plots but she employed contrivances. She employed eccentric characters. Her portrayal of the lower middle class results, according to Henry James, in "grotesque, fantastic, and romantic 'interference.' "[16] The structure is loosely woven, the account leisurely told, the conversations long-winded and inconsequential. "English novelists are really interesting to read but sometimes they get mighty tiresome," wrote Brunetière after giving an appreciation of George Eliot's better qualities.[17]

The novels of Meredith and Hardy extended well into the nineties and, in their later stages, bear very minor marks of continental influence. Yet neither of them had much to do with the changes that were to take place in the English novel. Both were closely bound to the English fiction which preceded them. In technique Hardy is the more obviously Victorian of the two.

Meredith and Hardy

"Mr. Hardy loves in plot the fantastic, the surprising, something to strike the imagination," says Joseph Warren Beach in an excellent analysis. "He is fond of ranging in that neutral ground where irony and poetry join hands . . . . where the cir-

[15] *The Development of the English Novel* (New York, The Macmillan Co., 1899), 251.
[16] *Letters of Henry James* (New York, Charles Scribner's Sons, 1920), 40.
[17] Ferdinand Brunetière, *Le roman naturaliste* (Paris, Calmann Lévy, 1896), "Le naturalisme anglais."

cumstances of men's lives combine in patterns which are bizarre and thought-provoking. His plots are often original to the point of incredibility. And yet he has no scorn of hackneyed motives —those popular plot-formulas which have piqued the curiosity and arrested the fancy of readers from time immemorial. The secret marriage; the 'squire of low degree,' favored by the heroine but not by her parents; the villainous, illegitimate son; the woman's fatal secret; the return of the absent lover, or relative, thought dead, to spoil sport for the living—each of these makes its appearance more than once, most of them three or four times, in the novels of Hardy."[18]

Shall we mention chance meetings, eccentric characters, overheard conversations, and what not? Surely the point is not to be contested.

Hardy's pessimism and his conception of the fragility of human nature do, indeed, link his writing with continental fiction of the time, and with English fiction of a date subsequent to 1880. Might it be suggested that he liked George Eliot and reacted against the philosophy of her writings? The matter is worthy of mention. Like George Eliot, Hardy describes *Under the Greenwood Tree* as "a rural painting of the Dutch School," and he invests the human soul with dignity. But George Eliot's novels seem to be written by one who believes in the reasonableness and sanctity of life, while those of Hardy show helpless men and women pursued by malign fates. "Justice was done," he remarks in a characteristic passage, "and the President of the Immortals (in Aeschylean phrase) had ended his sport with Tess."

Meredith, like Hardy, is an expositor of poetical conceptions. Although he read naturalistic works, his ways of thinking and writing were pretty well established when he published *The Ordeal of Richard Feverel* in 1859. With his usual enthusiasm he spoke on occasion both for and against the continental writers. Once in a ballroom he praised Guy de Maupassant as the greatest novelist who ever lived.[19] But he wrote to a friend,

[18] *The Technique of Thomas Hardy* (Chicago, University of Chicago Press, 1922), 14, 15.
[19] Arnold Bennett, *Books and Persons* (New York, George H. Doran Co., 1917), 137.

"O what a nocturient, cacaturient crew has issued from the lens of the Sun of the mind on the broader facts!—on sheer Realism, breeder at best of the dung-fly."[20] Here Meredith is less restrained than Hardy, who merely voiced a grave objection that critics found a similarity between his work and that of foreign realists.[21]

Temperamentally Meredith is a Tory, an idealist, a romanticist, and almost a sentimentalist in his respect for aristocratic virtues. "The art of writing novels," he says, "is to present a picture of life, but novel-writing embraces only a small portion of life." Like Henry James he has a leaning to the upper social strata, but unlike Henry James he was not progressively enamored of the beauties of a psychological reason and its pictorial possibilities. He was personally inclined, he says, "to prepare my readers for a crucial exhibition of the personae, and then to give the scene in the fullest of their blood and brain under stress of a fiery situation."[22] Here we have Charles Reade's "dramatic moments." The procedure, as Meredith says, necessitates the establishment of a " 'pitch' considerably above our common human."[23] To aid in the establishment of the "pitch," Meredith employs a language of dramatic intensity often reminiscent of the Elizabethan stage.

The tendencies here mentioned will help to draw the lines of demarcation. Actually the English novel written in the traditional vein is widely separated from the later realistic novel of critical inquiry. Moreover, Meredith and Hardy are not in the immediate stream of change. Meredith had few imitators. Hardy's influence was upon the regionalists, who in the early decades of the twentieth century were to play a minor, but not an unimportant role. The English novel was soon to make a wide break with the past, and plot, poetry, and rusticity were to be, at least for a time, outmoded. The first and strongest incitement to change was the influence of French naturalism.

[20] *Letters of George Meredith* (New York, Charles Scribner's Sons, 1912), 401.
[21] *Jude the Obscure* (Wessex edition; New York, The Macmillan Co., 1912), "Preface."
[22] *Letters of George Meredith*, 398.
[23] *Ibid.*, 399.

✗

❧ II ❧

NATURALISM
IN FRENCH FICTION

IT is hard for us to imagine the post-Victorian development of English fiction along strictly English lines. Perhaps the tendency would have been toward regionalism. Perhaps it would have been toward romantic realism and realistic romance in line with the effort of Blackmore, Stevenson, Haggard, and Kipling. Perhaps the "matter-of-fact romance" would have continued. Perhaps with the approach of the critical spirit in the twentieth century the tendency would have been toward satire.

As it so happened, the translation into English of French naturalistic novels furnished the occasion for a revaluation of the English novel's aims. Change was slow in coming. As will later be shown, the years 1885–95 were years of fierce controversy. But critical standards were altered, and the great figures of 1900–1917 were all in one way or another subject to strong naturalistic influence—Gissing, George Moore, Henry James, Arnold Bennett, Galsworthy, Wells, Maugham, Joyce.

Indeed, the naturalistic conception of fiction as a cosmic commentary—an outgrowth of Flaubert's theories—has generally prevailed in twentieth-century fiction. Up to World War I, writers in England were progressively concerned with the material details of human enterprise, the influence of circumstances upon individuals and classes, the mixture of qualities which make personality, the problem of fulfillment. Their spirit of inquiry was not that of the Victorians, and the presentation was based upon a logical sequence of events which could not have been of English origin.

There can be no adequate understanding of post-1885 English fiction without a knowledge of French naturalism. A million copies of translated naturalistic works were circulated in Britain before 1890, according to Ernest Vizetelly, whose father was chief publisher of the translations. Even in India during the nineties the translations crowded English novels off the market. English authors began to learn from naturalism, each in his own particular way.

The English modifications of naturalism produced the modern English novel. We shall later be interested in noting the temperamental limitations of English authors and the extent to which naturalism proved palatable to English taste.

The Victorian realists sought to present with conventional reticence the *matter* of life but allowed themselves full liberty to alter its typical *manner*. On the other hand, the French naturalists sought to portray both the *matter* and the *manner* of life. They would give the results of an impersonal study of representative men and women of their own time. In extreme cases their presentations were actually similar to clinical monographs. French naturalism is distinctive for its social consciousness. Since the effort was to reveal life, and therefore to expose it, the attitude of the author was necessarily critical. Man was a creature of circumstance, thwarted and degraded by certain specific causes. The novelist, taking his cue from experimental science, would become an experimental moralist by checking against the facts of life an observed or documented case of typical human behavior. The theories of Zola as propounded in *Le roman expérimental* were based upon the application of experimental science to physiology as developed in the writings of Dr. Claude Bernard.

Obviously since truth-telling was the aim, the naturalistic novelist would be brutally frank. He would give detailed descriptions of seductions, and in describing married life he would not stop at the doorways to bedrooms. He would describe the lives of harlots and he would enter houses of prostitution. He would expose vice and "foul passions." Equally important was the fact that the naturalists were debunkers of the romantic view. It served their purpose, therefore, to show that dreams and pleasant illusions are at variance with the harsh facts of life. The naturalists took pains to imply that God is unresponsive to prayers and to good intentions, and that violations of the moral code generally go unpunished. They treated the spirit and flesh as elements of the same central substance; today we would call them monists.

Certain phrases often applied to naturalism are misleading. It is sometimes said that naturalism is "literary photography," "a cross section of life." Obviously the terms are ill applied, for they exclude selection as a principle of composition. They exclude the alteration and grouping of material as it passes through the mind of the author, and the naturalists did not forbid rearrangement.

In striving to be impersonal the naturalists made painful efforts to conceal their temperamental likes and aversions. Yet Flaubert, who most nearly approached impersonality in his writings, realized the limits of any attempt and merely advised that the author extend as far as possible the moral horizon of his judgments. In perspective we see the naturalists as a group with humanitarian sympathies and a conviction of the cruelty and irrationality of human life. We see them aspiring to form and proportion; we see them bent upon showing the logical sequence of events; we see them stressing, often overstressing, motivation. We see them, within the limitations of their temperaments, endeavoring not to distort life; and we see them, bound by the spirit of a school, presenting selected aspects of life which give us a special and exceptional view of it. We realize now that this group spirit was characterized by a sympathy with the varied phases of human fallibility and a feeling that conventional valuations are awry. Even advocates of the naturalists admit a certain justification in Bouvier's unsympathetic comment that the naturalists' "principles of artistic conscience" were "hatred of the bourgeois, dislike of industrial

civilization and a normally regulated life, sympathy for out-
casts, eccentrics, law-breakers, and nomads."[1]

In form we note that the naturalists strove to show the direct
relation of cause and effect; that they attempted to expose the
influence of circumstance—though Zola was also concerned
with heredity; that they followed in the main Zola's precept in
Le roman expérimental—to show "what a certain 'passion,'
aroused under certain circumstances and in a certain environment, will result in as regards the individual and society."[2]

Surveyed in its general nature, the work of the naturalists
is distinctive for its exposure of the framework of society, for
its clarification of the springs of action, particularly among the
lower orders, for its exploration of the network of evils atten-
dant on industrial civilization, and for its vital presentation of
the masses in action. Walter Myers gives a convenient summary:

> Naturalism disdains literary graces and purports to tell the truth
> about life as it has been revealed by science. In telling the truth natural-
> ism professes to follow exactly the method of science, that is, collec-
> tion of detailed evidence, induction from this evidence, and imper-
> sonal setting forth of the conclusions. Unlike native British realism,
> naturalism opposes the use of any typification or idealization which
> will not serve to demonstrate that all men are by nature akin to the
> beasts, particularly in matters of sex. Moreover naturalism asserts, as
> Eliot and Meredith never did, the supreme importance of heredity and
> environment; and it finds its best material in the most degraded classes
> and in the revolting aspects of life.[3]

One should avoid too close a definition of naturalism. The
naturalists differed widely in their practices, and scarcely any
two French critics have agreed on who are the naturalists and
what naturalism really is.[4] Louis Cons, who has a closer knowl-

---

[1] Émile Bouvier, *La bataille réaliste* (Paris, Boccard, 1914), v.

[2] *Le roman expérimental* (Paris, G. Charpentier, 1881), 8.

[3] *The Later Realism* (Chicago, University of Chicago Press, 1927), 23.

[4] For a detailed exposition of the views of French critics see *L'Influence du natural-
isme français sur les romanciers anglais* (Paris, Marcel Giard, 1925), by William C.
Frierson, 26–28, or *Naturalism in French Fiction* (Columbus, Ohio State University
Bookstore, 1930), by William C. Frierson, 4–5.

edge of the French writers than Professor Myers, is wary of generalizations:

Naturalism is a label we put for convenience' sake on certain writers who differ widely from one another but who have in common a certain attitude towards Life and (this last point is very important) towards the Public. If I were obliged at the point of a sword to define this attitude, I would say it consists in admitting to the field of the novel all manifestations of life and in expecting the reader to stand the shock, or that naturalism is a literary anticipation of *Behaviorism* in that it describes life as a chain of reflexes responding to stimuli. Thus Zola, whose novels tend towards clinical monographs as a limit, is the typical Naturalist. Flaubert, Goncourt, Maupassant are less consistent Naturalists, for they still at times see Nature as a setting, as a landscape in which Man moves, and not exclusively as the inflexible Scheme of Things in which man is engulfed. In Maupassant we still hear the rustling of wind and water. In Zola, we hear only the swish of the whip of Man's Slavedrivers, Hunger and Sex.[5]

The divergences among the naturalists necessitate a somewhat careful treatment of the important figures in the movement. Each author extended the conception of the term "naturalism," and each author influenced English writers. It would be tedious in the course of this volume to pause for clarification of each separate influence. The exposition of the spirit and technique of individual naturalists made in this chapter will doubtless be valuable for reference purposes. Furthermore an effort will here be made to call attention to qualities of kinship. Insofar as possible the term "naturalism" will be extended to cover divergences within the school.[6]

[5] From a review of *L'Influence du naturalisme français sur les romanciers anglais*. *Journal of English and Germanic Philology,* October, 1928, 573.

[6] Only those naturalists who influenced English novelists are here treated. The typically naturalistic work of Huysmans was not translated into English and only one volume of Edouard Rod. No translations were made of Céard, Hennique, or Paul Alexis.

The question is often asked, How can you tell whether a certain work is or is not naturalistic? At the risk of oversimplification, I suggest that the problem may be approached as below indicated:

1. *Technique.* Is there a "theme taken from life"? (That is, is a social observation developed? Does the novel develop a social view, presented, for the most part, impersonally?) In default of a "theme," is there a more or less consistent development of a given situation which is not altogether improbable? Does the author stress material

We are not here concerned with the minor figures in the movement. Our concern is with the unifying tendencies among the masters. Naturalism as a literary label has become part of the international literary vocabulary, and the law of custom has bound inseparably the names of Flaubert, the Goncourts, Zola, and Maupassant. Let us first consider the ideas and purposes common to these writers.

Naturalism arose, on the one hand, from the psychological theories propounded by Taine and, on the other, from the influence of Balzac. These influences, of course, were dissimilar; that of Taine was direct, that of Balzac indirect. Taine expounded the great doctrine of "causes": "no matter if the facts be physical or moral, they all have their causes; there is a cause for ambition, for courage, for truth, as there is for muscular development, for digestion, for animal heat. Vice and virtue are products, like vitriol and sugar; and every complex phenomenon arises from other more simple phenomena on which it hangs. Let us then seek the simple phenomena for moral qualities, as we seek them for physical qualities."[7]

Balzac's influence was to inculcate the taste for document-like precision when dealing with the facts of life. We find in his writings a careful insistence upon the details of material circumstance, a concern with heredity, and a preoccupation with habits of mind. Nevertheless, we cannot call Balzac a naturalist, because naturalism is essentially a study of a significant phase of life. Balzac's studies are exceptional, oblique,

---

motives? is the treatment behavioristic? Can the book be called a study? (We must remember that a person wishing to give a liberal interpretation of naturalism might take Maupassant's view: that the literary artist has only to take up people at a certain phase of their development and lead them, by logical steps, to the next phase.) Are the individuals portrayed more or less creatures of circumstance? Are there brutal or unpleasant facts? Are the central characters rather imperfect? Is there an avoidance of dramatic technique?

2. *Spirit.* Is the author's view harsh, or at least critical and exacting? Is the author "social minded"? is he a scientific materialist? Is the account an exposé? Is the author's view at all despairing? does he suggest that humanity is tainted and perhaps imperfectible? Is the author devoid of national prejudices and critical of national institutions?

[7] Hippolyte Adolphe Taine, *History of English Literature* (Chicago, Bedfords, Clarke & Co., 1873), "Introduction," Section 3.

romantic. They testify to the endless variety of life, to the caprices of temperament, of obsession. Balzac is an expressionist who concerns himself with the naturalistic treatment of fevered and overbalanced minds. His stories are based upon conceptions rather than upon observation. Life furnished hints, starting points, settings. It was a tropical wilderness where he wandered, picking out strange multicolored flowers which he would arrange according to his own conceptions into a well-ordered garden. Sometimes nature's careless grouping would furnish him with an idea, but often he was too intent upon his own bizarre designs to seek guidance from nature.

Thus Balzac created the taste for reality in fiction without completely satisfying it. A closer approach to reality was made *Flaubert* by Flaubert when he published in 1857 *Madame Bovary*.

Before *Madame Bovary* was written, no novelist had taken the theme of his story from a human event of a seriously significant nature, analyzed the motives which had been the directing forces, and rendered the result of his investigation without partiality or prejudice, changing it only in so far as to make it fit in with a rationalized scheme of human action and a technical plan of dramatic effectiveness.

Flaubert attempted an objective and passionless rendering of naturally arranged human phenomena. "The artist should be in his work, like God in Creation, invisible and all-powerful," he writes in a letter. "He should be felt everywhere and seen nowhere. And then art should be raised above personal affections and nervous susceptibilities. It is time to give it the precision of the physical sciences by means of a pitiless method."[8] The new approach is associated in Flaubert's mind with a style of clarity and exactness. "I love before everything," he writes, "the nervous, substantial, clean phrase with swelling muscle, gleaming skin; I like masculine, not feminine phrases."[9]

[8] Gustave Flaubert, *Correspondance* (Paris, G. Charpentier, 1893), 80. Third series (1854–69). Letter to Mlle Leroyer de Chantepie, Paris, March 18, 1857. Impersonality, as Bouvier points out in *La bataille réaliste,* dates back at least as far as Champfleury. Flaubert's success popularized and established the method.

[9] Flaubert, *Correspondance,* 72. First series (1830–50). Letter to Louis de Cormenin, June, 1844.

But Flaubert did more than establish a new procedure in the method of writing novels. He adopted a spirit of approach to his material which was not without its influence. He would show human weakness and incapacity "in a fashion to set one musing"; he would "inspire a pathetic contemplation, like that of the stars." Humanity was tainted, cursed by God, and hence irresponsible: "However well we may feed the animal man, however thickly we may gild his stable, even though we give him the softest and most luxurious litter, he will ever remain a beast. The only progress upon which one can count is to make the beast less of a cannibal. But as to raising the level of his ideas, or inspiring the masses with a broader conception of God, I doubt it, I doubt it."[10] For humanity, therefore, he felt not love but compassion. "Tout comprendre est tout pardonner." "Christ's blood which stirs in us, nothing can extirpate that, nothing can drain its source; our business is not to dry it up, but to make channels for it."[11]

The persistent contemplation of human misery and the analysis and explanation of human action according to a mechanistic conception are the distinguishing features in the realistic writings of Flaubert and those of his associates and followers whom we gather loosely together under the title of "naturalists." "All human observers are sad and must be so," write the Goncourts. "They are but spectators of life, witnesses; they take part neither in what will deceive nor in what will intoxicate. Their normal condition is that of a melancholic serenity." And again, "The telescopic and microscopic researches of the present day, the exploration of the infinitely great and of the infinitively little, the science of the star and of the microscope, lead to the same infinite depth of sadness. They lead to the human thought to something far sadder to man than death—to a conviction of that nothing which is his lot even while alive."[12]

"Ah, the poor wretches, the poor wretches," says Maupassant after visualizing in reverie the forms of relief from life

[10] *Ibid.*, 373. Third series (1854–69). Letter to G. Sand.
[11] *Ibid.*, 131. Letter to Madame Colet.
[12] Les Deux Goncourts, *Idées et sensations* (Paris, A. Lecroix, Verboeckenhoven et Cie., 1886), 174.

22

taken by Paris' thousands of yearly suicides, "how well I have felt their anguish, how really I have felt myself dying their own death! I have been through every phase of their miserable lives. I have known all the sorrows, all the tortures that brought them there; for I have felt the deceitful infamy of life better than anyone has ever felt it before."[13]

"Que c'est triste, la vie!" are words uttered by a young painter standing beside the corpse of a woman who has killed herself. "Comme il y a des êtres malheureux! Je sentais peser sur cette créature humaine l'éternel injustice de l'implacable nature. . . . Et je comprenais qu'elle crût à Dieu, celle-là, et qu'elle eût espéré ailleurs la compensation de sa misère. Elle allait maintenant se decomposer et devenir plante à son tour. Elle fleurirait au soleil, serait broutée par les vaches, emportée en grain par les oiseaux, et chair des bêtes, elle redeviendrait de la chair humaine. Mais ce qu'on appele l'âme s'etait éteint au fond du puits noir."

Zola, for his part, had certainly no pleasant illusions about life. In moments of depression he was wont to think, with his own Dr. Pascal, that the only hope for humanity was regeneration through the injection of a serum! The exposure of human tares was his specialty, and no one, before or since, has found so many of them. Like the other naturalists, he had no pleasant illusions about an afterlife and considered death as "la déchéance au fond d'un cabanon, l'abominable décomposition de l'être."

Flaubert, the Goncourts, and Maupassant were humanitarians only artistically. They pitied and blamed not, but they were unconcerned with plans for human betterment. Zola, however, had faith in human progress, progress which was to be attained by pitiless truth and publicity. "If I were conducting a school of morals," he wrote in 1869, "I would hasten to put into the hands of my pupils *Madame Bovary* and *Germinie Lacerteux*, convinced, as I am, that truth alone can instruct and sustain generous souls." Enlightenment, therefore, exposure, and the further seeking of truth constituted a plan of action

---

[13] Guy de Maupassant, *Misti* (Paris, P. Ollendorff, 1912), "L'endormeuse."

to which he adhered with something of religious faith. He might well have spoken the creed of Dr. Pascal: "I believe that the pursuit of truth by science is the divine ideal which a man should prescribe for himself. I believe that all is illusion and vanity which does not contribute to the treasure of those slowly acquired truths which will never be lost. I believe that the sum of these truths, augmented continually, will in the end give to mankind incalculable power and serenity, if not happiness. Yes, I believe in the final triumph of life."[14]

In matters of technique there were many points upon which the naturalists agreed. Plots in the old sense were discountenanced and human action re-examined from what they chose to call a scientific point of view. If abnormal relations were considered, an attempt was made to generalize upon the abnormality—similar cases were investigated and the principles of conduct there determined were applied to a particular incident. Malice was largely eradicated from the characters; evil became a form of ignorance. Conflicts were portrayed in the lives of persons groping for happiness in blind and pathetic fashions. Simple, or at least uncultivated, types were generally chosen in order that universally recognized motives be attributed to them, and in order that the natural or physical aspects of life be shown as the controlling forces. Anything of a spiritual nature was but "a more finely-woven flesh." Startling or significant phases of life were selected for investigation, and the artist tried "not to belittle art for the sake of an isolated personality."

But differences are immediately in evidence. Flaubert chose to delineate character and its development through vivifying the mental processes of certain individuals. "What Flaubert strove to do in revealing scientifically the special quality of a certain human mind was to show the thoughts and sensations which ran through it, and to stress by repetition and rhythm the more significant ones," writes Paul Bourget. "Authors of monologues do this, and the author of *Madame Bovary* follows their procedure. His characters are associations of ideas which

14 Émile Zola, *Dr. Pascal* (New York, The Macmillan Co., 1898), 47.

24

walk."[15] Each thought or idea reveals, therefore, a significant trait of the person who conceives it, and the poetic qualities of the human soul are revealed through the rhythm and form by which its preoccupations are presented.

As regards the presentation of incidents, Flaubert is not to be distinguished from the other naturalists by the fact that his method is "scenic," but by the fact that his work is more "scenic" than theirs.[16] A rather evident feature is that the foreground rather than the background is made prominent. He portrays few landscapes and vistas; there are houses, streets, a chemistry shop, an inn, and, above all, people. Color, as in an impressionist's picture, is reflected. Speech, ideas, emotions, and customs—all have their interplay and effect. Figures are never isolated; there are no mere portraits; we are shown at close view a succession of scenes.

Sensitiveness and acuteness of vision account for the visual quality of Flaubert's work. "There is at present such a gulf fixed between myself and the rest of the world," he writes, "that I sometimes experience a feeling of astonishment when I hear even the most ordinary and casual things; there are certain gestures, certain intonations of voice which fill me with surprise, and there are certain silly things which nearly make me giddy." It was these startling and significant gestures and phrases which were to Flaubert the essence of pictorial art; they could stand for pages of careless description. "The unexpected is in everything," he told Maupassant. "The least object contains an unknown element or aspect. Find that."[17]

Perhaps the casual reader will note that the story of *Madame Bovary* is too interesting to be taken from life. Flaubert transformed his material[18] by elevating certain characters and by eradicating the artistic crudities of his material to fit in with a rational scheme of human action and a technical plan of dra-

[15] Paul Bourget, *Essais de psychologie contemporaine* (Paris, Plon-Nourrit, 1901), II, 165–66.
[16] Percy Lubbock, *The Craft of Fiction* (London, Jonathan Cape, Ltd., 1921), 73.
[17] Guy de Maupassant, *Pierre et Jean* (Paris, A. Michel, 1925), "Introduction," 22.
[18] William C. Frierson, "The Naturalistic Technique of Flaubert," *French Quarterly*, September and December, 1925.

matic effectiveness. It was in this way that he attempted to give "truth rendered by beauty."

The method of the Goncourts is in striking contrast to that of Flaubert. As the researches of Olin H. Moore conclusively show,[19] the Goncourts were unconcerned with consistent characterizations and with modifying human action so that it would seem reasonable. Believers in "l'illogique du vrai,"[20] they neglected unified effects. To quote Mr. Moore:

> The Goncourts, with their photographic method, often attempt to attribute to "A" as it were the *exact* finger-print of "X," the *exact* head of "Y," and the *exact* temperament of "Z." Their method would be less vulnerable if "A's" finger bore only an ordinary resemblance to that of "X." The difficulty is that the Goncourts, by renouncing the principle of selection in art, are prone to insist upon an *absolute resemblance*— their notes frequently being thrust into their novels without alteration. Thus their characters, though possessing features, living in surroundings, and speaking a language precisely such as have been observed in real life, and jotted down with infinite pains upon the author's pads, are far from being truly realistic. They are contrary to "nature," to "history," and to the medical science of which the Goncourts professed themselves disciples. Many a romantic character of the early nineteenth century novel, though improbable, was at least possible, while the characters of the Goncourts would seem, if our reasoning is just, to be in many cases impossible.

In reading the novels of the Goncourts, one feels that their practice was to write more in accord with documentary evidence than did Flaubert, but with less artistic comeliness of design. Abnormal and exceptional elements abound in both the characters and the story. There is much of newspaper veracity in their accounts, but one feels that these accounts often reveal no more significant aspects of life than do the daily papers.

[19] "The Literary Methods of the Goncourts," *PMLA*, XXXI.

[20] Les Goncourts, *Journal*, II, 219: "Le défecteux de l'imagination, c'est que ses créations sont rigoureusement logiques. La vérité ne l'est pas. Ainsi, je viens de lire dans un roman la description d'un salon religieux: tout s'y tient, depuis le portrait gravé du comte de Chambord jusqu'à la photographie du pape. Eh bien! je me rappelle avoir vu, dans le décor sacro-saint du comte de Montalembert, un portrait de religieuse, qui était le costume de comédie d'une de ses parentes, jouant dans une pièce du XVIIIe siècle. Voici l'imprévu, le décousu, l'illogique du vrai."

Their characteristic procedure is to portray human beings of a low order of intelligence who are made unhappy by an assembly of unfortunate circumstances. The influence of environment and incidents is, by inference, overstressed; the human will is all but obliterated.

Furthermore, the novels of the Goncourts take the form of chronicles. In the main there is an avoidance of epic or dramatic treatment. Incidents are related rather than portrayed, and the gradual development or disintegration of character is indicated by the delineation in separate chapters of incidents which may be supposed to have produced certain effects.

One strong point of similarity between Flaubert and the Goncourts, however, is their hypersensitiveness. In *Idées et sensations* we find the state of mind mentioned:

> I perceive that literature and observation, instead of deadening my sensibility has extended and refined it, developed it and laid it bare. . . . By observing and noting relations one becomes, instead of hardened, a sort of creature without skin, who is wounded by the least impression, utterly defenseless and seeping blood.[21]

In such states both Flaubert and the Goncourts sought for an unknown element or aspect of the least object, but their procedure was different. While Flaubert attempted an objective description of clarity and exactness, the Goncourts under the influence of a "forte fièvre hallucinatoire" sought to portray the scene or object in mind subjectively, in associating with the scene or object their own reactions to it. In order to record precisely their sensations they fashioned similes and metaphors of a certain originality, employing words outside of their usual connotations, and applying adjectives usually considered appropriate to one object as applicable to another.

Both Flaubert and the Goncourts seemed unconscious that they wrote to perpetuate their particular illusions of life—in the case of the Goncourts an illusion of life fostered by a rather dogmatic determinism; in that of Flaubert "une vision personelle du monde" in which the limitations and incapacity of

[21] Page 153.

humanity are the most evident features. It remained for Maupassant, Flaubert's pupil, to render his vision of life with humility. The "truth" which he portrays is consciously that which seems significant according to his particular temperament. Realism, he holds, should not be considered the portrayal of "reality" but that of personal visions of life. To decide which happenings are significant is the function of the artist. He elects and rearranges in accord with the dictates of his artistic temperament.

Maupassant was at great pains to refute the slander that the group of writers to which he belonged were bent upon giving a cross section of life. A photographic presentation of life would show it to be "brutal, made up of disconnected and unrelated segments, full of unexplainable, illogical, and contradictory catastrophes." Art, he says, consists in showing relations, in selection and regrouping with the aim of making visible a certain special truth which the artist feels to be significant and profound. Again he says:

> No one can claim to portray "reality." The truths that we see are the products of our conceptions, and therefore of our organs. Our eyes, our ears, our noses, our different tastes create as many truths as there are men on the face of the earth. And our spirits, receiving instruction from these differently constituted organs, analyze and pass judgment as if each of us belonged to another race. ... Each of us creates his illusion of the world, and the great artists are those who impose upon humanity their own particular illusions.[22]

Maupassant's particular illusion of life did not differ materially from that of the other naturalists—pity for, and scorn of, humanity's helpless blundering, hatred of sham and hypocrisy, and a sad or bitter acceptance of the imperfectibility of humanity and of the relentless influence of circumstance. But his vision was not rigid or uniformly severe. A pervading Gallic animalism by some strange magic tints the pitiful with the pathetic in his writings; the immensity and organic unity of creation seemed ever in his thoughts, lending perspective to

[22] *Pierre et Jean,* "Introduction."

the affairs of mice and men. Maupassant's theory was that the adroit grouping of "petits faits" would show the profound and concealed significance of happenings. But he did not depend upon the grouping alone for interpretation. A deft phrase or sentence, sometimes keenly insinuating, sometimes grimly pathetic, sometimes of a sophistical nature, gives point to his accounts; often carries suggestions of universality. And the artist must be a close and careful student of life.

He must show how the feelings are modified under the influence of environmental circumstance, how the sentiments and passions develop, how people love one another, how they hate one another, how struggles evolve in all the ranks of society, how within an individual the varied bourgeois interests fight for dominance—the interests of family and of money and of politics.[23]

Aside from *Bel-Ami*, which stands as the perfect example of the "experimental novel," Maupassant's stories are his most naturalistic writings. In them he could give expression to disconnected, unrelated "truths." But when he tried to associate the varied phenomena of life, as is necessary in a novel, he often evaded the artistic principle of detachment which Flaubert taught him. I refer in particular to *Mont-Oriol*, *Notre couer*, and *Fort comme la mort*. In these his personal sympathies are in evidence. He shows a fondness for the well-dressed and cultivated beau, and a leaning, rather conventionally French, toward the romance of intrigue. Even the sorrows and languors are romantic; the stark, naturalistic note of tragedy is lacking.

In two novels, however, he shows himself to be the detached and critical student of life. *Pierre et Jean* is a psychological portrayal. The author uses the magnifying glass upon a family situation. Social considerations are neglected and attention forced upon a soul tortured by the stain of illegitimacy upon his name and the dishonor reflected upon his father's household. Maupassant's other naturalistic novel, *Bel-Ami*, follows the procedure typical of Zola. A particular phase of society is exposed through the delineation of a life history. The

[23] *Ibid.*

author chooses for his central figure an ambitious and good-looking young journalist who is without delicate scruples. The journalist rises to a position of prominence through the influence of women, and the organic functioning of society is critically shown in a delineation of journalistic influence, political corruption, and feminine power.

We note that with the exception of *Bel-Ami*—which was written after Zola had attained a position of dominance in French fiction—the realistic work of Flaubert, the Goncourts, and Maupassant dealt largely with the nature of the human heart. Society was of importance in its relation to the individual. Zola looks through the other end of the telescope. Individuals are of importance in their relation to society.

As Henry James so ably points out, Zola's novels deal with Things in a gregarious form—classes, crowds, confusions, movements, industries.[24] Zola gives us individual life reflected in generalized terms; he shows the effect of character and passion in the lump and by the ton; and his particular talent lies in making his characters swarm, and in giving them a great central Thing to swarm about—"some highly representative institution or industry of the France of his time, some seated Moloch of custom, of commerce, of faith, lending itself to portrayal through its abuses and excesses, its idol-face and great devouring mouth."[25]

We may illustrate what is meant by "great central Thing" by specific reference. *Le ventre de Paris* deals with the process of feeding the huge city, with the great markets as the focal point of attraction; *Au bonheur des dames*, the spread of the mammoth department store showing "its ravage amid the smaller fry of the trade, of all the trades, picturing these latter gasping for breath in an air pumped clean by its mighty lungs"; *Germinal*, the coal miner and life in the underworld of the pits; *L'Assommoir*, drink among the lower orders and the depravity to which it may lead; *La Bête humaine*, the great railway;

[24] *Notes on Novelists* (New York, Charles Scribner's Sons, 1914), 43.
[25] *Ibid.*

L'Argent, finance, banking, and the French stock market; *La Debâcle*, the Franco-Prussian War; *Faute de l'Abbé Mouret*, a critical study of ecclesiastical life; *Vérité*, the evils of clerical influence and popular prejudice; *Nana*, the demimonde; *La Curée*, the decline of the second empire.

When we consider that one of the central features of Zola's labors was to assimilate an unbelievable variety of the details of human enterprise, a natural curiosity leads us to the moral theory underlying his portentous documentation. The theory, when we discover it, shows how closely Zola is allied in spirit to the other naturalists, for Zola was perhaps more conscious than the others of the variety of human taints and the well-nigh irremediable depravity brought about by man's inhumanity. Havelock Ellis adequately phrases this aspect of Zola's conception:

All are the victims of an evil social system, as Zola sees the world, the enslaved workers as well as the overfed masters; the only logical outcome is a clean sweep—the burning up of the chaff and the straw, the fresh furrowing of the earth, the new spring of a sweet and vigorous race. That is the logical outcome of Zola's attitude, the attitude of one who regards our present society as a thoroughly vicious circle. His pity for men and women is boundless; his disdain is equally boundless. It is only towards animals that his tenderness is untouched by contempts; some of his most memorable passages are concerned with the sufferings of animals. The New Jerusalem may be fitted up, but the Montsou miners will never reach it; they will fight for the first small, stuffy, middle-class villa they meet on the way. And Zola pours out the stream of his pitiful, pitiless irony on the weak, helpless, erring children of Men.[26]

But the hopeless vision above indicated could hardly have sustained Zola in the labors he imposed upon himself. I am disposed to consider him perfectly sincere in his suggestion, "Let us expose everything in order that everything may be healed." It is true, of course, that his hates become involved. "We naturalists are experimental moralists," Zola avowed. "We show through delineating a human experience how a passion works

[26] *Affirmations* (Boston, Houghton Mifflin Co., 1922), 155.

under certain circumstances. Whenever men understand the mechanism of this passion, they can reduce it or render it as inoffensive as possible. And thus the naturalistic novel is of practical moral value in that it takes the human mechanism apart piece by piece and then shows how the parts function under certain conditions. In time we can make generalizations and determine laws which have only to be applied if we wish to correct abuses and arrive at better social conditions."[27]

Although Zola's theories cannot be neglected in forming an estimate of his work, we would do well not to apply all the theories to all the work. When taxed for his aberrations, Zola would reply, "Yes, I admit it. I am just an old-fashioned romantic." "Oh my God," he once expostulated, "I laugh just as you do at this word 'naturalism.' I repeat it because we must give things new names so people will think them new."[28] And is not *Au bonheur des dames* a romance rather than an experimental novel? Nevertheless it may be said with all factors taken into account that Zola included the substance of life in his novels about as well as it could be done with due consideration given to interest and organic unity.[29]

Zola's most enlightened critical utterance is that "art is a particular corner of existence seen through a temperament." His own temperament was, of course, largely a product of literary influences. The remarkable fact, however, is that he was a person of sufficient capacity to assimilate Hugo, Balzac, the Goncourts, and Charles Reade without imitating any one of them. Zola's temperament was a strangely homogeneous compound of three outstanding qualities:

That part of Zola's temperament which is socialist-reformer is indicated by the painstaking portrayal of the varied forms of human error and the details of these great Things which tend to create it.

That part of Zola's nature which is sensationalist is shown by his tendency to write exposés and by his stressing of physio-

[27] *Le roman experimental* (Paris, G. Charpentier, 1881), 24.
[28] *Journal,* February 19, 1877, V, 314.
[29] See also Henri Martineau, *Le roman scientifique d'Émile Zola* (Paris, J.-B. Balliere et fils, 1907), 226.

logical factors. As Arthur Symons points out, there is everywhere in Zola's novels the "savor of plebeian flesh." Zola shows a preference for the crude and animalistic qualities. But the suggestion that Zola had in mind the sale of his books cannot be overlooked. Zola might have been either a humanitarian or a sensationalist; as a matter of fact, he was both.

That part of Zola's nature which is romanticist is indicated by the zest and color of his narrative, his sensationalism, the exaggerated accounts of scenes of squalor, and the thumping of the tom-toms in the spectacular displays of mass action and mass force.

We have noted that only Zola among the naturalists was intent upon social change and the alteration of individual behavior. Flaubert, Maupassant, and the Goncourts by probing into motivation with scientific detachment felt only "a pathetic contemplation like that of the stars." Their despair, and the despair of scientific agnosticism, was aptly phrased by the Goncourts: "The telescopic and microscopic researches of the present day . . . lead . . . human thought to something far sadder to man than death—to a conviction of that nothing which is his lot even while alive." It was largely Zola's individual incitement to a general investigation of industrial civilization which was to affect the social impulses of both the nineties and the Edwardian period; but underlying the specific urge to explore the social framework was a conception of man developed in the works of all the naturalists. According to this conception mankind is, in the words of André Maurois,

a confused crowd of poor human animals who think that they act freely, who suppose that they love, hate, judge, of their own responsibility, and who are in reality the toys of a few desperately simple physical and chemical laws. ... Such a pessimistic theory leads to a tender sympathy for men. This is true in the first place because one cannot keep from pitying those unfortunate animals who are always the victims of illusions without remedy, always committing in vain tasks that lead to nothing except death; and, in the second place, scientific fatalism, by making all moral judgments absurd, imposes upon the writer an admirable impartiality in regard to his characters.[30]

This view has been dominant in twentieth-century English fiction. It is needless to say, perhaps, that it has produced a revolution in moral and ethical values. It prepared the way for Freud and for fiction reflecting his ideas.

In the succeeding chapter we shall deal with the impact of French naturalistic novels on a somewhat startled England. During the eighties when the translations began to appear, Englishmen were not at all ready for a rendering of life that expressed a deterministic view, nor could they stand for the frankness of a detached and quasi-scientific probing. Not until the middle nineties was there any considerable acceptance of the view.

[30] "New Types of Fiction," *Nouvelles Littéraires*, Paris, March 6, 1926. Republished in the *Living Age*, April 17, 1926.

✍§ III §✍

THE ENGLISH CONTROVERSY
OVER NATURALISM

THE eighteen-nineties in England, as we have come to
see, were essentially years of ethical unrest, or experimentation, of imitation, and moral insouciance. But
they were also, as we have lately forgotten, years in which
Victorian doubt, soul-questioning, and moral fervor were not
at all lacking. That striking artistic creations should have resulted from such a troubled state of feeling is natural; and it
is also natural that these creations should be diverse and fragmentary. The eighteen-nineties, according to Max Beerbohm,
are not to be considered as a period at all but as a state of mind
—a rather tired state of mind demanding interesting novelties.
And novelty, rendered with a certain pagan gaiety by the
writers of the younger generation, announced the approach
of a new age. But the nation as a whole was not dominated
by the carefree agnosticism of certain younger writers. In all
of Britain there was not a public sufficiently interested to perpetuate either *The Yellow Book*, *The Savoy*, or *The Dome*
for longer than a few brief years. Indeed, the handful of cav-
aliers who revelled in the sophistries of Mr. Wilde laughed a
little too loudly. In the background there were serious and
troubled faces.

These serious and troubled faces have received inadequate
literary recognition. For the mass of literate late Victorians
were, in fact, rather irritated at the brilliant butterflies that flit-
ted across the landscape. They were still worried about souls,
more worried than ever; they were "healthily warding off the

intrusions of sterile pessimism"; and they were deeply concerned with international politics while trying to pierce the Veil. But the piercing of the Veil was no laughing matter, and they did not care to have it decorated by Mr. Beardsley with his gruesome designs.

And so the activities of the decade are viewed in proper perspective only when seen against a background of trouble. Being troubled, the late Victorians sought escapes in novels of adventure, in art for art's sake, and experiments in poetry; being troubled, they sang "Rule Britannia" and believed in the White Man's Burden; and being troubled, they read with no uncertain interest the pathetic and ironic narratives of troubled spirits in France who were exposing with relentless detail the material ingredients of the human soul.

But the reading of naturalistic fiction by Englishmen does not signify that they approved of it. Indeed the tenacity of the Victorian hold upon the public mind is shown by the controversy which raged from 1885 to 1895 over the translations of Zola, Flaubert, Maupassant, and the Goncourts. For Victorianism and naturalistic fiction are readily understood to be incompatible. We associate with Victorianism the belief in "higher selves" and "lower selves," a concern with spiritual values and free will, a tendency to look on the sunny side of doubt as well as of life, reticence in matters of sex, religious patronage, a chivalric attitude toward woman, Toryism, pride of race, and imperialism. With naturalistic fiction, on the other hand, we associate the insistence upon sex as a dominant force in human action, the negation of spiritual values, opposition to conventional religion, determinism, fatalism, internationalism, brutality, frankness, and a disregard for the sanctity of institutions, conventions, and womanhood.

To those who held to the Victorian tradition, therefore, naturalistic literature was iconoclastic and contaminating. It would "break the State, the Church, the Throne, and roll their ruins down the slope." It would "sap the foundations of manhood and womanhood, not only destroying innocence but corroding the moral nature." "How can we expect the young to escape spring blights," writes a critic, "if that beautiful and natural guard against them, the sense that calls the mantling blush to the cheek, be broken down by literature that is wantonly prurient?"

Other writers declared that naturalism resolved metaphysics into a process of "soul-making," that it destroyed our faith in the moral law, that its revelations of feminine mysteries made one feel "intrusive and unmanly." They suggested that the French writers did not reveal human nature, as they pretended to do, but "Gallic nature, which, we should do well to bear in mind, is human—with a difference." They decried the absence of spiritual ideals in Zola's works and concluded that "the visible when it rests not upon the invisible becomes the bestial." But Zola was not necessarily the chief culprit, for, we are told, "the underlings of the naturalist school are like dogs battening upon carrion offal. They imitate the master when he is offensive, and go beyond him in reeking foulness."

Not only were the Victorians hostile to naturalism at the dawning of the eighteen-nineties, but they became militant. They organized the National Vigilance Association with the intention of protecting the young from the spread of "pernicious literature" and conducted a campaign directed in considerable measure against the English translations of French naturalistic novels. The campaign, as we are informed, became the center of public attention. It resulted in two trials and two convictions of Henry Vizetelly, publisher, for the translation and sale of Zola's works as well as those of Bourget and Maupassant. The second trial ruined Vizetelly financially and resulted in a prison sentence of three months.

That the conviction (1889) bore the stamp of public approval is well indicated in the press comments which preceded the second trial. "Zola simply wallows in immorality," said one writer; "he gives full rein to filthy, libidinous propensities," avowed another; "his books are characterized by dangerous lubricity," wrote a third; "realism according to latterday French lights means nothing short of sheer beastliness," insisted a fourth; "the matter is of such a leprous nature that it would be impossible for any young man who had not learned the Divine secret of self-control to have read it without committing some form of outward sin within twenty-four hours after," protested a fifth. . . . We spare you the rest.

Strange as it may seem, no single voice was raised at this crucial time in defense of frankness and a stern treatment of life in literature. That these qualities were in demand by English readers of fiction is shown by the fact that the Vizetelly firm alone was accustomed to selling a thousand copies a week of Zola's translations, and that, as was estimated, a million copies of naturalistic works were in circulation. But the situation was an extremely delicate one. The white sanctity of Lady Britannia's garments had been ruffled and no gentleman could publicly condone the offense. Whatever excuses Messrs. Vizetelly and Zola may have had seemed unimportant in view of their disregard for good manners.

But though advocates of naturalism did not come to the front during, or immediately following, the Vizetelly trial, we may not suppose interest in the foreign fiction to have been discouraged by the taint of obscenity which the court verdict cast upon it. Such verdicts generally have the opposite effect. Moreover, the question of new artistic criteria for the novel became the subject for spirited private discussion. Thirteen publishers competed in supplying the demand for French naturalistic novels, and these novels, read in increasing quantities, continued to be maligned and liked. Two English authors, also, were stimulating interest in naturalism. George Moore was gradually rising into prominence with the publication of *A Modern Lover* (1883), *A Mummer's Wife* (1885), *A Drama in Muslin* (1886), *Spring Days* (1888), *Mike Fletcher* (1889), and *Vain Fortunes* (1890). Gissing, who had won little applause from *Workers in the Dawn* (1880) and *The Unclassed* (1884) began to interest the public when in *Isabel Clarendon* (1886) and *A Life's Morning* (1888) he became a disciple of Meredith. Thereafter he returned to a modified form of naturalism in *The Nether World* (1889) and *Born in Exile* (1892).

A change, at any rate, began to appear as early as 1890—not

a sudden change but the evidence of a new attitude. A defender of naturalism could not yet find a periodical to support him but he could at least strike a blow by ridiculing the feeble and sentimental attempts at narrative literature made by the mass of English writers; he could call attention to the evils resulting from conventionalism in fiction.

"In England the artist is either afraid to tell the whole truth, or else he is intellectually incapable of revealing the complicated mechanism of the human heart," says D. F. Hannigan in the *Eclectic* for May, 1890. "He barely hints at certain matters which the votaries of Mrs. Grundy consider it an indelicacy to speak about; and, whenever he attempts a bold piece of realism, he mars the effect of it by introducing some irrelevant bit of didacticism, intended no doubt to appease the virtuous indignation of the Pharisaic middle-class reader to whom the naked truth is unpalatable."[1]

"The sample English commodity which circulates in three volumes," writes a critic for the *Quarterly Review* of October, 1891, "is a conventional product, an institution like Saturday excursions to Brighton and Margate for half-a-crown, a refuge for distressed needle-women, a thing as native to our shores as Britannia metal and afternoon tea. The Homeric epithet, dedicated by long custom to its usage is 'trashy.' Our indigenous novel, taken in the bulk, contains little art and no science. And its art is well worn—a feeble echo of Rousseau with insular decorum stifling its too Gallic accents and reducing him to respectable inanity. It is a sentimental prude who would shriek and perhaps faint at the mere mention by bold Mr. Meredith of 'skeleton anatomy.'[2] Delighting in the love season, that carnival of egotism, our British Miss closes her record discretely when the wedding-bells strike, and she is—to use her own favorite expression—led to the altar by the hero whom she has

---

[1] "The Artificiality of the Novel," *Eclectic*, May, 1890.

[2] In the discursive first chapter of *Diana of the Crossways*, 1885, Meredith, in defending realism, referred to the skeleton anatomy of fact, which, he said, is necessary in fiction. "Instead of objurgating the timid intrusions of philosophy, invoke her presence, I pray you. History without her is the skeleton-map of events; fiction a picture of figures modeled on no skeleton-anatomy."

chased, or drawn on, from cover to cover, through a thousand pages. When the French satirist wanders in the forest of Mudie and glances at these strange, impossible creatures, he feels an overpowering sense of wonder and amazement, which tempts him to exaggerate the less desirable qualities of his own fiction in the hope of giving a redoubled shock, for there is nothing he so contemns as Rousseau turned Puritan. The 'everlasting pantomime' of rose-pink virtue squinting across the pages of it's prayer-book of vice, while it gambols within the measure of police-morality, is very laughable to him."[3]

In the next year, 1892, Edmund Gosse becomes more bold. "The Tyranny of the Novel," which appeared in the *National Review*, was virtually a plea that the novel, which had now taken precedence over all other forms of literary expression, enlarge its borders and extend its scope.

It is quite plain [writes Mr. Gosse] that to a certain extent the material out of which the English novel has been constructed is in danger of being exhausted. ... If we could suddenly arrive from another planet and read a cluster of novels from Mudie's without any previous knowledge of the class, we should be astonished at the conventionality, the narrowness, the monotony. ... What is the use of this tyranny which they [the novelists] wield if it does not enable them to treat life broadly and to treat it as a whole? ... The one living novelist who has striven to give a large, competent, and profound view of the movement of life is M. Zola. When we have said the worst of the *Rougon-Macquart* series, when we have admitted the obvious faults of these books—their romantic fallacies on the one hand, their cold brutalities on the other—it must be admitted that they present the results of a most laudable attempt to cultivate the estate outside of the kitchen-garden. In these books of M. Zola, as every one knows, successive members of a certain family stand out against a background of human masses in incessant movement. The peculiar characteristic of this novelist is that he enables us to see why these masses are moved, and in what direction. ...

Mr. Gosse then proceeds at some length to emphasize Zola's grasp of the mechanism of modern civilization, but he is on his

---

[3] "English Realism and Romance," *Quarterly Review*, October, 1891.

guard lest his words of commendation be taken as expressing unqualified approval of the Frenchman's work. "I would not be misunderstood," he says, "even by the most hasty reader, to recommend an imitation of M. Zola." Nevertheless, he adds, "the experiments of Mr. George Gissing and Mr. George Moore deserve sympathetic acknowledgment."

That Mr. Gosse felt decidedly sympathetic to the tendencies represented in the works of M. Zola is more amply shown in an essay entitled "Limits of Realism in Fiction," which he wrote in 1890. But this essay was never published in an English review. Mr. Gosse finally sent it to *The Forum*, an American publication. Later on, in 1893, he published it in England among the group of essays which he entitled *Questions at Issue*.

The fact that there had been created in England by 1893 a reading public sympathetic to an analytic examination of contemporary society is indicated by the publication in the *Contemporary Review* of that year of an article favorable to Zola and naturalistic art. "The Moral Teachings of Zola," by Vernon Lee, is really a hymn of praise:

> Genius can make its own terms [Miss Lee asserts]. You cannot beat it down or do without, for it offers a possession which outweighs all damage or disadvantage; the expression of what mankind is beginning to feel, the formula of what mankind is beginning to think. So despite all drawbacks, real or imaginary, Zola has had to be accepted. We may not enjoy and we may not approve; but unless we forego much knowledge of contemporary thought and feeling, and much practical benefit in consequence, we are bound, mature and thoughtful men and women, to read and meditate his works. The present moment is very propitious. Zola is not merely enthroned; he is beginning to be threatened with dethronement. We have long ago heard all objections of the generation which he shocked and horrified; we are now hearing all the objections of the generation which Zola himself produced by the force of imitation and reaction. It is universally admitted that Zola's books are full of horrors and indecencies, that the reading thereof must be attended by some disgust and perhaps some danger; also that they are not really scientific nor thoroughly realistic; and we know how he stands to Rabelais, to Victor Hugo, to Claude

Bernard. All these points having been discussed and settled, we are therefore at liberty to ask ourselves, each reader for himself, by what thoughts or feelings Zola has enriched his contemporaries, since, as I have remarked, the fact of his having been accepted, drawbacks and all, proves that he offered the world something it found worth possessing.

Zola's essential genius, according to Miss Lee, is exercised to show the moral incompetence of man in a complicated and naïf system of false weights and measures; he makes vivid

a network of tolerated mischief—a gigantic spider's web of lust, greed, vanity and sloth, of all the active and passive modes of indulging self while disregarding others—and into this is caught every inferior one of us, every inferior portion of ourselves. This network of complicated evil, this spiritual hell, which catacombs our life with its intricate circles, is what Zola has made us see and feel in his terrible set of novels. ... It is salutary to be horrified and sickened when the horror and the sickness make one look around, pause, and reflect.[4]

Equally important in establishing the date of this phase of the transition is the fact that an article by Arthur Waugh in the first issue of *The Yellow Book*, July, 1894, was concerned with protesting at the overenthusiasm for realism which English writers were showing. The acceptance of realism was, then, *un fait accompli*. The new school of fiction, writes Mr. Waugh, "will now be full of the sap of life, strong, robust, and muscular. It will hurry us out into the fields, will show us the coarser passions of the farm hand; at any expense it will paint the life it finds around it; it will at least be consonant with the want of taste which is falsely believed to be contemporary. We get a realistic fiction abroad and we begin to copy it at home." Such writing, Mr. Waugh states, is not "the sort of literature that will survive the trouble of the ages."[5]

Hubert Crackanthorpe, however, feels the victory secured, and in his reply to Waugh in the next issue of *The Yellow Book*

4 *Contemporary Review*, February, 1893.
5 "Reticence in Literature," *The Yellow Book*, July, 1894.

does not feel called upon to enter into the enthusiasms and extravagances of his fellow realists. "Time flits quickly in this hurried age of ours," he says, "and the opposition to the renascence of fiction as a conscious interpretation of life is not what it was; its opponents are not the men they were. It is not long since a publisher was sent to prison for issuing English translations of celebrated specimens of French realism; yet, only the other day we vied in doing honor to the chief figurehead of that tendency across the channel[6] and there was heard only the belated protests of a few worthy individuals inadequately equipped with the jaunty courage of second-hand knowledge." No one has to fight single-handed in the little bouts with the puritans, he continues; "heroism is at a discount; Mrs. Grundy is becoming mythological; a crowd of unsuspected supporters collects from all sides, and the deadly conflict of which we have been warned becomes but an interesting skirmish. Books are published, stories are printed in old-fashioned reviews which would never have been tolerated a few years ago."

As supporting the opinion that a change in the English attitude toward fiction had taken place, Crackanthorpe brings the testimony of Edmund Goose to bear.[7] "A public which has eaten of the apple of knowledge," he quotes Mr. Gosse as saying, "will no longer be satisfied with marionettes. . . . Whatever comes next, we cannot return in serious novels to the impossibilities of the old well-made plot, to the children changed at nurse, to the Madonna heroine and the God-like hero, to the impossible virtues and the melodramatic vices. In the future even those who sneer at realism and misinterpret it most wilfully will be obliged to put their productions more in accord with veritable experience. . . . There will still be novel-writers who address the gallery and who will keep up the gaudy old

[6] Referring to Zola's visit to England commencing September 20, 1893, in response to an invitation of the Institute of Journalists. The Institute of Journalists had invited the officials of various organizations, and Zola's invitation was addressed to him as *Président de la Société des Gens de Lettres.*

[7] "Reply to Waugh," *The Yellow Book,* October, 1894. The quotation from Edmund Gosse is taken from "Limits of Realism in Fiction," one of the essays included in *Questions at Issue,* 1893.

conventions . . . but they will no longer sign themselves George Sand or Charles Dickens."

To say that by 1894 the controversy was finally decided in favor of the realists would, however, be an exaggeration. Arnold Bennett wrote as late as 1917 that the orientation of English taste toward realism was still going on and that the transition of the English novel was not yet accomplished.[8] Above all, it would be unwise to suggest that the case for Zola had ever been won in England. Nevertheless, active hostility was replaced in some quarters by tolerance, in others by curiosity, and in others by sympathetic understanding. By 1896 the *Fortnightly* was willing to print an article favorable to Zola as well as one analyzing sympathetically the work of Edmond de Goncourt. "Now that the first burst of rage which greeted a new departure in literary treatment has somewhat died down," wrote R. E. S. Hart, "there may be more chance of modifying the harsh judgment for which the author [Zola] may have been as guilty as his critics in taking it." Mr. Hart does not consider it necessary to plead for Zola: "of the greatness and fertility of his genius there can be no doubt." He considers Zola's work as a whole, its scope, its tendency, its revelations; and Zola's social attitude he deduces from the explanations of Dr. Pascal—man is still in bondage but possesses the possibilities for his own release.[9]

Yetta Blaze de Bury, writing on the Goncourts for the same magazine, stresses the historical quality of their writing and their "restitutive curiosity" which makes them akin to Flaubert and Turgenev, "the polar bears of genius." Miss de Bury sees the Goncourts also as students of individual human specimens. Of *Germinie Lacerteux* she writes:

> It is the coexistence in this soul of morally morbid elements with others that are sound, the absence of contagion between the good and the bad, the inward flourishing together of poisonous plants with other perennial ones; it is the juxtaposition in the same ground of decomposition and vigor, of purulence and purity, which makes this study so

---

8 *Books and Persons,* 6.
9 "Zola's Philosophy of Life," *Fortnightly Review,* August 1, 1896.

singular and yet, we dare to say, so like truth.[10] [There is nothing of the controversy here.]

But although the active controversy was ended by 1896, the popular acceptance of French naturalistic art in England cannot, after all, be said to have taken place. Only a relatively small group of literati really accepted it; undiluted naturalism has never been congenial to the Anglo-Saxon temperament. Nevertheless, the facts presented here indicate that a change in critical opinion took place, and we may now survey the situation and mark the stages of the change. To begin with, the success which the first naturalistic translations enjoyed was largely due to their frankness and unconventionality. Consequently the dominant note in the protest before 1891—both popular and critical—was that of indignation at the crudities of the foreign work. There was, however, as has been noted, a strong objection on the part of the more philosophical Victorians to the mechanistic and fatalistic tendencies of the French naturalistic novel, and it is with this objection that we are here concerned. For although during the years 1890–93 there appeared in England no defender of naturalistic principles, the satirical criticisms of the sentimental and conventional tendencies in the English novel, which we have noted, were written by those who had accepted the lesson of the French fiction. Constructively the criticism was directed toward the creation of an English novel "more nearly in accord with veritable experience," a novel which would "show the complicated mechanism of the human heart" and be "a conscious interpretation of life." Beginning in 1893 we note a change in the attitude toward the tendencies of the foreign fiction and a more sympathetic feeling toward Zola shown in important reviews; we see Zola welcomed to England by the press as well as by English authors; we note the appearance of a new type of short story by English disciples of Maupassant; we witness the confident statements of young authors that a new attitude prevails in England with regard to fiction, and it

[10] "Edmond de Goncourt," *Fortnightly Review,* September 1, 1896.

seems not illogical to infer that a considerable number of Englishmen had undergone a change of heart.

Of course it may be suggested that, after French realism ceased to hold the public interest as a subject for controversy, indifference, and therefore tolerance, resulted. But facts indicate otherwise. George Moore became famous with the publication of *Esther Waters* in 1894—although *A Mummer's Wife* (1885), a much better novel, got only moderate notice when published. Richard Whiteing's *No. 5 John Street*, which is naturalistic in spirit and subject matter, was the center of public interest in 1895; and Percy White's *Corruption* (1895), Arthur Morrison's *A Child of the Jago* (1896), and Somerset Maugham's *Liza of Lambeth* (1897)—all naturalistic novels—were good sellers. Moreover, studies of marital incompatibility, for which the French novel supplied the technique as well as the demand, vied with the romantic novels of adventure for popularity between the years 1895 and 1900. Even these romantic novels, we learn from *The Sketch* of May 24, 1899, were not immune to the prevalent realistic influence, for they "stick fast to some hard facts and treat human nature of past epochs very much as if it belonged to the end of the nineteenth century." Finally, if further proof be needed, the Publishers' Catalogue will show that the demand for French naturalistic translations continued, if not increased, throughout the nineties.[11]

The realistic controversy died down, as we see, after a partial victory had been won for the principle of realism. But the victory secured for English realists no new license of expression in the matter of sex treatment. One result of the Vizetelly trial, as W. L. George tells us, was to make English publishers very timorous in accepting work which dealt too intimately with carnal relationships. When unconventional situations were treated, "a thick veil of ellipse and metaphor" was therefore necessary.[12] Nevertheless, in its more general aspects the influence of French naturalism exercised for a

[11] See also Frierson, *L'Influence du naturalisme français*.
[12] *Literary Chapters* (Boston, Little, Brown & Co., 1918), 127.

period of ten years before 1893 was of considerable importance. It created in England new standards of critical judgment; it focused attention upon the moral and social framework of contemporary society; it stimulated interest in a critical examination of human nature and suggested a wide and fresh range of human experience as subject for investigation.

~§ IV §~

THE MAUPASSANT SCHOOL
IN ENGLAND

BEFORE the eighteen-nineties the short story had not been taken seriously in England. George Sainstbury wrote late in 1887, "We are curiously behindhand in the short-story, or nouvelle properly so called, which is not a märchen, or a burlesque, or a tale of terror." The new short story appeared almost with suddenness, therefore, and it flourished with vigor. During the decade, writes H. G. Wells, "Short stories broke out everywhere." Mr. Wells mentions a list of some twenty-five writers who followed various gods, and continues, "I may be succumbing to the infirmities of old age but I do not think that the present decade [1910–1920] can produce any parallel to this list." "There was a tendency," he adds, "to treat the short story as if it was as definable a form as the sonnet. . . . It was either Mr. Edward Garnett or Mr. George Moore in a violently anti-Kipling mood who invented the distinction between the short story and the anecdote. The short story was Maupassant; the anecdote was damnable. It was quite an infernal comment in its way because it permitted of no defense."[1]

To concern ourselves with the twenty-five authors mentioned by Mr. Wells would not be especially useful. They imitated at random and made experiments of their own. Their writings, taken as a whole, show no single tendency other than that of variated effulgence. But the tendency to define the

[1] *The Country of the Blind* (Edinburgh, Nelson & Sons, Ltd., 1911), "Introduction."

story form, of which Mr. Wells speaks, is important. It aids us in sifting out from the heterogenous literary products of the time those which are significant in literary history. We select the Maupassant school because it was dominant, and because it presents a sharp deviation from the English tradition.

We can best emphasize this deviation, perhaps, by saying that the tendency of the English tradition was to stress what is "noble" in man's nature; to entertain while upholding the conventional code of social and moral values; and to divert the mind by accounts of unusual and bizarre happenings. Against such a background the attempt of the Maupassant school to show, in a spirit of artistic compassion freed from moral bias, the unromantic facts of life presents a sharp contrast. A new moral conception, we see, is present—a questioning, agnostic attitude; a different quality of spirit prevails—a comprehending charity. "In art," wrote Flaubert, "neither to provoke laughter nor tears nor lust nor rage seems to me to be the highest and most difficult object, but to act after nature's own fashion—that is, to set musing." This conception, we see, is dominant in the "episodic" short story of the nineties. The fiction of contemplation, of irony, and of compassion makes its appearance.

The new school followed the lead of Maupassant in narrating significant episodes of human life and conduct. No conventional idealization, no class distinctions, no heroes, no heroines, no villains, no Nemesis, no spiritual consolations are provided in the grim and pathetic revelations of contemporary tragedy which the short-story writers of the nineties provided. We find in their accounts a stern recognition of the cruelty, irrationality, and discord in life. The tragedy they present is that of human limitations. It is unrelieved and seems well-nigh unrelievable. No escape is provided, no sentimental balderdash, no moral tag. The gods on Mount Olympus have received word that something is amiss and have come down to look into the heart of things. Their decision is not altogether in man's favor, for he is warped by circumstance and the customs of society, driven on by irrational forces within him, shortsighted, often blind. And woman—she too is incompetent. The gods remain a little puzzled, a little sad. The human heart, they find, has lost its sacred fire.

Five volumes of short stories written in the Maupassant manner appeared simultaneously in 1893: *Wreckage*, by Hubert Crackanthorpe; *Mlle Miss*, by Henry Harland; *Keynotes*, by "George Egerton;" *Wreckers and Methodists*, by H. D. Lowry; and *Renunciations*, by Frederic Wedmore. Some of the titles, it will be noted, are significant. In 1894 *Discords*, by George Egerton, and *Tales of Mean Streets*, by Arthur Morrison, were published. 1895 is an important year, for during it there came from the press *Sentimental Studies*, by Crackanthorpe; *Episodes*, by G. S. Street; *Monochromes*, by Ella D'Arcy; *Dilemmas*, by Ernest Dowson; *English Episodes*, by Wedmore; *Grey Roses*, by Harland; *Women's Tragedies*, by Lowry; and *Celibates*, by George Moore. From 1896 to 1898 there appeared *Modern Instances*, by Ella D'Arcy; *Last Studies*, by Crackanthorpe; and *Of Necessity*, by H. M. Gilbert.

The fact that Englishmen cultivated by 1895 a temper of mind sympathetic to the naturalistic short story might be taken to indicate that the breakup of Victorianism had occurred. Such a conclusion as applied to the prevalent attitude toward fiction would, however, be erroneous. For Victorianism, like Puritanism, did not really break up; it merely became dispossessed of control. The public attitude toward fiction, the most popular of literary forms, would be slow to change. All we can deduce with honesty from the prevalence of a new attitude among the literati is that Victorianism as a literary force was well on the road to being supplanted. It is needful to specify that the new attitude was prevalent chiefly among the literati for we can hardly say that the writings of the Maupassant school attained a popular success in England. That they attained any success at all is the remarkable fact, for they are not for popular consumption; they are too nearly food for the gods.

The naturalistic short story flourished in England for only a few years—from '93 to '98. Various reasons for its decline might be indicated, but it seems probable that the authors found the financial returns disproportionate to the earnestness of their endeavors.

After *Discords*, George Egerton wrote in a lighter, less critical spirit. Morrison turned to detective stories and picturesque narrative. Lowry composed romances. Street returned to the essay. Harland, Hardy, and George Moore reverted to the novel. Moreover Dowson died and Crackanthorpe committed suicide. The Maupassant school flourished and then ceased to be. It remains in literary history as a distinctive phenomenon in a troubled decade and credits the nineties with having fostered a short story of artistic excellence unapproached in previous or subsequent English literature.

In a moment of enthusiasm George Moore once wrote, "Flaubert, Zola, Daudet, Goncourt, Bourget, Maupassant and Henry James have only taken and developed that part of Balzac which superficially they represent." A similar statement, with certain qualifications, may be made of the English followers of Maupassant. Lowry noted Maupassant's treatment of the peasants of Normandy and set himself to present incidents in the life of the Cornwall villagers. George Egerton took advantage of the elastic structure of Maupassant's *nouvelles* to reveal a personal attitude toward life quite similar to that of the Frenchman. Henry Harland recounted the observations of a detached and philosophic man of the world. G. S. Street indulged in satirical and ironic presentations of happenings in the upper social circles. Morrison concerned himself with the homely human animals whose lives are stunted by poverty. Dowson delineated in unromantic vein the affairs of the heart, while Ella D'Arcy and Henry James concerned themselves with temperamental reactions.

But Crackanthorpe alone can be said to have followed Maupassant in his various modes. His books are rightly entitled studies; they are studies of temperament, of sentiment, of artistic endeavor, of want, of suicide, of marital incompatibility and mortal frailty. They reveal the human heart as seen through the eyes of a tender but very cynical saint. The revelations are distinctive for the insistent material detail by which the presentation is vivified. But Crackanthorpe is not essentially the portrayer of externalities. He shows with deft delicacy the spider's web of sentiment that enmeshes the human soul. One would judge from reading his writings that circumstance determines only the least significant phases of existence. What appear to him significant are the affections, the aspirations, the sympathies, and the illogical emotional reactions which furnish the stimulus for some strange or striking act. In his writings Crackanthorpe reveals himself as possessed of a sensitive yet virile nature, given at times to chivalric as well as morbid moods.

... A well-born young writer and his wife drift apart. The wife finds no sympathy and understanding in the artistic circles where her husband moves. Her conservative nature provides no stimulus for his endeavors, and she does not comprehend the pain and sorrow that fill his soul at times; nor does she understand the consequent bohemian reaction. She keeps her old friends and her old ways while feeling a longing for the husband who can never be really hers. And he, oppressed by his wife's goodness and simple faith, takes a perverse pleasure in a liaison with the daring and gifted wife of a friend. But perversity alone is not responsible, for the free cameraderie, the consciousness of being above sin and guilt, makes of the liaison something strangely more sacred than the sentimental sanctity of more mundane affections. And in the daring and unconventionality of the woman the man is conscious of a lofty scorn which matches his own and which deifies her in a way. But mortal ears become irritably conscious of the celestial strains. The liaison is discovered and the discord of threatened divorce proceedings drowns out all other notes. The husband insists upon exposure, and the torrent of public vituperation is threatening those who sought an escape above the clouds... On a bridge of the Seine the writer seats himself to consider. He, strongest of mortals and hating the weakness of the rest, scorns all easy escapes. But she whom he reveres must not be tarnished, for the gold would then become as gilt and the luster of the sun would pass away. In the fullness of his resolve a fantastic, quixotic idea dawns upon him. Where before he had seen weakness he now saw strength. Suicide would cast a pall upon babbling tongues. The sanctity of her whom he loved would be respected since it could inspire sacrifice. Thoughtfully, bitterly, he filled his pockets with rocks, and then dived awkwardly into the Seine...

This is a true Crackanthorpe story. It is an imaginative account, written in the author's idiom, and concluding with the probable circumstances of his death at the age of thirty-one.

The story reveals a nature far from simple and a spirit out of tune with his times. "Bertie" Crackanthorpe, a slim and sensitive youth, was expelled from Cambridge during his first year for some boyish prank. Thereupon he went to France and joined a traveling circus as a bareback rider. Returning eventually to England and the patronage of his family, he began to write stories distinctive for their impersonality and unconcern with conventional values. He married a girl of his own station, but the relationship proved stifling to his spirit, and his wife proved unstable. In Crackanthorpe's stories women are shown to be clinging creatures who arouse aversion in man because of their unwillingness to aid him in fulfilling his aspirations. The foremost of Maupassant's disciples in England, he lived a life of revolt which fittingly terminated in the chivalric gesture of his death.

But though revolt was the dominant factor in Crackanthorpe's life, it was not a prominent feature in his writings. For Crackanthorpe as naturalistic artist would free himself from all personal sympathies. Like one of his characters, he would "walk abroad among London's grim unrest, savouring each fragile modulation of its dusky pageantry." He would show the contradictory forces and sentiments in man's nature, the crude and resistless logic of the emotions, the enslaving mystery of an ideal.

The precision and concentration of Crackanthorpe's phrasing deserves mention, for in these qualities, perhaps, he surpasses all previous writers of English fiction. He can draw a character in a line. A woman is troubled and "with doses of self-pity she assuaged her irresolution"; another possesses "that intelligent superciliousness of demeanor which passes for obvious superiority." Descriptive passages, moreover, reveal an intent perception enlivened by an appreciative sympathy. In *Vignettes, A Miniature Journal of Whim and Sentiment*, a landscape in Normandy is described:

A mauve sky, all subtle; a discreet rusticity, daintily modern, femininely delicate; a whole finikin arrangement of trim trees, of rectangular orchards, of tiny, spruce houses, with white shutters demurely closed. Here and there a prim farmyard, a squat church spire; and bloused peasants jogging behind rotund white horses, along a straight and gleaming road. In all the landscape no trace of the slovenly profusion of the picturesque; but rather a distinguished reticence of detail, fresh, coquettish, almost dapper.

The only revolt to be noted in Crackanthorpe's writings is that against the smug and commonplace. But with "George Egerton" (Mrs. Golding Bright) (Mary Chevalita) the case is different. Her genius lies in delineating with great vitality of style the temperamental reactions of an emotional and intelligent woman—a woman who can be none other than the impersonation of the author. George Egerton enthroned passion in English literature, and no English writer before the twentieth century treated the relationship between the sexes with greater freedom. Her attitude toward her unintelligent sisters is distinctly critical, and her attitude toward life is eminently that of the French naturalists. A poet in "The Regeneration of Two" speaks it for her:

I see a great crowd of human beings. Take all these men, male and female, fashion them into one colossal man, study him, and what will you find? Tainted blood; a brain with a thousand parasites sucking at its base and warping it, a heart robbed of all healthy feelings by false conceptions, bad conscience, a futile code of morality—a code that makes the natural workings of sex a vile thing to be ashamed of ... a code that demands the sacrifice of thousands of female victims as the cost of its maintenance, that has filled the universe with an unclean conception of things, a prurient idea of purity—making man a great sick man. Divide him into units again, drop them back into their proper places and look down at them; a hungry, ignorant crowd swarming like flies over a dust-heap for enough to keep them alive for the day.... And I see factory doors open and troops of men and women and children, apologies for human beings, narrow-chested, with the pallor of lead-poisoning in their haggard faces troop out of them; and as they laugh wearily their teeth shake loosely in their blue-white gums, and they are too tired to wash the poison off their hands before their scanty meals. And I said to myself, "Salvation lies with the women and the new race they are to mother." I sought out women I had heard of whose names were identified with advancement; and I found them no whit less eager to employ every seduction at their command to win men over to their particular narrow cause than their frivolous sister to keep them at her beck and call. And she who flaunted the white banner of purity calculated the cut of her evening frock, and enticed men to walk under her banner by the whiteness of her breast. And underneath it all I saw vanity, the old insatiable love of power that is the breath of most women's nostrils, or the psychological necessity of excitement that belongs to the wavering cycle of her being.

George Egerton was in revolt against the restraints of Victorianism. A pagan herself, she glorified the "new woman," freed from the trammels of the past, who fulfilled her own nature. Her pronouncements, indeed, occasioned the late Victorians some of their most severe shocks. "A woman does not care a fig for a love as deep as the dead sea and as silent," says a feminine character in "A Cross Line." "She wants something that tells her it in little waves at a time. It isn't the love, you know, it's the being loved; it isn't really the man, it's his loving!"

55

But the New Woman, George Egerton knew, was as yet a figment of the imagination. And so the idealized creature of *Keynotes* was replaced in *Discords* by her frail and incompetent sister.

Although the English followers of Maupassant were successful in writing *nouvelles* revealing unexplored regions of life, they do not all bear comparison with him. H. D. Lowry, for one, uncovered new material in the life of the Cornwall villagers, but he omitted to give point to his accounts by suggestions of universality. Lowry trusted a little too blindly in the interest of the facts of life. Nevertheless his stories present a significant departure from previous English fiction by their realistic treatment of villagers and rustics. Here, of course, Lowry touches the domain of Thomas Hardy. But Hardy's temperament makes him essentially an imperfect interpreter of village life. The sober depths of his nature are not quickened to active response by the discordant clamor of rustic humor, and when he occasionally hints the presence of bright skies, it is only for the sake of ironic contrast. Moreover, in Hardy's writings the jarring brutalities of lowly speech are smoothed over by deft stylistic strokes; the tone is even and well modulated. But Lowry, a less poetic writer and a more careful realist, reproduces the homely and clamorous rhythms of the folk music.

"The Two Processions" is one of Lowry's more successful tragedies. In the village of Pentreath a woman has sinned. When it becomes known that her child has been born, the villagers, in gibing mood, start in a procession to her home. Leading the procession is a cart bearing a rude woodwork arrangement to represent a gallows. From the gallows hang the effigies of a man and a woman. Those who follow the cart blow horns or beat on tin pots and kettles. They intend to make a demonstration around the home of the sinning woman —formerly a village beauty—and then to burn the effigies. But the procession is brought to a halt. A cart approaches from the opposite direction bearing the dead body of the illegitimate child and that of the mother, who has drowned herself. The abashed villagers with uncovered heads watch the death cart pass.

The jarring notes of rustic intolerance and superstition, the weird fancies, the bouyant, rough humor, and the unromantic sorrows of the Cornwall villagers furnish Lowry with his subject matter. The spirit of portrayal is that of mixed amusement and irony, tinged at times with pathos.

Those who read Lowry's stories will be struck by their distinctiveness and strange nature. Equally distinctive, but not at all strange to us, are the stories of G. S. Street. They are characterized by urbanity and ironic playfulness, but the manner has become familiar to us of late years through the writings of Michael Arlen. Street is less consciously aristocratic than Arlen, and his view of the older generation is rather genial.

More cosmopolitan than Street, less aristocratic, and more human is Henry Harland. An American by nationality, but in temperament a bohemian, his place in literature is naturally with a well-defined English group to which he was closely bound. Harland is best known as the editor of *The Yellow Book*. His stories are written in a light and graceful style, more personal than that of Street, less compressed than that of Crackanthorpe. His sympathies are broad, and he associates himself only casually with the English upper class. In his unguarded affection for Paris there is to be noted something of the American refugee, but Harland's delicate analyses of the shades of sentiment in an atmosphere of moral diffidence are not akin to anything west of the Atlantic. We can detect, furthermore, in his writings an undeniable American taint of kindness which blends strangely well with gentle Gallic irony and a pathos born of continental fatalism.

Ella D'Arcy, another member of the *Yellow Book* group, deserves a place beside George Egerton as an exposer of the weaknesses of her sex. But with Miss D'Arcy the "New Woman" did not exist. She showed her sisters to be vain and tyrannical creatures, hardly entitled even to the liberty which they possessed. In "A Marriage," Chatterton, the husband, wonders why "the gentlest, the sweetest, the most docile girl in the world" should change after the wedding into a woman who bullies her husband and insults his friends. "Marriage," he muses, "is the metamorphosis of women—the Circe wand which changes all these smiling, gentle, tractable little girls into their true forms." And as he continues his reverie he falls into despair as "the wife's cold heart, her little cruelties, her little meannesses, all her narrowness, all her emptiness of mind rise before him."

Miss D'Arcy was not a prolific writer. Indeed it seems that criticism of her sex was her only vital literary motive. No suggestions of moral laxity, no protests at current habits of thoughts, are to be noted in her stories. Sometimes, as in "Poor Cousin Louis," she follows Balzac in his treatment of eccentricity. At other times she flees into the realm of pure fancy. Nevertheless her insistence upon the narrowness and triviality of feminine interests is of sufficient importance in the literary history of the nineties to attract our interest. The intimate and unromantic detail which characterized her presentations forecast the unsentimental analyses of late English realists.

Morrison is fully discussed in Chapter VI. *Tales of Mean Streets* is available in the Modern Library edition. H. M. Gilbert, however, has virtually been forgotten. The concision of style and sternness of manner in his writings closely approaches that of Crackanthorpe in his more serious moods. Gilbert is chiefly concerned with the manifestations of the religious spirit in the lower middle class, and he is distinctive for the objectivity of his treatment. The characters and environment are sketched with crude vitality; and with remorseless precision the author shows how temperament, circumstance, and environment combine to produce inevitable, and often tragic, results.

The English realists of the nineties, as we have seen, hardly attained the lofty equanimity and compassion which was the artistic ideal of Flaubert. It may, indeed, be questioned whether

Flaubert himself attained it permanently, for the Christlike sympathy with human incapacity which is shown in *Madame Bovary* was replaced in *Bouvard et Pécuchet* by a diabolic indictment of human *bêtises*. Similarly the Goncourts could write a *Sœur Philomène* but were unable in *Germinie Lacerteux* to conceal their well-known disgust with vulgarity. Zola was mastered by his strong critical intelligence, and he hated more than he loved. But Maupassant, Flaubert's disciple, most nearly of all the naturalists was able to contemplate dispassionately the varied forms of human error and to extend immeasurably the limitations of his own personal sympathies. In this respect his English followers were able to apprehend him only imperfectly. Crackanthorpe approached him in spirit as did Harland. But George Egerton, Lowry, Morrison, Ella D'Arcy, and Gilbert were often moved as much by the critical as by the compassionate spirit, and here they suggest Zola. Sometimes, however, the Maupassant ideal is present, and sentiments of a comprehending charity pervade the realms of decay.

❧ V ☙

GEORGE MOORE : NATURALIST

> I came into the world apparently with a nature
> like a smooth sheet of wax, bearing no impress
> but capable of receiving any, of being moulded
> into any shape.—GEORGE MOORE, *Confessions of
> a Young Man.*

THE avowal is not as damning as it sounds. George
Moore had a genius for making the imprints his very
own. He assimilated writers and literary movements.
And he wrote novels which, if not the best in the language,
are at least the best of their particular genre. There is nothing in these novels to mark them as distinctly "Moore" novels,
in the sense that one might speak of a "Zola" novel or a "Dickens" novel. They are all different. One will seem to be a Zola
novel written just after Zola read *Madame Bovary* (*A Mummer's Wife*); another is pure Goncourt (*Esther Waters*); another an early Huysmans of the second period (*A Mere Accident*); a story of half-volume length is first-class Turgenev
("Mildred Lawson," from *Celibates*). Altogether the tracing
of varied influences in his work is an exciting adventure.

There is much good writing throughout Moore's novels,
but often he does not appear to be more than half inspired.
Part of this is due, no doubt, to the limitations of the naturalistic form; part to the fact that his interest may not be evoked
at will. But often, as in *Mike Fletcher*, "Mildred Lawson," *The
Lake*, and in later fiction with a historic background, Moore's
writing is of a very high order. As a critic he is of especial
value in bringing a fresh and continental view to bear on
English writers.

George Moore : Naturalist

George Moore must be interpreted at leisure. Summaries appearing in literary histories and histories of the novel do not take into account the variety of excellence which he attempted, the concessions he made to English taste, and his consistent search to find the proper form for narrative expression.

As suggested in the Introduction, two major influences transformed the English novel: naturalism, which changed the current of English thought and expression; and "spiritualistic naturalism" as it appeared in Huysmans' writings and was later to affect England through *Jean Christophe*. George Moore was the English pioneer who first adopted both of these modes of narration and explored the possibilities of each. Under naturalism and the "experimental novel" we may loosely classify *A Modern Lover* (1883), *A Mummer's Wife* (1885), *A Drama in Muslin* (1886), *Vain Fortunes* (1889), *Esther Waters* (1894), and "Mildred Lawson," from *Celibates* (1895). Under "spiritualistic naturalism," or naturalism of the spirit, we may put *A Mere Accident* (1887), *Mike Fletcher* (1889), *Evelyn Innes* (1898), *Sister Teresa* (1901), and *The Lake* (1905). Books like *The Brook Kerith* (1916) and *Héloïse and Abélard* (1921) are properly historical novels, the first with a naturalistic bent, the second containing many reminders of Huysmans.

George Moore's literary development occurred chiefly in Paris. He came there, as he tells us in *The Confessions of a Young Man*, full of curiosity, full of admiration for Byron and Shelley, and consumed by a desire to know art in its every phase. He lived in Paris off and on for some sixteen years, talking much with artists and writers, and experimenting with life. He found that he had no talent for painting, but he awakened to successive literary discoveries. Balzac, whom he considered as probably the greatest writer of all times, was his most lasting enthusiasm; but his awakening to Zola's theories of fiction dominated all else for many years. We cannot do better than to consider Moore's own account in the *Confessions:*

61

One day as I was waiting for M. Duval, I took up the *Voltaire*. It contained an article by M. Zola. *Naturalisme, la verité, la science,* were repeated some half-a-dozen times. Hardly able to believe my eyes, I read that you should write with as little imagination as possible, that plot in a novel or in a play was illiterate and puerile, and that the art of M. Scribe was an art of strings and wires, etc. I rose up from break-fast, ordered my coffee, and stirred the sugar, a little dizzy, like one who has received a violent blow on the head. ... The reader who has followed me so far will remember the instant effect the word "Shelley" had upon me in childhood, and how it called into existence a train of feeling that illuminated the vicissitudes and passions of many years, until it was finally assimilated and became part of my being; the reader will also remember how the mere mention, at a certain mo-ment, of the word "France" awoke a vital impulse, even a sense of final ordination, and how the irrevocable message was obeyed, and how it led to the creation of a mental existence ... And now for a third time I experienced the pain and joy of a certain inward light. Naturalism, truth, the new art, above all the phrase, "the new art," impressed me as with a sudden sense of light. I was dazzled, and I vaguely under-stood that my "Roses of Midnight" were sterile eccentricities, dead flowers that could not be galvanized into any semblance of life, pas-sionless in all their passion. ... I bought up the back numbers of the *Voltaire,* and I looked forward to the weekly exposition of the new faith with febrile eagerness. The great zeal with which the new master continued his propaganda, and the marvelous way in which subjects the most diverse, passing events, political, social, religious, were caught up and turned into arguments for, or proof of the truth of naturalism astonished me wholly. The idea of a new art based upon science, in opposition to the art of the old world that was based upon imagina-tion, an art that would explain all things and embrace modern life in its entirety, in its endless ramifications, be, as it were, a new creed in a new civilization, filled me with wonder, and I stood dumb before the vastness of the conception, and the towering height of the ambition. In my fevered fancy I saw a new race of writers that would arise, and with the aid of the novel would continue to a more glorious and legiti-mate conclusion the work that the prophets had begun; and at each development of the theory of the new art and its universal applica-bility, my wonder increased and my admiration choked me.[1]

---

[1] *Confessions of a Young Man* (New York, Modern Library, 1917), Chapter VI.

When, therefore, George Moore was forced to return to England and supplement his income, it was but natural that he should proclaim himself the English apostle of the new French school.

A Modern Lover is a story of a young artist, only moderately talented, who rises to fame and fortune through the influence of women. Compared with Maupassant's subsequent creation, *Bel-Ami*, Moore's lover is rather colorless and passive. Still he is a naturalistic "central character" rather than a hero and he possesses a sufficient quantity of nonheroic qualities. He is an amoral artist who lives only for his art, his emotions, and his success. Moreover, the chief feminine character is a woman of quality, who, to the immense surprise of English readers, tells lies with the greatest ease and facility. Liaisons are quite discreetly handled, and all that the reader sees are handclasps and two furtive kisses. Yet the remarkable fact is that as early as 1883 a liaison does take place in an English novel between two fairly nice and eminently respectable people, and the participants suffer no harm. As regards narrative technique, there are regrettable coincidences in the novel but in the main the trend of the story is logical and sound.

We wonder today how anyone could possibly object to *A Modern Lover*. The depths of even late Victorian conservatism among novel readers is indicated by W. H. Mallock, who wrote in 1892:

> In the English fiction of today it is a universal rule that the men, and especially the women, with whom the reader is invited to sympathize, shall all stop short of one another at a certain point, whatever may be their dispositions or circumstances. It is also a rule equally universal that any grave transgression of the conventional moral code shall entail on its transgressors some appropriate punishment, or, at all events, that it shall not end in their happiness.[2]

George Moore, it seems, did offend these rules. Two ladies living in the country wrote to the director of circulating li-

---

[2] *A Human Document* (London, Chapman and Hall, 1912), 24–25.

braries that they disapproved of *A Modern Lover*. Consequently George Moore's three-volume work was withdrawn by Mr. Mudie from his list of approved writers.

Moore then persuaded Vizetelly and Company to publish *A Mummer's Wife* in a single volume. When this novel had reached its fourth edition he felt that he had gained sufficient prominence to become the critic of the Mudie-sponsored three-volume system, which put the author at the mercy of the circulating libraries. In *Literature at Nurse or Circulating Morals*, a pamphlet, he aimed a broadside at Mr. Mudie, arbiter of literary taste for the empire:

... Instead of being allowed to fight, with and against the thoughts and aspirations of men, literature is now rocked to sleep in the motherly arms of the librarian. That which he approves is fed with gold; that from which he turns the breast dies like a vagrant child; while in and out of his voluminous skirts run a motley and monstrous progeny, a callow, a whining, a puking breed of bastard bantlings, a race of Aztecs that disgrace the intelligence of the English nation. Into this nursery none can enter except in baby clothes; and the task of discriminating between a divided skirt and a pair of trousers is performed by the librarian. ... To analyze, you must have a subject; a religious or sensual passion is as necessary to a realistic novelist as a disease is to a physician. The dissection of a healthy subject would not, as a rule, prove interesting, and if the right to probe and comment on humanity's failings be granted, what becomes of the pretty schoolroom with its piano tinkling away at the "Maiden's Prayer," and the water-color drawings representing mill-wheels and Welsh Castles? ... Let us renounce the effort to reconcile these two irreconcilable things—literature and young girls. ... And that the nineteenth century should possess a literature characteristic of its nervous, passionate life, I hold is as desirable, and would be as far-reaching in its effects, as the biggest franchise bill ever framed. ... When a young girl is seduced through the influence of a novel, it is by a romantic story, the action of which is laid outside the limits of her experience. A pair of lovers—such as Paul and Virginia—separated by a cruel fate, whose loves are apparently nothing but a long cry of yearning and fidelity, who seem to live, as it were, independent of the struggle for life, is the book that more often than any other leads to sin; it teaches the reader to look for a false ideal, and gives her—for men have ceased to read novels in England —erroneous and superficial notions of the value of life and love.

We note that Moore concludes his able indictment with a moral simper. The one writer of the time who might have been consistently an exponent of superior art-forms in the novel thus weakens his position. But the attempt to palliate, to soften the effect of his work, occurs more than once. In *Spring Days* omniscience avows: "A man's struggles in the web of a vile love are as pitiful as those of a fly in the meshes of a spider."[3] Moore tried to make *Evelyn Innes* palatable by calling it "a love story, the first that has appeared in the English language." He lightened the tone of his work when he composed *A Drama in Muslin*. He made a heroine of Esther Waters. What is the explanation? It is obviously Moore's desire to succeed as a novelist, of which he tells us fully in the *Confessions:*

> I boldly confess that I then desired notoriety. I walked the streets mad; I turned upon myself like a tiger. "Am I going to fail again as I have failed before?" I asked myself. "Will my novel prove as abortive as my paintings, my poetry, my journalism?" I looked back upon my life. "Would it be the same to the end?" I asked myself a thousand times by day and a thousand times by night. We all want notoriety, our desire for notoriety is hideous if you will, but it is less hideous when it is proclaimed from a brazen tongue than when it hides its head in the cant of human humanitarianism.[4]

Not only this, but Moore tells us in six glowing pages of his attempt to force a duel with a young lord for the sake of the notoriety that would result. The frankness of his confessions makes some atonement. Moore was at least honest with himself.

Let us continue with the naturalistic novels. *A Mummer's Wife* is an excellent piece of work, of far more distinction than the dull *Esther Waters* that later caught the public's attention. The story is that of a woman who abandons her invalid husband in order to follow her lover, the director of an Opera-

---

3 *Spring Days* (London, Vizetelly & Co., 1888), 361–62.

4 Modern Library edition, 216. (We are imagining, of course, that in this and the following paragraphs Moore is speaking through his impersonation.)

Bouffe company. She partakes of the gay life of the traveling entertainers, falls under the influence of drink, and later descends to debauchery and poverty.

Kate's literary loves are much like those of Emma Bovary, and not unlike those of the Victorians. Moore mentions a novel that pleased Kate in particular:

It concerned a beautiful young woman with a lovely oval face, who was married to a very tiresome country doctor. This lady was in the habit of reading Byron and Shelley in a rich, sweet-scented meadow, down by the river, which flowed dreamily through smiling pasturelands adorned by spreading trees. But this meadow belonged to a squire, a young man with grand, broad shoulders, who day after day used to watch these readings by the river without venturing to address a word to the fair trespasser. One day, however, he was startled by a shriek: in her poetical dreamings the lady had slipped into the water. A moment sufficed to tear off his coat, and as he swam like a waterdog he had no difficulty in rescuing her. Of course after this adventure he had to call and inquire, and from henceforth his visits grew more and more frequent, and by a strange coincidence, he used to come riding up to the hall-door when the husband was away curing the ills of the country-folk. Hours were passed under the trees by the river, he pleading his cause, and she refusing to leave poor Arthur, till at last the squire gave up the pursuit and went to foreign parts, where he waited thirty years, until he heard Arthur was dead. And then he came back with a light heart to his first and only love, who had never ceased to think of him, and lived with her happily for ever afterwards.

Kate's mother-in-law disapproves of books because they cause "such a sighing after richness and pleasure," but Kate has little else to sustain her in the dreary days of her marriage. Nevertheless Kate is a good and devoted wife to the husband whom she does not love.

George Moore's thesis is that too radical a change of living conditions is likely to produce disastrous effects. As he explains it, "the life that up to seven-and-twenty knew no excitement, no change of thought or place, now knows neither rest nor peace." The foreword of the novel was taken from Duruy's *L'Introduction Générale à l'Histoire de France*:

"Change the surroundings in which a man lives and in two or three generations you will have changed his physical constitution, his habits of life, and a goodly number of his ideas."

At this stage of his writings, George Moore was an out-and-out disciple of Zola. In the preface to the English edition of *Pot-Bouille* (*Piping Hot*), which appeared in the same year as *A Mummer's Wife*, he writes:

> Emile Zola is to me a great epic poet, and he may be, I think, not inappropriately termed the Homer of modern life. For he, more than any other writer, it seems, possesses the power of seeing a subject as a whole, can divest it at will of all side issues, can seize with a firm, logical comprehension on the main lines of its construction, and that without losing sight of the remotest cause or the furthest consequences of its existence. He has alone conceived and constructed the framework of a complex civilization like ours, in all of its worse ramifications.

Like Zola, George Moore can give us the atmosphere and feeling of a human enterprise. The world of traveling entertainers in *A Mummer's Wife* becomes a separate and distinct world of its own with its own laws and customs. The novel is the happy result of note-taking, for to prepare himself for writing this book Moore spent several weeks traveling with a group of actors. The world of artists was well enough handled in *A Modern Lover*, but it is nowhere comparable to the world of the Opera-Bouffé company. A certain genius is further shown in the portrayal of Dick Lennox, director of the company. He is a dynamic character, virile, devoid of scruples, but humanly likable. He marries Kate eventually but feels no particular responsibility for her. George Moore has no especial talent for creating vital characters. Dick Lennox is, like Mike Fletcher, one of the exceptions.

A Drama in Muslin is a different kind of writing. Moore was determined to become popular and to force the circulating libraries to use his books. So he would write something in the vein of Jane Austen, and he would arrange for serial publication in a newspaper. The husband-hunt in a Dublin castle atmosphere was the theme he now selected. Documentation would be a simple matter since, as an Irish landlord and a bachelor, he had an entree; and his naturalistic interests might be centered upon the analysis of varied universal types of young womanhood. Moreover, in the structure of the novel which he envisaged there would be opportunity for social criticism directed against the uncultivated aristocracy; against the effect of the Catholic religion upon the rich, who accepted it as a form, and the poor, who groveled under its mysteries; against social displays; and against the ugliness of an ill-planned social order.

Like the novels of Jane Austen, *A Drama in Muslin* is not altogether a satire. Moore is fairly well pleased with his bevy of young ladies, and he permits them a considerable amount of lively, casual chatter as well as some love-making. But, as Stuart Sherman points out, the destiny of each young lady is carefully linked with her physical equipment:

> From Alice Barton's "thin arms and straight hips and shoulders" Mr. Moore proves her "natural powerlessness to do aught but live up to the practical rectitudes of life, as she conceived them to exist"; and accordingly Alice is married to a prosaic doctor, and lives a life of dull British respectability. The "amorous plentitude" of arm and bosom in her sister Olive and her extremeties flowing into "chaste slenderness" mark her out for vapid and futile pursuit of a titled husband. May Gould is a round, soft-limbed girl: "the soft, the melting, the almost fluid eyes, the bosom large and just a bit falling, the full lips, the absence of any marked point or line, the rolling roundness of every part of the body announced a want of fixed principle, and a somewhat gross and sensual temperament." May gives and takes pleasure as opportunity offers, and fares as prosperously as any of her friends. Cecelia, having a deformed body, necessarily conceives of life as a "libidinous monster crouching in a cave, with red jaws dripping with foul spume." She abhors equally Alice's honest marriage and May's *liaisons:* "It is the same thing; one seeks a husband, another gratifies herself with a lover. It is the same thing. Where's the difference. It is animal passion all the same."[5]

[5] *On Contemporary Literature* (New York, Henry Holt and Co., 1917), 138.

Since his theme is not a tragic one, Moore is ever alive to life's little ironies. Of the Dublin debutantes who have been passed over the first season he writes:

> Still they must fight on to the last, there is no going back—There is nothing for them to go back to. There is no hope in life for them but the vague hope of a husband. So they keep on to the last, becoming gradually more spiteful and puerile, their ideas of life and things growing gradually narrower, until, in their thirty-fifth or fortieth year, they fall into the autumn heaps, to lie there forgotten or be blown hither and thither by every wind that blows—poor old women who have never lived at all.

A particular advance of George Moore's handling of descriptive effects is to be noted in this novel. Sometimes he follows Zola as he did before. Of a castle ball he writes:

> An hour passed: perspiration had begun to loosen the work of the curling irons; dust had thickened the voices, but the joy of existence was in every head and limb.

The change which now appears is that he achieves the "brilliant adjectival effects" which he admired in the works of the Goncourts, and, later, in the writings of Huysmans. It is his first release from the sober naturalistic formula which he had formerly prescribed for himself. Consider his description of the manufacturing district of Northwood:

> Sharp as the teeth of a double saw were the interminable gables, and not a ray of light glinted against the black windows. So black was everything that even the spire of the church remained a silhouette in the liquid sunlight that was poured as out of a diamond vase from the long pale space of sky which rose behind the hills of western Cozney.

Huysmans is more definitely invoked in describing the atmosphere of Dublin:

> The Dublin streets stare the vacant and helpless stare of a beggar selling matches on the doorstep. And the feeble cries for amusement are those of the child beneath the shawl for the red gleam of a passing soldier's coat. On either side there is a bawling ignorance of plaintive decay. Look at the houses! Like crones in borrowed bonnets some are

fashionable with flowers in the rotting window-frames—others languish in silly cheerfulness like women living on the proceeds of a pawnshop; others—those with the brass plates on the doors—are evil smelling as the prescriptions of the threadbare doctor, bald as the bill of costs of the servile attorney. And the souls of Dubliners blend and harmonize with their conatural surroundings.

What may we finally say of *A Drama in Muslin?* On the whole it is somewhat important. It is probably the first "impersonal" social study that appeared in English fiction. And all of its material is native. In this regard it contrasts with *A Modern Lover* and *A Mummer's Wife,* which, with certain exceptions, show continental characters in an English setting. But *A Drama in Muslin* is a native naturalistic study in a lighter mode.

Spring Days and *Vain Fortunes* we may consider as distinctly minor works. *Spring Days* concerns itself with the loves of the son and three daughters of a rich distiller. The distiller is much preoccupied with seeing that the marriages of his children do not result in draining his private fortune. As Moore describes his effort, he intended to write "the tale of a city merchant who is worried about his daughters—a sort of comic King Lear."[6] He also intended to "recreate Jane Austen's method"[7] and to write a book suitable for serial publication in *The Evening News.* The novel taxes the reader's credulity and it exposes Moore's weakness as a writer of love stories. As the story progresses, attention is centered on a romantic and ineffectual artist, Frank, who loves one of the distiller's daughters, Maggie. But Frank is a vain creature who poses with pistols and daggers when Maggie will not have him, and he even attempts suicide. Later, after the two are engaged, Frank is easily offended, and a sentimental, protective love for a barmaid overpowers him. He is about to get reconciled to the distiller's daughter when the yearning for the barmaid becomes too strong to resist.

[6] Joseph Hone, *The Life of George Moore* (New York, The Macmillan Co., 1936), 145.
[7] *Ibid.,* 148.

Spring Days was badly received. A writer for *The Academy* declared it was the worst novel ever written. Moore's inability to judge his own work is shown by the fact that he persisted in saying for a time that the novel "is the best thing I have ever done."[8]

Vain Fortunes is about a struggling dramatist whose adopted daughter is in love with him. Wedded to his work, he is hardly conscious of the girl's love, only knowing that she is jealous of his interest in his work. He inherits a fortune and marries his housekeeper, who is his critic. The adopted daughter commits suicide.

Here are an inherited fortune and a suicide—not the best material for a naturalistic study. It was a hasty work, written in the winter of 1890–91 and destined for serial publication in the *Lady's Pictorial*. We recognize the Strindberg theme. The novel is earnest but mild. The significance of the novel is that it begins a new phase. The evenness of tone and the psychological preoccupation of *Vain Fortunes* is continued in an intensified form in "Mildred Lawson," the half-novel which appeared in *Celibates*. Moore had now discarded Zola and the more typical naturalists. In this work he is little concerned with milieu and determinism; he is bent upon a psychological portrayal of a subclassification of the human species. Turgenev obviously comes to mind, especially since Turgenev describes Mildred Lawson's type much better than does George Moore:

> Valentina Mikalovina was clever, not ill-natured ... rather good-natured on the whole, fundamentally cold and indifferent ... and she could not tolerate the thought of anyone remaining indifferent to her. She was full of that charm which is peculiar to egoists; in that charm lies no poetry or true sensibility, but there is softness, there is sympathy, there is tenderness. Only these charming egoists must not be thwarted; they are fond of their power and will not tolerate independence in others. Women like Valentina excite and work upon inexperienced and passionate natures; for themselves they like regularity

---

[8] *Ibid.*

and peaceful life. Virtue comes easy to them; they are unmoved, but the constant desire to sway, to attract, and to please lends them mobility and brilliance. Their will is strong, and their very fascination depends in part upon this very strength of will. Hard it is for a man to hold his ground when for an instant gleams of secret softness pass unconsciously, as it were, over a bright pure creature like this; he waits expecting that the time is coming and now the ice will melt; but the clear ice only reflects the play of the light, it does not melt, and never will he see its brightness troubled! ... Flirtation cost Valentina little; she was well aware that there was no danger for her and never would be.[9]

Mildred breaks with her fiancé and leaves the country house of her brother in order to find wider fields to conquer. We gather that she is beautiful and intelligent. She has an independent income. First she studies art in London and permits a young artist to fall in love with her. But she does not respond to his love and goes to Paris. Here she becomes bored and finally discouraged. Consequently she joins two feminine friends who are painting in the provinces, and, feeling the need of a conquest to appease her soul, succeeds in attracting the lover of one of her friends. But, the conquest having been made, she wearies of it and cultivates a French family of high social station. She goes with this family to Paris and is launched into society. She must create a sensation wherever she is, and she is not at all above lies and exaggerations.

On the advice of her French friends, Mildred makes bad investments and loses her fortune. Realizing that she has been deceived, she returns home to her brother. But now that she has lost her fortune, her former fiancé does not press his suit ... Later her brother dies and she inherits his property. The former fiancé begins to show interest again, but Mildred sees that the love he formerly had for her is dead. Alone and lonely she surveys the wreck of lives, her own included, which have resulted from her ill-defined ambitions and her impervious nature.

[9] Ivan S. Turgenev, *Virgin Soil* (London, Heineman, 1907), 156.

Again we must refer to Stuart Sherman:

> Mildred Lawson in *Celibates* is a study of <u>unchaste chastity.</u> The vital force in her is represented as just strong enough to make her lascivious and just feeble enough to keep her "chaste." She has a queasy appetite for artistic expression and a life of passion: she toys with art and abandons it to toy with and torment a series of lovers; not virtue but timidity and impotence inhibit her desires. .... She is a Vestal vampire—one of the most noxious and noisome creatures in English literature.[10]

"Mildred Lawson" is a careful and expert piece of work. It has the distinctive quality of being well molded.

Esther Waters was published in 1894. As soon as it appeared, according to Arnold Bennett, "the most conservative critics praised it with all the fervor of their souls." Bennett adds that George Moore's popularity began with this novel.[11]

Just why this should be would seem at first glance a mystery. *Esther Waters*, the life history of a servant girl, is about as dull and unpleasant a book as was ever written. The fact that Esther has an illegitimate baby and later marries a tuberculous man who runs a "pub" gives little significance to a monotonous life of drudgery.

There are, of course, several good reasons for the novel's popularity. In the first place, people had started reading George Moore. By 1895, twenty editions of *A Mummer's Wife* had appeared. In the second place, as we have seen, the year 1894 marked a change in the English attitude toward fiction. Finally, Esther is a heroine, and, like Tess, a "pure woman." The novel is a story of a struggle against heavy odds.

We will note that this book belongs properly to the very early period of George Moore's writings. The kinship to *Germinie Lacerteux* is obvious, but the author seems to have eliminated more improbabilities than did the Goncourts. At least as far back as the publication date of the *Confessions*

---

[10] *On Contemporary Literature*, 148.
[11] *Fame and Fiction* (New York, E. P. Dutton & Co., 1901), 235.

(1888), and we imagine several years before, Esther's creator was busy examining the "slavey" in his boarding house:

> Emma, I remember you—you are not to be forgotten—up at five o'clock every morning, scouring, washing, cooking, dressing those infamous children; seventeen hours at least out of the twenty-four at the beck and call of the landlady, lodgers, and quarrelling children; seventeen hours at least out of the twenty-four drudging in that horrible kitchen, running up stairs with coals and breakfasts and cans of hot water; down on your knees before a grate, pulling out the cinders with those hands—can I call them hands? The lodgers sometimes threw you a kind word, but never one that recognized that you were akin to us, only the pity that might have been extended to a dog. And I used to ask you all sorts of cruel questions, I was curious to know the depths of animalism you had sunk to, or rather out of which you had never been raised. And you generally answered innocently and naively enough. But sometimes my words were too crude, and they struck through the thick hide into the quick, into the human, and you winced a little; but this was rarely, for you were very nearly, oh, very nearly an animal: your temperament and intelligence was just that of a dog that has picked up a master who may turn it out at any moment. Dickens would sentimentalize or laugh over you; I do neither. I merely recognize you as one of the facts of civilization. ... Poor Emma! I shall never forget your kind heart and your unfailing good humor.[12]

Mr. Hone mentions that soon after the publication of *A Drama in Muslin* (1886) Moore became interested in writing a novel about servants. It seems likely that *Esther Waters* was written, at least in part, some eight or ten years before it was published, and that the state of English critical opinion and George Moore's fame are responsible for the publication at a later date.

Strangely enough, *A Mere Accident*, which portrays a religious obsession, was the fourth book George Moore published, coming immediately after *A Mummer's Wife*. It owes something to Huysmans and begins the second phase of Moore's writings. Nevertheless the religious theme which Moore here

[12] Modern Library edition, 133–34, 137.

attempts was dropped with the publication of this book and not resumed for fourteen years. It is true that in *Mike Fletcher* and in *Evelyn Innes* we have much of Huysmans' dislike of humanity and his disgust with vulgarity. But religious preoccupation as a central theme was abandoned for fourteen years.

That George Moore abandoned the theme is not surprising. Perhaps more surprising is the fact that he ever attempted it, and that he attempted it for a second time after the lapse of fourteen years.

Matters of literary influence often surprise the scholar. Knowing Moore's propensity to assimilate, one would carelessly assume that Maupassant's *Bel-Ami* provided inspiration for *A Modern Lover*. But Moore's work preceded that of Maupassant by two years, and we must assume that Maupassant was the borrower. In *A Mere Accident* one notices that Moore gives us lyrical and despairing passages on human grossnesses and a search for spiritual tranquillity in following the observances of the Catholic Church. But though the lyrical and despairing passages may well be reflections of Huysmans— and George Moore all but tells us this in the *Confessions* —Huysmans' *En route* was published nine years after *A Mere Accident!*

It is true that the conclusion of *A rebours* would forecast either *A Mere Accident* or *En route*. Des Esseintes, a bundle of nerves, returns to Paris to seek tranquillity in the church. "Lord, take pity on the Christian who doubts, on the sceptic who would fain believe, on the galley-slave of life who puts out to sea alone, in the darkness of the night, beneath a firmament illuminated no longer by the consoling beacon-fires of the ancient hope." It took Huysmans twelve years to think out his subject. George Moore made a stab at it right away.

John Norton, the young squire in Moore's account, has a temperamental aversion to life which came from neither satiety nor any physical weakness. The aversion is quite real, although

John Norton seems somewhat too young for the meditations credited to him:

> Few among men ever realize the truth of things, but there are rare occasions, moments of supernatural understanding or suffering when we see life in all its worm-like meanness, and death in its plain stupid loathsomeness.[13]

He goes to an exhibition and

> it seemed that all the back kitchens and stair-cases in England had been emptied out—life-tattered housewives, girls grown stout on porter, pretty-faced babies, heavy-handed fathers, whistling boys in sloppy clothes, and attitudes curiously evidencing an odious domesticity. Till then I had never realized the foulness of the human animal but there his foulness was overshadowed by his stupidity. The masses, yes, I saw the masses and I fed with them in their huge intellectual style.[14]

John Norton's revulsion and his sickness of soul is not alone responsible for his determination to separate himself from the world and lead an ascetic life. He has a tangible fear of the fires of Hell. But no separation from life is possible in the country home of his mother, with whom he lives. So he betakes himself to a university and arranges his room like that of a monastery. He makes friends with Jesuits, comes more and more under their influence, and begins plans for converting the country home into a monastery. While carrying out these plans he falls under the influence of a young girl. His interest in her destroys his ascetic leanings.

The story so far might well fit into what Huysmans called "spiritualistic naturalism," but Moore introduces a complication. Returning home one day, the young girl is attacked by a tramp, who rapes her. Hating the sight of men, she goes to her room and refuses to leave it. When Norton, much agitated, calls to inquire about her, she sends word that she is willing to see him. On his appearance, however, she jumps out of a window and is killed. John Norton decides to give up his

---

[13] *A Mere Accident* (London, Vizetelly & Co., 1887), 56.
[14] *Ibid.*, 57–58.

former plans. He goes into the world of men, resolving to make the world his monastery, whatever that may mean.

A Mere Accident was soundly panned by the critics, and justly. Moore himself soon lost confidence in the novel. It is connected neither with social interpretation nor with a true "soul crisis." The story is here mentioned in some detail in order to emphasize the difference between naturalism and the dramatic portrayal of soul-sickness, which is the main concern in the books of Moore's second period.

Is a "spiritualistic naturalist" a naturalist? He is probably not, yet he has strong naturalistic propensities. Huysmans, who expressed aversion for life more strongly than Flaubert, the disgust with nature more powerfully than Maupassant, the baseness of human nature with more feeling than the Goncourts, is, in spirit, their successor. Moreover, as Lalou tells us, "the translation of the most spiritual realities into concrete images and phrases permits us in the last analysis to call Huysmans a naturalist."[15] But only the writers of autobiographies are as personal as Huysmans. Let us examine in some detail Huysmans' theories of fiction, since they influence not only George Moore but Rolland and Joyce, and through them the English life-novel of the years 1910–17.

"It is most certain," declared Durtal, "that when naturalism confines itself to monotonous studies of mediocre people revolving amid interminable inventories of rooms and fields it tends to complete sterility if one is honest and clear-headed; and, if one is not, to most painful repetitions and the dullest of all possible stories." But Durtal could not quite see how you could give up naturalism without returning to the high-flown ditties of the romantics, to the downy verbiage of Cherbuliez and Feuillet or else to the lachrymose stories of Theuriet and Sand!

We must, he said to himself, retain our regard for document-like veracity, for the precision of detail, and continue to employ the fibrous and nervous language of realism. But we must also plumb the depths

---

[15] R. Lalou, *Histoire de la Littérature française contemporaine* (Paris, G. Crés, 1924), 73.

of our souls and not try to explain every mystery as some form of a physical malady. If we give ourselves this liberty, we would have a novel of both soul and body, and concern ourselves with their reciprocal reactions. There is no getting around the fact that we must follow the highway that Zola has established. But it is also necessary to trace a parallel path in the air, another road by which we may reach the Beyond and the Afterward, in short to achieve a spiritualistic Naturalism. What a splendid accomplishment this would be![16]

Durtal sees a consummate revelation of such spiritual naturalism in Matthias Grünewald's crucifixion at Cassel—"the Christ who was at once a putrid and unaureoled corpse and yet a manifest god bathed in invisible light, the union of outrageous realism and outrageous idealism."[17] "Thus from triumphal ordure Grünewald extracted the finest mints of delectation, the sharpest essences of tears."

It is interesting in approaching the works of Moore's second period to note his reaction against his former masters. He tells us:

> With Balzac I had descended into the nether world of the soul and watched its afflictions. Then there were minor awakenings. Zola had enchanted me with theory; Flaubert had astonished me with the wonderful delicacy and subtlety of his workmanship; Goncourt's brilliant adjectival effects had captivated me for a time, but all these impulses were crumbling into dust, these aspirations were etiolated, sickly as faces growing old in gaslight.[18]

> Art is not nature. Art is nature digested. Art is a sublime excrement. Zola and Goncourt cannot, or will not understand that the artistic stomach must be allowed to do its work in its own mysterious fashion. If a man is really an artist he will remember what is necessary, forget what is useless; but if he takes notes, he will interrupt his artistic digestion, and the result will be a lot of little touches, inchoate and wanting in the elegant rhythm of synthesis.[19]

[16] *La-bas* (Paris, G. Crés, 1912), Chapter I.
[17] Havelock Ellis, Introduction to Huysmans' *Against the Grain* (New York, Illustrated Editions Co., 1931), 37.
[18] *Confessions*, 184.
[19] *Ibid.*, 105–106.

By 1888 Moore could say of Zola's writings, "Only the simple crude statements of a man of powerful mind, but singularly narrow vision."[20] Several years later, in 1891, he was so hostile as to speak of "the mud-banks and shallow shores of naturalism."[21]

In the *Confessions* we get a full acknowledgment of Moore's debt to Huysmans when he speaks of *A rebours* as "that prodigious book, that beautiful mosaic." He continues, "In hours like these a page of Huysmans is as a dose of opium, a glass of some exquisite and powerful liquer. . . . Huysmans is quite right, ideas are well enough until you are twenty, afterwards only words are bearable. . . . Huysmans goes to my soul like a gold ornament of Byzantine workmanship; there is in his style the yearning charm of arches, a sense of ritual, the passion of the mural, of the window."[22] Much later Moore said of Zola, "Huysmans and I lie on the floor and kick up our heels when we think of him."[23]

Returning to Moore's other novels of his second period, we pick up with some pleasure a little-known volume, *Mike Fletcher*. Though it is "spiritual naturalism," the religious preoccupation is not present. Instead the author allows himself a liberty of expression second only to the *Confessions* in describing Mike Fletcher's states of soul—feelings of love and yearning and satiety and despair. And, in his best mode, he employs a poetic prose of color and variety. Furthermore, Mike is a character whom George Moore likes. He is virile and lovable; he is hearty and without any particular moral sense; he is sensual and possessed of delicate sensibilities.

Mike writes feature articles for one of the magazines which herald the "New" ideas of the nineties. He is often self-indulgent, and his spurts of activity are caused by financial necessity. There is no littleness in Mike; he is not even shrewd.

---

[20] *Ibid.,* 74.
[21] *Impressions and Opinions* (London, T. W. Laurie, 1912), 58.
[22] *Confessions,* 190–91.
[23] Hone, *Life of George Moore,* 144.

His generosity of nature and his warmheartedness facilitate his conquest over women.

On the death of one of his former mistresses, Mike inherits her property in the country. He is now able to enjoy every caprice and gratify every sensation. He gives himself to his desire but, strangely, his new life brings him little satisfaction. He is haunted by the memory of a former love, Lily, and he resolves to find her. Hearing that she is suffering from consumption, he makes a thousand-mile journey. They meet and resolve to go away together, but the girl is sinking fast, "her deciduous beauty, now divided from the grave by only a breath, beautiful and divinely sorrowful in its transit."[24]

Lily dies and Mike goes to live among the Arabs for two years. Feeling at length that he has recovered from his sorrow, he returns to London again to seek new sensations. But "there was no taste in him for anything; he had eaten of the tree of knowledge, and with the evil rind in his teeth wandered an exile beyond the garden."[25] "Oh, for rest," he cries. "I am weary of life. Oh, to slip back into the unconscious whence we came and to pass forever from the buzzing of the Midges. To feel the sharp, cruel implacable externality of things melt, vanish, and dissolve. The ordinary run of mortals do not see into the heart of things, nor do we except in terrible lucid moments; then seeing life truly, seeing it in all of its monstrous deformity, we cry out like children in the night."[26] He finds that nature has arranged to crush those who lose touch with humanity; "for now I know," he concludes, "that man may not live without wife, without child, without God."[27] Like a gourmet, he longs "to taste of the dark fruit of oblivion." He dresses for the evening with careful detail and then puts a bullet in his head.

We like in *Mike Fletcher* the monologues which continue from page to page, the echoes of Schopenhauer, and the grave

24 *Mike Fletcher* (London, Ward and Downey, 1889), 249.
25 *Ibid.*, 261.
26 *Ibid.*, 259.
27 *Ibid.*, 261.

and sombre tonal quality of the last quarter of the book. But externals are treated casually. Mike's satiety might have been more convincing if his search for sensations had been revealed more openly.

A novel of this type properly concerns itself very little with milieu; nevertheless George Moore gives us a good picture of the turbulent nineties:

> All institutions, especially the Royal Academy, Drury Lane Theatre, and Eton College, were held to be symbols of man's earthiness, the bar-room and the music hall as certain proof of his divine origin; actors were scorned and prize-fighters revered; the genius of courtesans, the folly of education, and the poetry of pantomime formed the theme on which the articles which made the center of the paper were written. Insolent letters were addressed to eminent people, and a novel by Harding, the hero of which was a butler and the heroine a cook, was in the course of publication.[28]

We constantly regret the restraints under which George Moore wrote. *Mike Fletcher* might have been a great novel. But the sensualities of the sensual Mike are virtually omitted and a character which Moore created with fervor does not live his full life on Moore's pages. "If I ever write a great novel, it will be Don Juan," said the author in a letter. *Mike Fletcher* was the book, and the author spoke of giving readings from it in America.

But America, according to Moore's American publisher, would not buy one single copy. And the author was not consoled by the small commercial success in England, for the critics, even those to whom Moore had read fragments, were dead set against the finished product. It is little wonder that Moore decided not to try any more Don Juan books. "My next novel," he wrote Madame Lanza, "will be more human. I shall bathe myself in the simplest and most naïve emotions, the daily bread of humanity."[29] Moore next gave his attention to a play concerning workmen, *The Strike at Arlingford*, and to *Esther Waters*.

[28] *Ibid.*, 40.   [29] Hone, *Life of George Moore*, 161.

In spite of the intermission, the continuity between *Mike Fletcher* and the *Evelyn Innes–Sister Teresa* story is not broken. Both are spiritual biographies and both are discreet handlings of unconventional relationships. Perhaps Moore felt that he had gone far enough in making Evelyn the mistress of the man who developed her into a great singer, and that he need not go into detail about the love situation. What makes it worse is that George Moore in the preface calls his book a love story, "the only prose love story in the English language." He explains that a love story is one in which love is the only theme. As for love, we do not see that Evelyn or any other woman would have been spontaneously attracted to the austere and philosophic Sir Owen. Neither the author nor Sir Owen nor Evelyn ever unbends.

Evelyn Innes and *Sister Teresa* are, as Moore explains, really the halves of a single volume. Evelyn has the background, intelligence, looks, and talent to make her a great singer. Sir Owen sees this; sees also that she has every quality for a highly civilized mistress. We appreciate the highly civilized nature of Sir Owen. We appreciate his highly civilized intent to develop every quality of Evelyn and to develop not merely the voice but the woman. We are convinced of the successive stages by which Evelyn rose to fame. But as to the love affair, we are merely willing to admit that it is the most highly civilized one in the English language and let it go at that. *Sister Teresa* also fails us somewhat. It is not that the atmosphere of the nunnery lacks anything. It is not that Evelyn lacks devotion. It is merely that successful opera singers in England do not enter convents.

Altogether the religious phase of Evelyn's life is more convincing than her love affair. George Moore can make us feel a convent atmosphere—perhaps because the windows of his study overlooked the cloisters of a nunnery. He can make us feel devotion. And he gives up some sense of the cold wind that blows between the worlds. Evelyn feels its permeating influence:

The nuns do not succeed any better than I; all screens are unavailing, for the wind is about everywhere—a cold searching wind which prayers cannot keep out; our doorways are not staunch—the wind comes under the actress's dressing-room and under the door of the nun's cell in draughts chilling us to the bone, and then leaves us to pursue our avocations in peace.

There are various endings to the different editions. In perhaps the best one, Evelyn is only moderately successful in her attempts at expiation. The consolations of religious contemplation are perhaps not as great as those of human service. So she departs.

The historical novels, *The Brook Kerith* and *Héloïse and Abélard,* are properly outside the limits of this study of transitional influences. And yet I cannot forbear mentioning that Moore the Naturalist is everywhere present in *The Brook Kerith.* Jesus, a former carpenter, joins the monastic order of Essenes and absorbs their teachings. He hates insincerity and hypocrisy sufficiently to stage a revolt against the Pharisees. Lifted up in pride he feels himself the Son of God. He is saved from death by an admirer, the rich Joseph of Arimathea, who procures the yet-living Jesus from a corruptible Centurian and has him nursed back to health. Afterwards Jesus becomes a shepherd again, humbly regretful of the pride which had lifted him to claim kinship with God. And yet Moore credits Jesus with his miracles.

As to *The Lake,* it is the "spiritualistic naturalism" of a post-Huysmans George Moore. We recall that the *Confessions* were very strongly pagan. Rarely does the George Moore of that period reach toward pantheism, yet occasionally we note an authentic strain:

I had not thought of the simple and unaffected joy of the heart of natural things; the color of the open air, and many forms of the country, the birds flying—that one making for the sea; the abandoned boat, the dwarf roses and the wild lavender; nor had I thought of the beauty of mildness in life, and how by a certain avoidance of the wilfully passionate, and the surely ugly, we may secure an aspect of temporal life that is abiding and soul-sufficing.

The Lake is pure pantheism. Father Gogarty virtually drives from the village an unmarried expectant mother. Later she writes to him and brings him a vision of far places and the joys of human life. He rediscovers nature and the influence of trees and flowers and forest. He finds that "he and the trees were one, for there is but one life, one mother, one elemental substance out of which all has come." Life, he decides, "is oriented like a temple, there are in every existence days when life streams down the nave, striking the forehead of God." Chastity is an evil because "woman is life." Father Gogarty leaves the church and George Moore, having finally expressed a vision which we may really call his own, retired to the realms of literary criticism and historical romance.

As we have seen, George Moore reflected his generous enthusiasms by imitating widely, but his place in English literary history is that of an innovator. His early naturalistic novels were read with mild interest even before the controversy over naturalism was well under way. By the time that naturalism was winning wide popular acceptance in England George Moore had become disgusted with it. His spiritual biographies—*A Mere Accident, Confessions of a Young Man, Mike Fletcher, Evelyn Innes, Sister Teresa,* and *The Lake*—were influential in shifting English interest from social to personal problems. They helped bring about the vogue of the life-novel in the years 1910–17. The paganism of the *Confessions* gave him prophetic standing in the war-conscious years of the twenties. And if, as H. G. Wells forsees, the novel is to give place to biography and autobiography, George Moore will be abreast of the new tendencies with his trilogy, *Hail and Farewell,* which includes *Ave* (1911), *Salve* (1912), and *Vale* (1914).

⊷§ VI §⊷

THE REACTION AGAINST DICKENS : I

RUDYARD KIPLING, ARTHUR MORRISON

W. SOMERSET MAUGHAM

RICHARD WHITEING

WHEN Dickens portrayed a thief, a rogue, or a gravedigger he presented him as an individual, an oddity, not a type. The social order, sound except for specified abuses, contained quite a few scoundrels, but nice people in any locality were not very far away. Then, too, the atmosphere of poverty in Dickens' works was not necessarily malign. Some of the most admirable people were poor. Depravity among rich and poor was present but it was exceptional; the social organization was askew here and there but a fundamental good order prevailed.

What distinguished the portrayal of poverty and depravity among the English followers of Zola during the nineties, however, was that whole classes of people did not differ materially from the individuals selected for inspection. A rogue was associated with other rogues, with a great many rogues, and when they were put all together they didn't look at all comical. Depravity was still presented in a lively manner and the depraved were hardly conscious of their sins. But there is something just a little bit ghastly in the good-humored delineation of a social infection. Moreover poor people, not very much unlike, were grouped together, and their social situation was evaluated. So poverty was merely poor and degrading. By indicating this with a Dickens-like freshness, several English disciples of Zola obtained some striking effects.

All this is not naturalism. It is often satire. It is often the attempt to make squalor so squalid that it is exciting—but Zola himself could not withstand this temptation. The point of view is, however, naturalistic, particularly when the author delights in the genial manifestations of his characters' animality.

Not very many books of this type were written. Not many were required. The awful lesson was very easily learned. The point is that nobody could read any of these books and persist in looking upon poor people as picturesque.

Rudyard Kipling, I believe, is responsible for establishing the tone of this new kind of fiction. He wrote only one story to prove his point, but "The Record of Badalia Herodsfoot" is more effective than anything Zola ever did in a like number of pages. For Kipling "conventionalizes" the varied forms of human baseness and casually refers to them in a genially tolerant fashion as if nothing else is to be expected. If the characters justify themselves in accordance with the code of the locality, it is all right with Kipling.

On account of the influence of this story, we might consider it in some detail:

Badalia's husband, after beating her unconscious, has left her for "a pan-faced slut in Hennesy's Rents." In the absence of her husband Badalia looks after herself "with a mangle, some tending of babies, and an occasional sale of flowers."

Badalia has qualities which make her somewhat better than the rest of the squalid inhabitants of Gunnison Street, London, and these are brought to the attention of the Reverend Eustace Hanna when she upbraids him for his careless dispensation of charity. The preacher has just left supplies for an invalid prostitute who is living with her dissolute mother. "You give Lascar Loo custards," she tells him, "you give her blankets. Go on home. Her mother, she eats them all and drinks the blankets. ... Lascar Loo don't never smell of them even."

The curate, though ignorant of life, is not so unintelligent as to be heedless of good advice. He appoints Badalia the dispenser of a weekly grant—a trust to be held for the benefit of Gunnison Street. She keeps a book of her careful dispensations and reports weekly to him.

In her thrifty disposal of the funds she holds in trust, Badalia finds opportunity of extending her activities. "She, magnifying her office, faced the drunken husband; coaxed the doubly shiftless, thriftless girl-wife into a little forethought, and begged clothes when and where she could for the scrofulous babies that multiplied like the green scum on the untopped water-cisterns."

Badalia might have successfully escaped the fights and scrapes that resulted from her just distribution of charity. But Tom, her husband, who has taken to drink during the confinement of his "new wife," returns to demand money of Badalia—the trust fund which he has heard that she keeps. On being refused he chokes her and throws her against the bed. "Her forehead struck the bed-post and she sank, half-kneeling to the floor. It was impossible for a self-respecting man to refrain from kicking her; so Tom kicked with the deadly intelligence born of whiskey. The head drooped to the floor, and Tom kicked at that till the crisp tingle of hair striking through his nailed boot with the chill of cold water warned him that he might as well desist."

Badalia is dying, and a Catholic priest brings a sister to attend her. "Then he stood at the landing and bit the flesh of his fingers in agony because he was a priest trained to know, and he knew how the hearts of men and of women beat back at the rebound, so that love is born out of horror and passion declares itself while the soul is quivering in pain." Badalia dies, but not before she tells that it was a stranger who attacked her.

Kipling does not disparage the efforts of the social workers, although he is conscious of their immense task. "There exists," he says, "a very close brotherhood in the ranks of those whose work lies in Gunnison Street. To begin with, they have seen pain—pain which no word or deed of theirs can alleviate—life

born into death and death crowded by unhappy life. Also
they understand the full significance of drink, which is a
knowledge hidden from very well-meaning people, and some
of them have fought with the beasts of Ephesus. They meet
in unseemly hours in unseemly places, exchange a word or
two of hasty counsel, advice, or suggestion, and pass to their
appointed toil, since time is precious and life hangs in the
balance of five minutes."

Thus Kipling, in a spirit of compassion not unmixed with
humor and sentiment, portrays the life of the lower orders.
The union in his account of pathos and a cruelly genial humor
will later be shown as reflected in the work of Morrison,
Maugham, and Whiteing. These writers follow Kipling even
in subject matter: the prevalence of wife-beating among the
poor and the unwillingness of neighbors to interfere; the concealment of all crime from officers of the law; the existence of
depraved old women who bear little love for their offspring;
the ineffectual sincerity of social workers and the practice of
the poor in fooling them; and, finally, the laxity of poor people's morals.

ARTHUR MORRISON

Tales of Mean Streets and *A Child of the Jago* are essentially naturalistic. Each of the *Tales* crudely reveals some form
of human irrationality and folly. *A Child of the Jago* is concerned with the influence of environment upon the son of a
low and not especially clever criminal. The son grows up no
better and no worse than the rest of the inhabitants of the
Jago. He is killed one day in a gang fight shortly after his
father's execution for murder.[1]

Morrison follows English writers in creating his poor folk
as full of bravado, humor, the zest of life, and animal warmth.
But often there is a sterner rendering. We see hate, slothful-
ness, greed, and depravity. Morrison draws no lesson and

---

[1] There is little of naturalism in his other works of fiction. After writing *Tales of
Mean Streets,* Morrison wrote detective stories for two years. *A Child of the Jago*
was followed by realistic novels and stories in the Dickens manner, depicting noble-
hearted poor folk. A book of ghost stories appeared in 1897.

preaches no sermon. He accepts the low creatures' depravity as he accepts their bravado. Like Flaubert he would believe that the cannibal who eats his fellow man is as innocent as the child who sucks his lollipop. He writes with droll sympathy and even enthusiasm, almost as if he, too, were one of the creatures he describes.

We recall that one of the English critics spoke of the French writers as showing "Gallic nature, which we should do well to bear in mind, is human,—with a difference." Morrison would seem to laugh good-naturedly as he gives his reply: "I would show you our own *canaille*. We have our due proportion of worthless old men who sponge on their wives and mothers, depraved old women, worn-out harlots with kind hearts, mountebanks, conscious and unconscious hypocrites, thieves, rogues and drunkards. They are generally not susceptible to ethical compunctions but show a laudable attempt to keep out of trouble. They are generally proud of something, even if it is their especial variety of villainy."

Morrison lays on his depravity in heavy daubs. Not even Zola has pictured a community of such riotous squalor and misery, and one so full of crime, as Morrison shows us in his slums. The author even finds it necessary to lay the scenes of *A Child of the Jago* in the past so as to be free from restraint in picturing the vileness of the locality. He is essentially a journalist and does not hesitate to claim the documentary veracity of his book of ghost stories.[2]

Tales of Mean Streets is concerned with incidents from the lives of English working people. The book is of necessity milder in tone and less concerned with criminality and violence than *A Child of the Jago*. Yet it depicts the East End as "an evil plexus of slums that hide human creeping things; where filthy men and women live on penn'orths of gin, where collars and clean shirts are decencies unknown, where every citizen wears a black eye, and none ever combs his hair."[3]

---

[2] *The Dorrington Deed Box* (London, Ward and Lock, 1897), "Preface."
[3] *Tales of Mean Streets* (Modern Library Edition), 1, "Introduction."

Morrison describes the passing of a day in the working quarter. It begins with the night watchman's knocking to awaken the workers at half-past five. "The knocking and the shouting pass, and there comes the noise of the opening and shutting of doors, and a clattering away to the docks, the gasworks, and the shipyards. Later more door-shutting is heard, and then the trotting of sorrow-laden little feet along the grim street to the grim board school three grim streets off. Then silence, save for the subdued sound of scrubbing here and there, and the puny squall of croupy infants. After this a new trotting of little feet to docks, gasworks, and shipyards with father's dinner in a basin and a red handkerchief, and so to the board schools again. More muffled scrubbing and more squalling, and perhaps a feeble attempt or two at decorating the blankness of a square hole here and there by pouring water into a grimy flower-pot full of dirt. Then comes the trot of little feet toward the oblong holes, heralding the slower tread of sooty artisans; a smell of bloater up and down; nightfall; the fighting of boys on the street, perhaps of men at the corner near the beer-shop; sleep. And this is the record of a day in this street; and every day is the same."[4]

Nobody laughs here—life is too serious a thing; nobody sings. There was once a woman who sung—a young wife from the country. But she bore children, and her voice cracked. Then her man died, and she sung no more. . . . Where in the East End lies this street? Everywhere. The hundred and fifty yards is only a link in a long and mightily tangled chain—is only a turn in a tortuous maze. This street of the square holes is hundreds of miles long. That it is planned in short lengths is true, but there is no other way in the world that can more properly be called a single street, because of its dismal lack of accent, its sordid uniformity, its utter remoteness from delight.[5]

Morrison's stories, however, are not as sober as his preface. To note his vigor we might consider one story in some detail.

[4] *Ibid.*, v.   [5] *Ibid.*, xv.

Like the folk of Dickens, Morrison's poor people are not conscious of the squalor they live in. "Lizerunt" will serve our purpose well.

The author introduces his chief character in the following manner: "Somewhere in the register was written the name of Elizabeth Hunt; but seventeen years after the entry the spoken name was Lizerunt. Lizerunt worked in a pickle factory, and appeared abroad in an elaborate and shabby costume, usually supplemented by a white apron. Withal she was something of a beauty. That is to say, her cheeks were very red, her teeth very large and white, her nose was small and snub, and her fringe was long and shiny; while her face, new-washed, was susceptible of a high polish. Many such girls are married at sixteen, but Lizerunt was belated, and never had a bloke at all."

Lizer's love affair begins one day as she walks along the street. "Billy Chope, slouching in the opposite direction, lurched across the pavement as they met, and taking the nearest hand from his pocket, caught and twisted her arm, bumping her against the wall.

" 'Garn,' said Lizerunt, greatly pleased. 'Le' go!' For she knew that this was love."

This was not the first overture that had been made to Lizer, for two days before "Sam Cardew threw an orange peel at her, but went away after a little prancing on the pavement."

Billy takes Lizerunt to the fair on Whit Monday at Wanstead Flats. "The pair walked and ran with arms about each other's necks; and Lizerunt thumped her bloke on the back at proper intervals; so the affair went regularly on the whole." A fight between her bloke, Billy, and Sam Cardew springs up, and Billy is beaten. Whereupon Lizerunt proudly goes off on the arm of her new bloke, Sam.

But Billy does not remain passive. "Two nights later Lizer was going home with a jug of beer when somebody sprang from a dark corner, landed her under the ear, knocked her sprawling, and made off to the sound of her lamentations." The next evening a gang of seven or eight fall upon Sam

Cardew with sticks and belts and beat him until he is speechless and still.

Sam lies at home for nearly four weeks, and when he stands up again it is in many bandages. Lizer comes to see him but before long gets tired of Sam and his bandages and his grunts and groans. Billy sees Lizer looking in a window filled with fashionable plush and feather hats and offers to "sport her one." Shortly afterwards she marries him.

Billy does not work but extorts his spending money from his mother, who does mangling, and from Lizer. He beats them both from time to time. He beats Lizer immediately before she has her first child and again several hours afterwards. Lizer is irate with the young doctor who takes her part.

Lizer has three children before she is twenty-one and is discharged from the pickle factory. In order to meet her husband's exactions and to feed her children she does charing.

Billy's mother dies and sufficient money is not forthcoming to pay household expenses and to buy drink. Thereupon Billy forces Lizer out into the street at night to get money as best she can and "as plenty others does."

A Child of the Jago begins with an exhortation:

Woe unto the foolish prophets, that follow their own spirit, and have seen nothing!

Because, even because they have seduced my people, saying, Peace; and there was no peace; and one built up a wall, and, lo, others daubed it with untempered morter:

Say unto them that daub it with untempered morter, that it shall fall: there shall be an overflowing shower; and ye, O great hailstones, shall fall; and a stormy wind shall rend it.

Lo when the wall is fallen, shall it not be said unto you, Where is the daubing wherewith ye have daubed it?—Ezekiel 13: 3, 10-12

Scarcely anyone works in the Jago—only a few women who do sewing and make matchboxes. Stealing is the general occupation of the male population, and the varieties of theft

range from snatching apples to acts of violence. Consider
the atmosphere:

> Old Jago Street lay black and close under the quivering red sky;
> and slinking forms, as of grey rats, followed one another quickly be-
> tween the posts in the gut by the High Street, and scattered over the
> Jago. ... On the pavement some writhed wearily, longing for sleep;
> others, despairing of it, sat and lolled, and a few talked. They were not
> there for lack of shelter, but because in this weather repose was less
> unlikely in the street than within doors; and the lodgings of the few
> who nevertheless abode at home were marked here and there by the
> lights visable from the windows. For in this place none ever slept
> without a light, because of three sort of vermin that light in some sort
> keeps at bay; vermin which added to existence here a touch not to be
> guessed by the unafflicted, who object to being told of it. For on them
> that lay writhen and gasping on the pavement; on them that sat
> among them; on them that rolled and blasphemed in the lighted
> rooms; on every moving creature in this, the Old Jago, day and night,
> sleeping and walking, the third plague of Egypt, and more, lay un-
> ceasing.

The story itself is important only as it reveals the base condition of what is virtually an outlaw community. Dickey, son
of a criminal, makes some slight effort to break away from
this Jago of thieving and gang fights and wife-beatings and
police raids, but in the end he succumbs.

RICHARD WHITEING

Before Richard Whiteing attempted fiction he had published a guidebook of Paris and another work interpreting
the customs and nature of Parisians. Before he wrote his second
novel he had translated into English three volumes of Maupassant's stories.

In spite of his French sympathies, however, Whiteing is
no naturalist. He is eminently a satirist who takes a critical
view (and generally a naturalistic one) of England and things
English. The story itself is a simple affair of a man or woman in
an unfamiliar place; but the discoveries and reflections of the

central character are startling. Through his impersonation the author expresses his amazed horror of the British Empire and feudal system, the class distinctions, the Christian religion, and, most important, the depravity of human nature brought about through an improvident industrialism.

Whiteing wrote three socially introspective novels: *The Island* (1888), *No. 5 John Street* (1889), and *The Yellow Van* (1903). Of these, *No. 5 John Street* is by far the best known. *The Island,* however, provides a good introduction through its satire on the self-glorifying literature of imperial Britain and the extension of British culture to the remote parts of the empire.

The gods of Chance direct Whiteing's hero, who finds London and Paris equally repellent, to a small island of the Pacific. Here he is charmed by the islanders' simple generosity and friendliness, and by the order and reason behind their simple customs. But he finds that they are studiously mastering British culture, just as the imperial storybooks say. They express to him their veneration for the aims and interests of England. "They seem to see human life not at all as a mere struggle but as a great race for a crown of virtue, in which Britain was first and their little island so decidedly nowhere that they could afford to sink rivalry in admiration." "I winced," says Whiteing's hero, "and I winced, and winced again."

When Vittoria, a splendid savage Venus, desires to know about the "blessed Sabbaths in England," the narrator is moved to reflection: "O my England, my England! why cannot I speak of a thing we must honor so? Why rather do I pray for strength to keep the secret of thy Sabbaths well! Dread day of the division of the classes, weekly vision of the Judgment, in its utter separation of the social sheep and goats, never one flock, alas! at any time but now so clearly two. In this dark hour of remembrance I hear the hoarse clappers of thy meeting houses, vainly fanning the stagnant air in cities of the spiritually dead. I see thy funereal processions of the elect, wending to and from the conventicles, past groups of coster-boys who wait for the opening of the houses and expectorate on the pavement in patterns of the dawn of decorative art. It is all before me, the dingy squalor of thy miles of shuttered marts, the crying contrasts of thy summer finery, more hurtful to the eye than thy week-day rags."

The narrator makes notes for a speech to be delivered to the natives concerning the English people, but he finds himself including matter hardly fit for them to hear: "Nightfall brings the whole slum together, at the universal rendezvous, from every near or distant scene; men, and those who were once maidens, mumbling age and swearing infancy, stand six-deep before the slimy bar, till the ever-flowing liquor damps out the fiercest fires and the great city is once more at rest. The imagination of him that saw Hell could hardly picture the final scene."

In *No. 5 John Street*, Lord ——,the narrator, is the Agent General sent from The Island as a representative for the approaching Jubilee, being specially instructed to testify to the Queen the patriotic joy of the islanders and to acknowledge their huge debt to England for moral example and for the numerous presents of hymnbooks and sewing machines which she had sent them as grants-in-aid. As a Report on British Manners and Customs is entailed in the duties of the Agent General, Lord —— decides that he must live for six weeks among the great mass of the English working people in order to submit a well-authenticated report.

Accordingly he settles at No. 5 John Street, announcing to his friends that he is going to the Caspian Sea. The author, without overmuch enthusiasm or disgust, gives a vivid account of his discoveries in the underworld. Facts give their own interpretation, for the most part, but occasionally the author summarizes. On one occasion he considers the debased journals which specialize in stories of vice and crime. "These," he says, "in their innumerable varieties, form the mirror of life for the slums. They should be carefully stored in our private archives, for they will be priceless to the future student of manners. They show how remote from the surface we yet are in our ascent from the bottomless pit of taste. They represent the visible world as the incarnation, under an innumerable variety of forms, of the Universal Cad in the dual nature of woman and of man. The creative spirit moves upon the slime, and we have organizations and institutions."

The author leaves the reader in no doubt as to his own sympathies and reactions. He is violently antireligious and humbly humanitarian. One Sunday he records that the missionaries give never a thought while tampering with our souls to the "ever-present suggestions of every kind of defilement which litter the filthy streets of the filthiest capitol of civilization—unswept because it is the Lord's day." He considers the effect of religious teachings on a person called "Holy Joe": "He has cut down his human nature to the irreducible minimum of aspiration and of claim. ... A wise legislature would endow him as an object lesson on the efficacy of those counsels of perfection addressed to his class ... a broken man bent with spiritual privations more than with age and want, and a missing link between the sick and solitary ape and the most piteous developments of anti-social humanity."

Lord —— returns to society—ostensibly from the Caspian Sea. But the social life of the upper classes is now as new a subject for observation as John Street. The dear, charming life of the leisure class calls him and he responds, but with eyes opened to its ridiculous aspects. Its sentimental aspirations to uplift the masses, its search for a new religion, its utter indifference to the vital interests of the multitude, its care to set the proper example to the lower classes—all are the butts of his satire. And, above all, there is the pretentious spectacle of vainglory—the matchless Jubilee!

The author discusses remedies fully and suggests democracy. But the suggestion is made with little hope. Despair is in the writer's heart, and despair is written into his story. Yet he is contrite and would acknowledge close kinship with "the beer-swilling crew, who are but an organized appetite." He concludes: "Happy the dreamer though, for all that, to whom it is given to learn a final secret without the inconvenience of dying! Yet such the awakening to the sense of life, toil, purpose, the depression of failure, that one would send in one's resignation as a human being ere the vision fades."

We need concern ourselves little with *The Yellow Van*, since the book deals with the upper classes. Whiteing again employs a personification—Duke Allonby's American bride. This lady finds the country with its feudal manners and institutions so picturesquely perfect that she would like to put it under a glass case. Nevertheless she protests: "The inherited deference, the peak of the cap as an institution, almost an act of faith! The paltry village education of manhood and womanhood. The social system a kind of worship of ancestors, and mostly other people's ancestors at that! The pettiness of it all—my God, the pettiness! Anything better than that, even the fierce millions striving at the leash for they know not what, but at least for the good of muscle and nerve."

Whiteing's democratic feelings are everywhere present in his satirical chronicles, and he has a Rousseauistic concern for the betterment of the heart:

> Efficiency is too narrowly construed, even by the best of us. . . . The soul must still be master from first to last. By all means learn the job of your workshop, whatever it may be, founding a science or cooking a beefsteak. But your head and your hands are not enough; the true source and sustainer of all the powers must still be the heart. . . . I wrote *John Street* in the hope of giving this organ a lift to its place.[6]

The author advocates individualism, "but not that of the Wild Jack Ass whose kick is death." The statement of his general philosophy is rather vague. He values

> blessedness, the sweet of adversity for the building up of character, self-control, self-denial, the old beatitudes, no matter what their theological setting, the new birth of the spirit into its real self-hood, in one

[6] *My Harvest* (London, Hodder and Stoughton, 1915), 331–32.

word, all that differenciates the finished article from the mere mistakes of the potter, these, I think, in their struggle for the old ethical pattern, are going to be the note of a new time.[7]

W. SOMERSET MAUGHAM

Liza of Lambeth (1897) was Mr. Maugham's first novel and the most naturalistic account that he has written. And yet no French writer ever attempted a naturalistic novel like this one, with its genial good humor that makes the cruel situations and the satire all the more biting. Maugham's characters are vibrant, self-assertive, pugnacious, immensely hearty, and self-confident. The story is sad, but the author would not for a moment suggest that it is serious. The reader discovers the seriousness for himself after he has finished the book.

Liza is the best of her set of factory workers. She is boisterously animal, boisterously human, like every other creature in the baby-infested dinginess of Vere Street, Lambeth, London. She has a drinking, boastful, complaining, and sometimes kind mother, and a nice lad, who wants to marry her, for a lover. Then there comes into her life a big, hairy, married man, Jim, who is just her sort, openhearted and a good fellow. Jim is no dainty technician in the matter of love. He is masterful, overpowering, but withal kind. All the love-making he does is to kiss Liza, hold her hand, and hug her now and then until one Saturday night he carelessly avows, "Yer know, Liza, I love yer—fit to kill." With them there is only a small gap between friendship and love. Jim takes Liza to a melodrama, gets her to drink two pints of beer, sits and hugs her on a street bench for two hours, and then

> "Liza," he said in a whisper, "Will yer?"
> "Will I wot?" she said, looking down.
> "You know, Liza. Will yer?"
> "Na," she said.

He asks her twice more and she doesn't answer. Then he gives

[7] *Ibid,* 318–19.

her a good-natured blow in the stomach. "Come on," he says, and leads her off.

Unlike other English heroines who are seduced, Liza is monstrously happy. She meets Jim in parks when it is warm, and she sits with him in railway stations when it is cold. They try to avoid observation, but the inhabitants of the street find out. Liza is snubbed, and Jim's wife makes his life miserable. They want to go away together, but Jim won't leave his children, nor Liza her mother.

Jim's brawny wife lies in wait for Liza and the two have a fight. A crowd forms a ring and some men take it upon themselves to be referees and judges. Both women are torn and bloody when Jim comes up and stops the contest. Liza returns home, tells her mother of a fight with "a woman," and is acclaimed by the mother as a worthy daughter. To celebrate the occasion the two women get drunk.

Liza was "in a family way," as she said, before she became drunk. The drink makes her feverish, and the doctor is called. He says that Liza will die. Jim comes in to weep by the bed while the mother and the midwife sit drinking in the corner, bragging and talking of funerals and deaths, insurance and husbands.

Not all the book is sad. The characters are both humorous and the object of humor. Consider an incident taken from a holiday outing. A couple is detached, and their antics are described in a chapter entitled "The Idyll of Coyden and Phyllis." The Idyll concludes as follows:

The faithful swain took out of his pocket a short clay pipe, blew through it, filled it and began to smoke, while Phyllis [who had just drunk a pint of beer] sighed at the thought of the cooling liquid gliding down her throat, and with pleasing recollection gently stroked her stomach. Then Coyden spat, and immediately his love said,

"I can spit further than that."

"I bet yer can't."

She tried and did. He collected himself and spat again, further than before. She followed him, and in this idyllic contest they remained until the tooting horn warned them to take their places in the van.

We read these writings and at best are only cynically amused. Unconsciously our thoughts revert to social causes and influences. We think of education and amelioration. When we read Dickens again, we think of what Dickens has omitted. We feel that Dickens gives us good entertainment, but that he does not face the normal realities of life.

ᵛᵍ VII ᵍᵛ

THE REACTION AGAINST DICKENS : II

GEORGE GISSING

A SECOND PHASE of the reaction against Dickens came from a novelist who admired him and loved his works. But continental writers had sobered George Gissing by giving him a preoccupation with social maladjustment and tragedy. Moreover he himself was maladjusted and wrote novels to express the pain of his own experience and the social ideals that filled his mind. Not having the talent or the coherent social conceptions of his follower, H. G. Wells, his novels are not eminently effective.[1] The novel-form he uses is an anomalous thing with a well-defined social background and with central characters strangely undetermined by conditions. One of these generally voices the author's complaint.

Two quotations especially well interpret the spirit of Gissing's reaction against Dickens. In a letter of November 3, 1880, he wrote:

for one cannot, of course, compare my methods and aims with those of Dickens. I mean to bring home to people the ghastly condition (material, mental, and moral) of our poor classes, to show the hid-

[1] Writing in 1925, Austin Harrison indicated the main line of Gissing's effort: "When Gissing began to write, the England that Dickens depicted had hardened into the modern institutionalism of Victorian wealth, smug decorum and industrial success. It was utterly indecent to think socialistically or even to question the absolutism of things that seemed so dreadfully successful and shed such radiance. But, unlike Dickens, Gissing would not make concessions. He conscientiously set out to write about poverty and the life of the submerged truthfully, in direct opposition to Dickens's method. He attempted to show the side of life omitted by Dickens—the side that did not laugh and had got consciously tired of being laughed at. He knew the lower middle class as well as Dickens, but he could not harlequinize or symbolize his types—hence his failure. . . . Gissing always said that Dickens had made him feel he was really necessary." —"Signposts of Fiction," *Contemporary Review*, July, 1925.

eous injustice of our whole system of society, to give light on the plan of altering it, and, above all, to preach an enthusiasm for just and high idealism in this age of unmitigated egotism and "shop." I shall never write a book which does not keep all these ends in view.

The second quotation follows:

The novel of every-day life is getting worn out. We must dig deeper, get into untouched social strata. Dickens felt this but he had not the courage to face his subjects; his monthly numbers had to lie on the family tea table. . . . Not virginibus puerisque will be my book, I assure you, but for men and women who like to look beneath the surface . . .[2]

Gissing further differs from Dickens in that rewards and punishments are not handed out in accordance with a character's deserts. He is no votary of Nemesis. He appreciated Dickens' love of his better characters but thinks that Dickens carries solicitation too far:

The kindliness of the author's spirit, his over-flowing sympathy with poor and humble folk, set one's mind in a sort of humble music which it is good to live with; and no writer of moralities ever showed triumphant virtue in so cheery a light as that which falls on these humble people when rascality has got its deserts.[3]

In Gissing's writings we may not expect naturalistic novels. The view of the masses of the poor is naturalistic, but there is rarely a social observation consistently developed or a central theme at all. Most often the interest in "character" and in the author's impersonations is dominant. True, our interest in *Workers in the Dawn* is focused upon a tragedy: a young man who marries a woman grossly unsuited to him will be unhappy. But this theme is developed only in the third volume of a three-volume work. Similarly we read *The Nether World*, looking in vain for a unifying idea. A rather villainous father breaks up the marriage of the heroine, his daughter,

---

[2] *The Unclassed* (London, Chapman and Hall, 1884), II, 33. Weymark makes this statement, but he is evidently the author's impersonation.

[3] George Gissing, *Critical Study of the Works of Charles Dickens,* (New York, Greenberg, Inc., 1924), 153.

with the hero. The father inherits money, deserts his daughter, and goes to America, where he loses the money in speculation. The hero marries a girl he should not have married, and the heroine resigns herself to a life of toil. Only when the two meet near the conclusion of the book does the author tell us in plain English what the events signify:

> In each life little for congratulation. He with the ambitions of his youth frustrated; neither an artist or a leader of men in the battle of justice. She no savior of society by the force of a superb example; no daughter of the people holding wealth in trust for the people's needs. Yet to both was their work given. Unmarked, unencouraged save for their love of uprightness and mercy, they stood by the side of those more helpless, brought some comfort to hearts less courageous than their own. Where it abode it was not all dark. Sorrow certainly awaited them, perchance defeat in even the humble aims that they had set themselves; but at least their lives would remain a protest against those brute forces of society which fill with wreck the abysses of the nether world.[4]

This is good writing but it is special pleading. And it is special pleading for a hero and a heroine of Victorian breed. Obviously Gissing has learned little about construction from the naturalists. Frank Swinnerton ably evaluates his rather unsatisfactory art:

> He was Victorian in his notions of construction. Many threads go to make up most of his books, threads interwoven with, for the most part, sincere regard for not improper interrelation. . . . It gives the appearance of too greatly diffused interest. . . . The result, as Mr. Arnold Bennett well says, "is that he seems never to centralize the interest. His pictures have no cynosure for the eye.[5]

Our interest is therefore with Gissing's vision. What is distinctive in his treatment of the poor?

Essentially it is his hatred of grossness, of vulgarity, and of poverty itself. At times it amounts to an aristocratic contempt:

> I am no friend of the people. As a force, by which the tenor of the

---

[4] *The Nether World*, (London, Smith and Elder, 1889), 391–92.
[5] *George Gissing*, (New York, Mitchell Kennerley, 1912), 166.

time is conditioned, they inspire me with distrust, with fear; as a visible multitude, they make me shrink, aloof, and often move me to abhorrence. For the greater part of my life, the people signified to me the London crowd, and no phrase of temperate meaning would alter my thoughts of them under that aspect. . . . Every instinct of my being is anti-democratic, and I dread to think what our England may become when Demos rules irresistibly. . . . Right or wrong, this is my temper. But he who would argue that I am intolerant of all persons belonging to a lower social rank than my own would go far astray. Nothing is more strongly rooted in my mind than the vast distinction between the individual and the class. Take a man by himself, and there is generally some reason to be fond of him, some disposition for good; mass him with his fellows in the social organism, and ten to one he becomes a blatant creature, without a thought of his own, ready for any evil to which contagion prompts him. It is because nations tend to stupidity and baseness that mankind moves so slowly; it is because individuals have a capacity for better things that it moves at all. In my youth, looking at this man and that, I marveled that humanity had made so little progress. Now, looking at men in the multitude, I marvel that they have advanced so far.[6]

I knew the poor and I knew that their aims were not mine. I knew the kind of life (such a modest life!) which I should have accepted as little short of the ideal, would have been to them,—if they could have understood it,—a weariness and a contempt. To ally myself with them against the "upper world" would have been mere dishonesty or sheer despair. What they at heart desired, was to me barren; what I coveted was to them forever incomprehensible.[7]

These selections are taken from a work written fourteen years after *The Nether World*. Nevertheless they have a definite interpretative value. "Nine out of ten" are like their fellows, but Gissing concentrates upon the tenth man or woman. Otherwise he gives a view of poverty characterized by its utter despair. Mad Jack, a preacher of the sidewalks, expresses it in lyrical fashion when he rails at the workers:

This life you are now leading is that of the damned; this place to which you are confined is hell! There is no escape for you. From poor

---

[6] *Private Papers of Henry Ryecroft* (Modern Library Edition), 39–40.
[7] *Ibid.*, 164.

you shall become poorer; the older you grow, the longer you will sink in want and in misery; at the end there is waiting for you, one and all, a death in abandonment and despair. This is Hell—Hell—Hell![8]

The author describes a locality:

> The slum was like any other slum; filth, rottenness, evil odors, possessed these dens of superfluous mankind and made them gruesome to the peering imagination. The inhabitants, of course, felt nothing of the sort; a room in Shooter's Gardens was the only home that most of them knew or desired.[9]

He describes a train journey through the district:

> Over the pest-stricken regions of East London, across miles of a city of the damned, such as thought never conceived before this age of ours; across streets swarming with a nameless populace, cruelly exposed to the light of heaven; stopping at stations which it crushes the heart to think should be the destination of any mortal; the train made its way beyond the outmost limits of dread, and entered upon a land of level meadows, of hedges and trees, of crops and cattle.[10]

Gissing inhabits his Nether World with a sufficient quantity of appropriate inhabitants, brutalized by their surroundings. But, like Dickens, he centers attention upon men and women whose inherent good qualities are in strict contrast to the prevailing sordidness. Flowers bloom on his rubbish heaps. Unlike Dickens, however, he not only doubts the fundamental soundness of the social order but the integrity of the universe. In default of a remedy he could but offer a personal protest, "If I hold apart . . . it is because I believe the world is better, not worse, for having one inhabitant who lives as becomes a civilized being."

Most of Gissing's novels are concerned with working people and slum life: *Workers in the Dawn* (1880), *The Unclassed* (1884), *Demos* (1866), *Thryza* (1887), *The Nether World* (1889). Dostoievski influenced him in *Isabel Clarendon* (1886). Meredith's influence is quite obvious in *A Life's Morning* (1888) and *The Crown of Life* (1899). *Born in Exile*

---

[8] *The Nether World*, 211–12.   [9] *Ibid.*, 178–79.   [10] *Ibid.*, 109.

(1892) is somewhat autobiographical and is a continuation of the tendency earlier expressed in *Workers in the Dawn* and *The Unclassed*.

Aside from the essays of Gissing the Latinist in *The Private Papers of Henry Ryecroft* (1903), Gissing will live in literary history as a good hater. People write about what pains them, he once said. He himself was pained to the point of hatred by "the hideous injustice of our whole system of society." No English writer before him or since has portrayed with as much loathing the irremediable squalor and degredation of the poor. The genial optimism of admirers of Dickens is shaken.

In an evaluation of Gissing we must be discriminating. He has nothing of the modern spirit of eager inquiry. He constantly judges "our poor unhappy world from the point of view of a literary young man of high ideals." Frank Swinnerton tells us that he was a conscious malcontent, not a revolutionary. We find protest where we look for analysis; we find social rebellion tapering off into discussions of culture. There is nowhere a firm grasp of life or philosophy or novel-structure. Everything he wrote is dated. And yet he did more than any other writer before Wells to call attention to the evils of the social system. He altered the naturalistic novel to provide for interludes of social philosophizing. Weygandt gives a list of English writers whom Gissing influenced—Bennett, W. L. George, Walpole, Oliver Onions, J. D. Beresford, and Allan Monkhouse. Weygandt concludes, "No English writer not of first power has, during the past twenty years, had so wide and deep an influence as Gissing."[11]

[11] Cornelius Weygandt, *A Century of the English Novel* (New York, The Century Co., 1925), 438.

⊸§VIII §⊱

HENRY JAMES'S VERSION
OF THE EXPERIMENTAL NOVEL

HENRY JAMES, son of a cultured clergyman, was born in Northampton, Massachusetts, in 1843. His first trip to Europe was made at the age of twelve. His acquaintance with the continental currents of thought began with his next sojourn when he pursued his studies, first at Geneva, and later in London, Paris, and Bern. His education was not entirely in the hands of European teachers, however, as he also studied in New York, Albany, and Newport. When twenty-six years of age he visited Europe for two months, and when twenty-nine for two years. In 1875, when he was thirty-two years old, he again came to Europe, this time to make it his home.

The year 1875-76 was eventful for Henry James. During part of this time he was located in Paris, cultivating the acquaintance of Turgenev, Flaubert, Daudet, Maupassant, and Zola. In spite of the value of these connections, however, he decided not to remain permanently in France. He doubted that an American could take root and flourish on French soil. Consequently he moved to London, resolved to make that city his permanent headquarters.

His pre-European work has a passing interest for us here, chiefly for a mention of early influences. That of Hawthorne is obviously present in certain stories—"The Last of the Vererii," "De Gray," "The Romance of Certain Old Clothes" —and, as Carl Van Doren points out, "other works came near to achieving the considered sobriety of George Eliot, whom he admired, and he tucked himself as far as he could under the mantle of Balzac."[1] Hawthorne has been credited with shepherding James into the European environment and lending him a framework on which to drape his emotions until he discovered his own power to build up an imaginative structure.[2]

Roderick Hudson (1876) was James's last work before he made Europe his home. We note that he is already preoccupied with the "international situation," and that, except for the ending of the book, he is already a pretty fair "experimental" novelist. Let us consider the book in brief summary in order to compare it with James's later development: A young American who has shown some ability in sculpture is freed from the drudgery of a lawyer's office in Northampton by a benefactor and is sent to Rome to follow the bent of his genius. In Rome he makes his acquaintance with the requisites of the artistic life, which demand that he purify himself of all vestiges of nationality. The process of changing his ideas is a painful one, and while he is undergoing it, Hudson falls glamorously in love with the beauty of Christina Light. Christina and her mother have a greater complexity of character than that with which the young American is familiar. This complexity is dependent upon a calculating shrewdness which approaches unscrupulousness. Hudson does not know that the mother and the young girl are traveling all over Europe in search of a rich husband, and he does not understand the unkind treatment given him. His interest in his work becomes demoralized. But this is not the end of the story. The end of the story is reached only when Hudson falls over a cliff in Switzerland.

In revising his novel for the definitive edition, Henry James permits himself a joke. Hudson hears that his American benefactor has been nobly stifling a yearning for his (Hudson's)

---

[1] *The American Novel* (New York, The Macmillan Co., 1921).
[2] Rebecca West, *Henry James* (London, Nisbit and Ltd., 1916), 25.

sweetheart. "It's like something in a novel," comments the Hudson of the first edition. "It's like something in a bad novel," comments the Hudson of the definitive edition. How unfortunate that James did not reserve this comment for Hudson's melodramatic demise!

The ending of this novel is purely arbitrary. It is the kind of thing Zola laughed at—authors dropping bricks on their characters' heads at convenient moments.

Henry James had learned his lesson by the time he published *The American* in 1877. The theme of James's study as announced in the preface of the definitive edition (New York) is, "the situation, in another country and an aristocratic society, of some robust but insidiously beguiled and betrayed, some cruelly wronged compatriot; the point being in special that he should suffer at the hands of the person pretending to represent the highest possible civilization and to be of an order far superior to his own." A strong and affable American explores Europe and eventually presents himself at the house of the Bellegardes, an ancient royalist family. His subsequent desire to marry the widowed daughter, Claire de Ceintre, results in the family's hastily sending her away to a convent. The American is indignant at the occurrence but utterly powerless until he discovers a family secret. He finds out that Madame de Bellegardes, supported by her son, had long ago caused the death of her husband by refusing him medicine when ill. The American plans revenge by exposure of the secret. But so great is the gulf between himself and the Europe he has discovered, so great a gulf is there between the moral structure of these people and that of his own nature, that he feels the satisfaction from revenge would be insignificant and decides to let the matter drop.

The ending of this story is not in accord with the practice of English or American novelists. A writer of romance would have caused the American to rescue his well-beloved; Hawthorne might have shown Madame de Bellegardes terrified by the remembrance of her crime; George Eliot would have rendered homage to Nemesis by letting the secret be found out by someone who would put the machinery of the law in motion. But the novel of James ends when the logical conclusion of a certain set of circumstances is reached.

It is unfortunate that the letters of Henry James written between 1875 and 1876 are not published. We should like to get his first impressions of the Paris group. No doubt much of *Notes on Novelists* (1878) was written during the year in Paris and the contacts provided there inspired the chapters on Balzac and Flaubert. "Flaubert is of the school of Balzac; the brothers de Goncourt and Emile Zola of the school of Flaubert." James's mature evaluation of the naturalists is not expressed until 1884, when he wrote to William Dean Howells from Paris:

> I have been seeing something of Daudet, Goncourt, and Zola, and there is nothing more interesting to me now than the effort and experiment of this little group, with its truly infernal intelligence of art, form, manner—its intense artistic life. They do the only kind of work that I respect; and in spite of their ferocious pessimism and their handling of unclean things, they are at least serious and honest. The floods of tepid soap and water which under the name of novels are being vomited forth in England, seem to me, by contrast, to do little honor to our race.

Later James was to express more clearly his temperamental aversion to the practices of the naturalists. He was able, he writes, "to see little entertainment from watching a wayfarer enter an alley that we know to have no issue" and for witnessing the spectacle "for the very sake of the face he may show us on reappearing at its mouth."[3] He criticizes Balzac and all French men of letters for their hatred of the *bourgeoisie*.[4] *Madame Bovary* was to him a disagreeable novel; "everything in the book is ugly."[5] He objects to Zola because "he presents us with a decoction of 'nature' in a novel unfit for the pur-

---

[3] *Notes on Novelists*, 272.
[4] *French Poets and Novelists* (London, Macmillan, 1878), 102.
[5] *Ibid.*, 206.

pose, a receptacle lamentably, fatally in need of scouring (though all scouring, apparently, would be really ineffective) and in which no article intended for intellectual consumption should be served up."[6]

The American appeared three years before *Le roman expérimental* was published. Yet Edmund Gosse considers it an experimental novel, "the first in the English language." And if *The American* is an experimental novel, why not *The Europeans, The Bostonians, The Ambassadors, The Portrait of a Lady?*

Gosse's use of the term "experimental novel" does not, of course, mean to imply that James was a follower of Zola in anything but theory. And even then the term "experimental novel" refers only to the principle of logical deduction and "follow through" that Zola and the other naturalists posed as a primal requisite. No doubt when Zola published *Le roman expérimental* he expounded the theories which had been developed by the naturalists in Paris, and with which Henry James was thoroughly familiar. The experimental novelist would "show what a certain 'passion,' aroused under certain circumstances and in a certain environment, will result in as regards the individual and society." Henry James's own contention (after his stay in Paris) was that the author should take his *donnée,* or situation, and work it out to a logical conclusion. There is one chief difference in the theories. Zola would show the logical outcome of events on both "the individual and society." James was little concerned with the influence of events upon society at large.

And so we may loosely classify the major portion of James's fiction as experimental novels. But James, though wanting a logical conclusion, could not bear that a conclusion be forseen. Like the naturalists, he approved of note-taking, but he felt that no amount of documentation would infallibly predict the decisions of highly refined intelligences. Thus results the suspense generally characteristic of James's work and the

[6] Introduction to *Nana* (London, Vizetelly & Co., 1884), xiv.

excitement which comes from speculation on decisions that hang in the balance.

As James grew older, the passion for the highly differentiated and "exquisite" grew upon him. He progressively chose rarer and more highly specialized "cases" which piqued his curiosity and provided neat exercises for artful concealment of the pattern in his mind. It is well known that he went too far. The daemon of the highly rarefied eventually led him to a region where cold logic alone exists. He ascends with one reader to a plane which is not life, and where there is neither wisdom nor warmth nor poetry. Some bleak god of plaster casts sits enthroned before a delicately molded and immaculate assemblage of Higher Perceptions, Noble Ideals, Tender Restraints, and Unsung Heroisms—with a few stage gargoyles in the background.

But André Gide has, I believe, written the best depreciation of Henry James so far composed:

He lets only just enough steam escape to run his engine ahead, from page to page: and I do not believe that this economy, this reserve, has ever sagaciously been carried further. The proportion remains perfect between the propulsive force and the drawing out of the narrative. No wonder, since nothing really alive nourishes him, and James only extracts from his brain what he knows to be there, and what his intelligence alone has put there. The interest is never in the outpouring, but is solely in the conduit. His work is like that of the spider, who ceaselessly widens her web by hanging new threads from one chosen support to another. Doubtless I shall praise him for taking his stand always on the same data of a problem. The skillfully made network spun out by his intelligence captivates only the intelligence; the intelligence of the reader, the intelligence of the heroes of his books. The latter never seem to exist except in the functioning of their intellects, they are only winged busts; all the weight of the flesh is absent, and all the shaggy tangled undergrowth, all the wild darkness.[7] ...

We must avoid the temptation of considering in too much detail the extravagances which Henry James permitted him-

[7] "Henry James," *The Yale Review*, March, 1930.

self. The extravagances are present and therefore deserving of mention. Those who are interested in his tendency to elaboration should by all means read his stenographer's account,[8] for the tendency to elaboration progressed with James's discovery of the convenience of dictation. Our interest here must be centered on the main tendencies of the author's more important work. We turn, therefore, to the author's "world."

The "world" of Henry James is not to be confused with the segments of industrialized society treated in different novels of the naturalists. It is rather a plane of existence inhabited by people who are worldly in the very best sense of the word; who are "really fine and complicated," to use James's own expression. To be "fine" one must have a richly developed consciousness and the delicate powers of discrimination. A "fine" sentiment is aristocratic rather than epicurean—it is often the gentlemanly fine. So James's people make "fine decisions"—that is, humanly fine decisions, for God and abstract ideas of right do not enter. The matter of the author's sympathy is, of course, purposely concealed for a time. In the last analysis, however, it will be seen that he is infallibly on the side of the highly civilized and exquisite.

As opposed to the "fine" there is Evil, in rather well-acknowledged guises. But what surprised Henry James's contemporaries was that Satan should be given high social privileges, and that the elect and highly differentiated were often mindful of his blandishments. Wrote the critic for *The Sketch:*

> That a portion of the world on which all hopes hang should be made suspect, should be shown to have the loathsome disease of sin knit in with their tender fibers, not in the guise of mere naughtiness and weakness, not merely in the germ, but in full-blown strength— these are intolerable thoughts.[9]

One wonders to what extent Henry James introduced Evil merely for the purpose of drama. His interest sometimes seems

---

[8] Theodora Bosanquet, *Henry James at Work* (London, The Hogarth Press, 1924).
[9] May 30, 1898.

rather scientific; and yet there is truth in his stenographer's version:

> When he walked out of the refuge of his study into the world and looked about him, he saw a place of torment, where creatures of prey perpetually thrust their claws into the quivering flesh of the doomed, defenceless children of light. He had the abiding comfort of an inner certainty (and perhaps he did bring that from New England) that the children of light had an eternal advantage; he was aware to the finest fibre of his being that the "poor sensitive gentlemen" he so numerously treated possessed a treasure that would outlast all the glittering paste of the world and the flesh; he knew that nothing in life mattered compared with spiritual decency.[10]

In *Longman's Magazine* for September, 1884, Henry James published his essay "The Art of Fiction." I mention the date because of the similarity to Maupassant's article on the novel which was published as a preface to *Pierre et Jean* in 1888. Maupassant is the borrower.

Says Henry James:

> The subject-matter of fiction is storied up like that of history in documents and records, and if it is not to give itself away, as they say in California, it must speak with assurance, with the tone of the historian. .... The novel in its broadest definition is a personal impression of life; that, to begin with, constitutes its value, which is greater or less according to the intensity of the impression.

The author's production of the illusion of life depends on his choice of details, and in this respect according to James, "he competes with his brother the painter in *his* attempt to render the look of things, the look that conveys their meaning, to catch the color, the relief, the expression, the surface, the substance of the human spectacle." James recommends note-taking and says that the author "cannot possibly take too many, he cannot possibly take enough." But "art is essentially selection," and "it is a selection whose main care is to be typical, to be inclusive."

---

[10] Bosanquet, *Henry James at Work*, 32.

James does not see that a novel, being a picture, "can be either moral or immoral." The English novelists have a moral timidity in refusing to face the difficulties with which the treatment of reality bristles. The attempt to include "adventure" in the novel would bring it back "to the hapless little role of being an artificial, ingenious thing—bring it down from its large free character of an intense and exquisite correspondence with life." "A psychological reason is, to my imagination, an object adorably pictorial; to catch the tint of its complexion— I feel as if that idea might inspire one to Titanesque efforts."

Henry James did more than introduce in England the beauties of a psychological reason, for he introduced the beauties of a not overdogmatic logic, and he showed the possibilities of a logical art-form in the novel. He cultivated with considerable success the art of making the minute, if not important, at least exciting. If, as Wells suggests, his dexterity sometimes reminds one of a hippopotamus trying to pick up a pea, it is also true that much of his writing is not overcomplicated and that he is largely responsible for the more formal developments of the novel in the postwar years. As an innovator he at least prepared the way for stream of consciousness, and he is responsible for postwar concern with "time-sequence"—a mode in which all exposition is handled through refraction. During the extended years of his writing his quiet influence advanced the position of fiction as a serious artistic medium. People were always a little bit in awe of him.

❧ IX ❧

THE EIGHTEEN-NINETIES

GENERALITIES ON ITS FICTION

MOST of the novels and stories so far mentioned were produced during the nineties, although the writings of the more important novelists—James, Moore, and Gissing—began much earlier and extended into the twentieth century. A startling new conception—in fact a great many new conceptions—of the novel had become widely prevalent. It seems advisable at this point in our study to treat the diffused nature of the English response. Here our interest becomes associated with the time-spirit. For the English response was not confined to imitation. Change was abroad in the land and a new fiction was needed to keep pace with the shifting current of values.

From several excellent books which have been written on the eighteen-nineties we gather that the breakup of Victorianism resulted in such an intellectual and emotional stir as England had not experienced since the awakening to the Italian Renaissance. The tendency was toward new endeavor in following the widest variety of interests. Holbrook Jackson sees in the diversity of experimentation a broad ethical awakening. "Anybody who studies the thoughts and moods of the Eighteen-Nineties," he says, "cannot fail to observe their central characteristics in a widespread concern for the correct—that is, the most effective, the most powerful, the most righteous— mode of living. . . . Life aroused curiosity. People became enthusiastic about the way it should be used. . . . It was an epoch of experiment."[1] W. G. Blaikie-Murdock in a short book entitled *The Renaissance of the Nineties* states that the chief tendency was toward agnosticism. Osbert Burdett in *The Beardsley Period* speaks of the decade's vision of light which men believed "would lift the fringe of the horizon and prolong the cycle of the hours."[2] J. M. Kennedy would extend the limits of the "period"; "The artists of the period 1880–1905," he writes, "were caught up in a torrent of materialism, atheism, idealism and romanticism."[3]

That the last decade of the century was one of diverse leanings is evident from a mention of its literary interests. Nietzsche, Schopenhauer, Ibsen, the Celtic Revival, the French symbolists and naturalists with their English followers, the romantic fiction of Kipling and Stevenson, the novels of Hardy and Meredith, the dramas of Shaw—all these were the concerns of the nineties. There were, furthermore, a number of "new" preoccupations. The adjective "new" was used to indicate extreme modernity and was applied to a wide variety of subjects. There was the "New Hedonism," the "New Fiction," the "New Paganism," the "New Voluptuousness," the "New Remorse," the "New Spirit," the "New Drama," the "New Woman," and the "New Revelation."[4] The *National Observer* changed its name to *The New Review*, and a weekly paper with humanitarian tendencies entitled *The New Age* began to appear. Magazines expressing the new tendencies of thought suddenly made their appearance: *The Yellow Book, The Savoy, The Parade, The Pageant, The Evergreen, The Chameleon, The Hobby Horse, The Rose Leaf, The Quarto,* and *The Dome*.[5]

Several observations are in order. In the first place, since the nineties was a period of uncertainty and curiosity, it was congenial to the social introspection of naturalism and to inno-

---

[1] *The Eighteen-Nineties* (London, Grant Richards, Ltd., 1922), 14.
[2] Osbert Burdett, *The Beardsley Period* (London, John Lane The Bodley Head, 1925), 94–95.
[3] *English Literature* (1880–1905) (London, Low, Marston & Co., 1913), "Introduction."
[4] Jackson, *The Eighteen-Nineties*, 22–23.   [5] *Ibid.*, 36.

vations in technique. In the second place, a strong tendency running counter to naturalism was apparent in the romantic works of Kipling, Stevenson, and Rider Haggard, and in the rejuvenated historical romance which won a wide public during the last five years of the century. In the third place, even interest in "serious fiction" was divided. Hardy and Meredith were looked upon by many as "the greatest" novelists. Yet the range of those influenced by the naturalists was wide, and the critical approach was undoubtedly responsible in part for the flood of novels treating marital incompatibility. Finally, and in order to give us a still broader perspective, we must keep in mind a prosaic fact, so obviously neglected in the enthusiastic chronicles dealing with the nineties, that a large mass of the English public was influenced by neither Nietzsche, Zola, Ibsen, nor the French symbolists. They were reading Tennyson, Dickens, Thackeray, and George Eliot, as well as the sentimental-romantic novel of surprises which, then as now, was present in abounding quantities. Transition in literary art-forms is never thorough. And in the novel, more than in other forms, it affects a fringe.

The fiction of the eighteen-nineties shows us the beginnings of transition. What is significant from this point of view is the number of both new and established writers who participated in it. In general we may say that "transition" involves, on the one hand, a progress in truth-telling in the light of the broad cosmic view opened by scientific materialism; on the other, a technique, or a variety of techniques, which makes the truth-telling plausible. As we glance through the minor fiction of the nineties we notice certain strong tendencies aside from the revival of romance and aside from the interest in Hardy and Meredith: first, a concern with degradation and the life of the poor; second, an interest in themes of marital incompatibility; third, an inclination to present themes taken from life —or, if you will, social observations consistently developed. Certain writers broke away from the tendencies of their earlier work.

A Capful o' Nails (1896), by David Christie Murray, is a study of the poor taken from firsthand observation. "In its main lines the tale is quite true," writes Murray in his introduction, "and, in my childhood, many of its people were familiar to me. I have written of what I knew, and I have nowhere exaggerated by one hair's breadth. Much is amended nowadays, but the truth, even today, is stern and mournful, and may well make an Englishman ashamed." The story is that of a fight by the father of the narrator for justice, fair treatment, and education in behalf of his fellow nail makers who live near the brick kilns between Castle Barfield and Quarrymoor. The father is aided with funds by a curate, but his effort to lift the people out of their stagnant mental condition meets with failure; "he could not free the slaves who were in debt and quaking before their masters." A school is established, but the workers send their children only if paid to do so, and they murmur against their fellow nail maker for setting himself up to be better than his neighbors when he turns schoolmaster. The sentiment against him grows, and on an occasion when he tries to quiet a mob he is beaten to death. The people are left in bondage, remembering their would-be deliverer as a man who deserted his class for gain.

Edwin Pugh, admirer of Dickens and first-rate employer of cockney dialect, goes deeper than his master into scenes of degradation. In *A Man of Straw* (1897), a man follows a prostitute into her den: "They descended cautiously to a foul smelling passage. There was a noise of scurrying vermin. In a room close at hand a woman was shrieking at a drunken lover, and beating his prostrate body with her hand. The sound of her thumping punctured her jeremiad. The man was either dead or senseless for he made no protest."[6] At a music hall the audience joins in with the chorus in singing a popular number: " 'The Gorgonzola Cheese' was mouthed by the wizened youth and sung by the audience. Drunken boyhood, sodden womanhood, foul age, howled and shrieked it from the gallery; men

6 Edwin Pugh, *A Man of Straw* (London, Heineman, 1897), 329.

in greasy evening dress and debauched women hummed it from the stalls."[7] Pugh shrinks from no subject; he treats with equal impartiality diseases ranging from "religiosity" to the more venal ones. He would lift "the fringes of a curtain hanging from heaven to earth, hiding a world where people play with life."

Unholy Matrimony (1899), by John Le Breton (Mr. Murray Ford and Miss Harte-Potts), is typically naturalistic. A curate and Rose, a barmaid, are left behind at a picnic. Rose plays the curate, David, for a compromise, and he marries her to save her reputation. The marriage turns out badly; "Rose's sturdy and combative animalism irritated and disgusted David, gradually transferring his coldness and aversion to sympathetic contempt." The wife proves to be a drunkard and later kills her child. David is driven out of the church and Rose becomes more and more debased from drink. The author divulges with some insistence the evil of drink among the lower classes. David drifts into the shipping business, which is explained in full naturalistic detail.

Of more importance, however, in showing England's awakening to the problems of poverty was a series of articles written by Robert Harborough Sherard for *Pearson's Magazine* and later published in book form as *The White Slaves of England* (1897), *The Cry of the Poor* (1901), and *The Child Slaves of Britain* (1905). Sherard based his articles largely on the stories and accounts of workmen. He traveled as a trespasser, he says, living among the poor and asking no favors of their employers. Everywhere he found "unclean beds, coarse food, foul sights and fouler odors, evil talk and harrowing tales. . . . There came a time when body and soul revolted and great was the yearning to return to the upper air."[8] "The workmen seemed to have little or no interest in my work, experience had made fatalists of them all; they have forgotten how to hope; of all their stirs and alarms nothing has come and they expect noth-

[7] *Ibid.*, 67.
[8] *The Cry of the Poor* (London, Digby, Long & Co., 1901), 12.

ing but the 'grubber' [workhouse], struggling on with a resignation and a courage that is little short of sublime."[9] Responsibility is difficult to place, but the author concludes: "Instability of employment, excess of population, early marriage and too large families; these are often the cause of the squalid misery of the slums."[10] "The great success which has attended on M. Zola and Mr. Arthur Morrison is due without a doubt to the fact that these writers, realists of fact as well as of fiction, are known to speak the truth."[11]

As previously explained, the new liberty of thought and expression which attended the first phase of the transition, the critical attitude toward life, the awakened curiosity of the novel-reading public—all prepared the way for studies of marital incompatibility. Perhaps *A Doll's House* and the Feminist movement had a great deal to do with the matter. During the last five years of the century a frank discussion of temperamental disharmony was a distinguishing feature of the English novel. Representing the effort of minor writers the following novels might be mentioned: *Disillusion* (1894), by Dorothy Leighton; *The Sentimental Sex* (1897), by Gertrude Warden; *The Duenna of a Genius* (1898), by M. E. Francis (Mrs. Bluddell); *Bam Wildfire* (1898), by Helen Mathers; *Some Unoffending Prisoners* (1899), by "John Fulford."

What interests us especially in isolated novels of the later nineties is that the precepts of *Le roman expérimental* were beginning to be widely known. Characters in these novels enjoy great freedom of action, and the voice of Nemesis, the goddess of the Victorian novel, becomes feeble and inarticulate.

Corruption (1895), by Percy White, is concerned with the affairs, political and amorous, of an unscrupulous, ambitious, capable, and attractive politician. To this extent the book echoes *Bel-Ami*. Paul Carew is, in the eyes of the world, "a political Launcelot without a blemish." But in reality he is

---

[9] *The White Slaves of England* (London, James Bowden, 1897), 24–25.
[10] Sherard, *The Cry of the Poor*, 14.
[11] Sherard, *The White Slaves of England*, 17.

in the power of a rich brewer who lends him money, and he is not at all sincere with the motley crew of socialists and labor sympathizers who depend upon him for leadership in Parliament. He has for mistress the wife of a well-known sportsman. Carew makes no attempt to justify his actions; they seem, he says, "to have been mapped out for the amusement of invisible spectators. Destiny plays the call-boy. I am growing used to my part." He sees that a step in his advancement would be his marriage with the brewer's daughter, and he brings the matter to pass. But he tells his mistress that if their secret is discovered, he will leave the country with her. He is forced to keep his promise when a discharged servant sells the information. The pair go to the Mediterranean but are unable to marry because Carew's wife will not divorce him. Later he returns to England alone in order to look after his interests, leaving his mistress to amuse herself with Prince Ferdinand. On his return there is a scene, following which his mistress runs away with Prince Ferdinand and Carew rejoins his loving wife preparatory to resuming his career.

But a summary hardly suffices to indicate the comparatively new type of central character which the author introduces. Carew refers to *Le Disciple*, saying that it is a "dangerously fascinating book." "I confess to some sympathy with the neurotic pessimist who is the hero," he avows. "He was the victim of the desire of the age from which we all suffer. Directly a man is convinced of his insignificance in this lath and plaster civilization and flies to science and sociology for comfort, he begins to take even his love as a problem."

Other novels may be mentioned in brief summary. *George Mandeville's Husband* (1894), by C. E. Raimond, is the study of a fat, selfish, sentimental woman writer who neglects her child. The child, who is not fond of the mother, dies. But the mother imagines that she adored the child and paints her in terms which show that she does not even remember what the child looked like. *A Deliverance* (1898), by Allan Monkhouse, tells of a strong-willed, high-minded woman who tries to keep up the courage of her dying lover in order that his end will be worthy of him. But the man does not want to have his courage kept up; he wants to relax, to groan, to weep, and to tremble. Finally he sends the woman away, although he loves her, and calls to him a weaker creature who will allow him the privileges of weakness. *Rachel* (1899), by Jane Find-later, is concerned chiefly with a preacher possessed of a certain mystic fire who is forced continually to invent new visions for the crowds who look to him for light and leading. *Within Bounds* (1898), by Ethel Coxon, is a story showing the deadening effect of teaching upon teachers. *Two in Captivity* (1899), owes much of literary inspiration to *Thérèse Raquin*.

It seems not amiss to suggest that new criteria of artistic excellence had been established for fiction in England, and that twentieth-century novelists might accept them or not as they pleased. What, then, are the naturalistic criteria of excellence which became in a measure accepted in England before the beginning of the twentieth century? Or shall we rather ask, What did the English writers learn during the eighties and nineties that they did not know before?

Well, they learned the importance of approaching life from a questioning, agnostic point of view; that the structure of society is of inexhaustible interest to those who would examine it; that the novel should be a conscious and critical interpretation of life; that all is not well with the world nor with the institutions of society which reveal man's improvidence and incapacity; that poverty is a disease and that no good end will be served by calling it by any other name. And man? He is certainly not a noble creature—but still, not unhuman; willing unselfishly to aid his neighbor, but moderately covetous nonetheless; ambitious and successful, but not overscrupulous; a creature capable of love, but not altogether discriminate in his affections; pious, but subject to impiety; honest, sometimes, but frail.

As to construction, the English learned that the novel might be simplified to the level of the best intelligences; that there need be no hero, heroine, villain, or plot if the portrayal is honest and revealing; that the novel need not be conclusive, but, whatever the author's vision of a set of circumstances and people, we must be content with the vision and not require a philosophy.

❧ X ❧

ORIENTATION, 1900–1915

REALISM VS. ROMANCE

THE most obvious fact about English novels at the turn of the century is that there were so many of them. When the three-volume novel became extinct about 1895, the novel-buying public was vastly increased. In less than a century a remarkable change had occurred. Only eighteen new novels were accepted by the British museum in 1820, and two thousand were accepted in 1900. In 1903 exactly 1,859 new novels (no reprints) were published in England.[1] "The novel has spread like a prairie fire," wrote G. K. Chesterton in 1902. "Space itself is becoming a nightmare merely because there is so much of it."[2]

Between 1900 and 1904 controversy centered on the romance vs. realism issue. Critics were loosely divided, some advocating realism and some welcoming the new romance, with advocates of romance sometimes joining the opposition to declaim against puerile extravagance. Andrew Lang, romanticist, naturally approved the romantic swing as a reaction against naturalistic brutality: "the tendency to a new licence seems to have expended itself."[3] A writer for the *Edinburgh Review* held that readers really liked "imagination rather than truth"; that the "battle instinct" and the love of rough-and-

---

[1] H. Cuthbert Hadden, "The Plague of Novels," *Fortnightly Review*, June, 1904.
[2] "The Over-Production of Novels," *Pall Mall Magazine*, May, 1902.
[3] "Evolution of Literary Decency," *Blackwoods Magazine*, May, 1902.

tumble adventure survived in the sex that did the fighting; that it was not for the critic to say "nay" if the public liked Hall Caine's vision of the monstrous wickedness that goes on in London's hospitals or Marie Corelli's vision of society as the haunt of wicked peers and abandoned peeresses, or Mary Cholmondeley's melodramatic social situations.[4] Chesterton persuasively argued for plot in novels:

> The evolutionist may think life is a race, and the Buddhist may think it a wheel, but neither of them at the bottom of their souls has any doubt that life is a three-volume novel. In the light of this it is sufficiently absurd that any hyper-aesthetic critics should have taken to sneering at plot in novels. A man may surely be permitted to read a novel because there is a plot in it when he is engaged in living a life in the face of every obstacle because there is plot in it.[5]

A writer for the *Fortnightly* wanted "beauty, humor, charm, and joy" in the novel, and he took Zola to task for the absence of these qualities in his works.[6] Further belated criticism of Zola appeared in the *Quarterly Review*. Zola was rather expertly compared with Hugo, but his pessimistic vision was regretted.[7] Walter Sichel celebrated the romantic reaction against "the sterner writers" although he was not inconsiderate of their merit.[8]

It would seem from these opinions that the critical view was in opposition to the realistic tendencies, but such was not altogether the case. Sichel, who celebrated the return of romance, was critical of the deluge of romances. Hadden in the *Fortnightly* felt that "not one out of every thousand" of the current product had the chance of immortality:

> Plots are incoherent when they are not hackneyed, characterization limp and feeble; the dialogue is imbecile and superficial; in short the whole performance is not worth the ink and paper expended on it. ... Reviewers are heartily sick of these miserable "romances."[9]

4 "Some Recent Novels of Manners," July, 1900.
5 "The Over-Production of Novels."
6 Cecil G. Brown, "Realism," September, 1902.
7 "The Novel of Misery," October, 1902.
8 "Some Phases of Fiction," *Fortnightly Review,* August, 1902.
9 "The Plague of Novels."

A writer for the *Quarterly Review* found "the relation between the merit of novels and their popularity has never been of a kind so anomalous, so independent of any serious literary standards, as it is in our country at the present moment."[10] Chesterton, after his usual elaborate fooling, confessed that "the atmosphere of plutocracy and fashion, the mere romance of the drawn sword, and the everlasting kailyard are pretty well exhausted."[11]

On the "plus" side for the realists was the admission that Zola "photographs the idealist";[12] favorable comment on Gissing, Stephen Crane, and Frank Norris;[13] some belated praise for *The Woman Who Did;*[14] and a dialogue by D. F. Hannigan which flaunts the realists' banner. In Hannigan's article the character who expresses the views of the author calls Thackeray the worst of snobs and Kipling an imperialist snob. The novel of the future "will possess the verisimilitude of Defoe, the scientific exactitude of Flaubert and Zola, the masculine plain-speaking of Maupassant."[15]

Perhaps we could call it a draw. There is, of course, no need of choosing a dominant tendency. In literary history the significance of the controversy is that the new realism, of a species akin to naturalism, was not submerged. The advocacy of romance in England was nothing new, but the criticism of romance and the continuation from the nineties of pro-naturalistic sentiment reveal the permanence of a new critical outlook. Furthermore we get from a hostile comment of Sichel in 1902 a penetrating picture of the inroads of naturalism:

There are problem plays everywhere. ... The post-nuptial phase of love and marriage are alone treated. ... Melodrama is vamped up in the guise of a problem play with the dissenting deacon taking the villain's part instead of the conventional attorney. ... In the great mass

---

[10] "The Popular Novel," July, 1901.
[11] "The Over-Production of Novels."
[12] Sichel, "Some Phases of Fiction."
[13] "The Novel of Misery."
[14] Richard Le Gallienne, "On Grant Allen," *Fortnightly Review,* December, 1899.
[15] *Westminster Review,* May, 1900.

of serious fiction man is a machine. Heredity, necessity, encompass him. ... There is a growing lack of reverence in modern fiction. It is naked but not ashamed. Nothing for it is common or unclean. ... The reign of the fireside is over. ... The modern novelists, partly in the spirit of fashion, partly from cosmopolitan conventions which increased communicability stereotypes, ignore it and prefer passion to affection. ... So fiction is cosmopolitan and exhales no flavor of the soil. ... There is a lack of finality in our recent novels. ... Ours is eminently a self-conscious era. ... Scientific psychology is no longer the nebulous hypothesis it was once.[16]

THE NOVEL OF IDEAS

Although it has seemed advisable to deal separately with the years 1900–1904 because of romantic and counter-romantic currents, there is little reason for a division of the years 1904–15. Sometime between 1906 and 1909 romance passed from fashion; sometime around 1910 British writers began to be less objective. In the main we note three tendencies: (1) the liking for ideas in the novel; (2) the triumph of Wells, subjectivism, and the life-novel; and (3) the general Russian influence.

The predominant tendency of the English novel for the years 1900–1915 was to give expression to ideas—social, political, and philosophical. The tendency was not a new one in English fiction. What was new was that the horizon of the writers was broader. Novelists and public were actively critical of past valuations. They were deeply concerned with new ways of living and new ways of thought. A humanitarian, a cosmopolitan, an urban consciousness prevailed.

Thus we find one critic telling us that the love interest has been subordinated and that novelists have acquired a sufficient sense of proportion to recognize that readers may be interested in politics, sociology, or Votes for Women.[17] Another asks for more political novels.[18] A third suggests that the appeal

---

16 "Some Phases of Fiction."
17 E. L. Lacon Watson, "The Modern Novel; Some Tendencies," *Dial*, October, 1913.
18 "Novels with a Philosophy," *Edinburgh Review*, January, 1906.

of novels lies not so much in the story as in the range of ideas that they represent and illustrate; that we learn by close contact with actualities; and that "there is no experience for which a man or woman may not in the end find cause to be thankful, provided that it is experience not of stagnation but of life."[19] A fourth critic remarks, "Fiction is becoming what poetry was once truly said to be—a criticism of life."[20] A fifth feels that "all novels should be contributions toward the liberal education of their readers."[21] Even Zola is no longer criticized, and when, as is rare, a critic decides to write about crudity in fiction, he chooses English works as the subject of his invective.[22] Zola even comes in for occasional praise: "His earnestness and sincerity, his extraordinary force, courage, and emotion carry conviction and compel readers to go along with him against their will."[23] Gissing is acclaimed a social philosopher:

In a series of books he exhibits Demos as it really is, with its virtues and aspirations faithfully represented, its faults and passions undisguised, while he more particularly depicts in action the development of Socialist agitation and notes its effect upon various minds.

The critic continues,

The public will not study sociology, much less visualize the conditions and problems that set out and make them bear any real meaning. It is exactly this that the novelist can do for "the man in the street."[24]

Even W. L. George, who attempted impersonality in most of his works, came to the conclusion, "Ashamed as we are of writing novels with a purpose, we can no longer write novels without a purpose."[25]

Obviously something has happened to British critical opin-

19 "Insular Fiction," *Edinburgh Review,* January, 1907.
20 *Ibid.*
21 "Ugliness in Fiction," *Edinburgh Review,* April, 1908.
22 *Ibid.*
23 E. B. Harrison, "Some Thoughts About the Novel," *Nineteenth Century,* November, 1913.
24 Norman Bentwich, "The Novel as a Political Force," *Nineteenth Century,* November, 1906.
25 "Form in the Novel," *Living Age,* April, 1914. Included in W. L. George's *Literary Chapters.*

ion. A critic for the *Westminster Review* of 1911 gives Zola the chief credit,[26] but the influence of H. G. Wells, who was influenced by Zola, seems definitely predominant.

Both as social philosopher and as novelist Wells came into early popularity. Between 1901 and 1905 three volumes of his social prophecy appeared serially: *Anticipations, Mankind in the Making, Modern Utopia.*[27] *The English Review* published *Tono-Bungay* between 1906 and 1908. Between 1905 and 1908 full-length articles about Wells appeared in the *Fortnightly*, the *Contemporary*, the *Quarterly Review*, and the *Nineteenth Century.*[28] Wells's intention was generally acclaimed. A critic in 1906 welcomed *Kipps* as expressing Wells's idea that "the whole framework of society is absurdly adjusted."[29] The *Edinburgh Review* in 1907 appraised the beauty of Wells's co-operative world as against life "sordidly repulsive and hopelessly depressed." Wells is quoted as saying, "Our laws and customs are like a record of some nasty-minded lunatic's inventions."[30] The *Quarterly Review* liked him because, "far from despising those whom the stern socialist of the vegetarian school considered dull and base, he exerts all the might of his imagination to exalt the humble and put down the mighty."[31] But the influence of Wells as an exponent of ideas, and of ideas in the novel, did not depend upon critical opinion. His widely read novels and his manifestoes best conveyed his principles of composition. His paper delivered to the Times Book Club in 1912 is but one of his many militant utterances:

> We are going to write about it all. We are going to write about business and finance and politics and precedence and pretentiousness

[26] C. O. French, "The Romance of Realism," April, 1911.

[27] "Anticipations," *Fortnightly Review*, 1901; "Mankind in the Making," *Fortnightly Review*, 1902–1903; "Modern Utopia," *Fortnightly Review*, 1904–1905.

[28] J. B. Crozier, "Mr. Wells as a Sociologist," *Fortnightly Review*, September, 1905; J. A. Hobson, "The New Aristocracy of Mr. H. G. Wells," *Contemporary Review*, April, 1906; "The Ideas of Mr. H. G. Wells," *Quarterly Review*, April, 1908; W. H. Mallock, "Persuasive Socialism," *Nineteenth Century*, May, 1908.

[29] "Novels with a Philosophy."

[30] "Insular Fiction."

[31] "The Ideas of Mr. H. G. Wells."

and decorum and indecorum, until a thousand pretences and ten thousand impostures shrivel into the cold, clear draught of our elucidations. We are going to write of wasted opportunities and latent beauties until a thousand new ways of living open to men and women. We are going to appeal to the young and the hopeful and the curious, against the established, the dignified, and defensive. Before we have done we will have all life within the scope of the novel.[32]

The importance of Wells in developing the vogue of the subjective novel of ideas can hardly be overemphasized. He adapted the naturalistic subject matter to nonnaturalistic ends. Stuart P. Sherman evaluates his significance:

You are no realist, Mr. Wells. . . . But you have been a brave myth-maker and a heartening poet to the Intellectuals of your time. You have turned an entire generation of novelists and readers from contemplating the fatal forces of heredity and environment and instinct to considering the god-like power of an intelligent will to control instinct, environment and heredity.[33]

SUBJECTIVISM AND THE LIFE-NOVEL

The limits of Victorian "objectivity" are evident. It never was really objective. I do not refer to the personal intervention of George Eliot and Thackeray but to the tendency of the Victorian novelist to mete out rewards and punishments in accordance with conventional moral evaluations, and to create heroes and heroines as the incarnation of the various social and domestic virtues. The new word "impersonality," which the naturalists brought to England, demanded the complete efface-ment of the author and the exclusion of his personal sym-pathies. Heroes and heroines were to be replaced by "central characters" of mixed qualities, and the conclusion of the novel would be the logical result of a given set of circumstances. Moore, James, Bennett, Galsworthy, Conrad, W. L. George —all attempted impersonality, and under their guidance the

---

[32] Republished in *Experiment in Autobiography* (New York, The Macmillan Co., 1934), 417.
[33] *Critical Woodcuts* (New York, Charles Scribner's Sons, 1926), 107.

English novel became more objective than it had ever been. Yet a change in critical opinion began to appear around the year 1910, and in the four years that followed, the "subjective" came into vogue.

As regards fiction, the "subjective" obviously means that the author's personal views are aired in his works. Often a convenient "register" speaks for the author, and the author's valuations are generally to be seen through the characters sympathetically presented. The novels of Wells did much to bring about the reaction against objectivity, but contributory influences are those of Butler, Rolland, and the Russians.

In 1909 we find the *English Review* commenting editorially in words that could easily have been those of Wells:

> It is obvious that the author, being the creator of his characters, *may,* if he will, create himself. ... He will be attempting to give the world as he sees it—a world all the more interesting to the measure of his personal value. He too, will *constater,* not colour, the life of which he treats.[34]

In the same year the *Contemporary Review* protests against objectivity:

> It is easy to name, let us say, twenty writers of almost equal merit who have thoroughly mastered their craft, but whose work in spite of considerable powers of thought and observation leaves the reader without any feeling of definite contact with a personality.[35]

The chief protest, however, is expressed by Wells himself. Writing in 1911 for the *Fortnightly* he not only endorses the "exhaustiveness" of *Jean Christophe* and the "discursiveness and variety" of Bennett's work, but he comes out with a clear-cut statement that the novel must reflect the novelist's vision and that in the contemporary view the individual instance is of more importance than the generalization:

> The novel should not, like the short story, aim at a concentrated impression. ... The novel by comparison is like breakfasting in the

[34] January, 1909.
[35] "C. T." Literary Supplement of the *Contemporary Review*, December, 1909.

open air on a summer morning; nothing is irrelevant if the author's mood is happy, and the tapping of the thrush upon the garden path, or the petal of apple-blossom that floats down into my coffee, is as relevant as the egg I open or the bread and butter that I bite. . . . Nearly all the novels that have, by the lapse of time, reached an assured position of recognized greatness, are not only saturated with the personality of the author, but have, in addition, quite unaffected personal outbreaks. . . . The novel has almost inseparable moral consequences. . . . Even if the author attempts or affects the impartial, he cannot avoid, as people say, putting ideas into his readers' heads. The greater his skill, the more vivid his power of suggestion. And it is almost equally impossible for him not to betray his sense that the proceedings of this person are rather jolly and admirable, and of that, rather ugly and detestable. . . . The novel is not simply a fictitious record of conduct, but also a study and judgment of conduct. . . . The conflict of authority against criticism is one of the eternal conflicts of humanity. . . . And today while we live in a period of tightening and extending social organization, we live also in a period of adventurous and insurgent thought, in an intellectual spring unprecedented in the world's history. . . . The essential characteristic of this great intellectual revolution amidst which we are living today consists of the reassertion of the importance of the individual instances against the generalization. . . . We have small respect for abstract principles and abstract rules.[36]

A writer for the *Academy* of March, 1913, leaves no doubt as to the prevalence of Wells's influence:

Since Mr. H. G. Wells' first attempt to construct his unconvincing Socialist Utopia in fictional form some ten or fifteen years ago, the employment of the novel for propagandist purposes of every variety has increased by leaps and bounds.

Two years and eight months separated the pronouncement of Wells from the beginning of the World War. During those years the life-novel or spiritual biography was establishing a new form for the novel in England. The new development did not cease with the advent of the war, but the progressive intensity of the conflict finally brought it to extinction.

The life-novel is virtually a new form or mode of writing

---

[36] "The Contemporary Novel," November, 1911.

in England since it is a semi-autobiographic account dealing with a person's life from birth to his discovery of the world. Early influences and the pain of youth are stressed. Generally the central character achieves, in some measure, an understanding of life.

The separate influences of Butler, Wells, and Romain Rolland in the creation of the English life-novel will be considered in a later chapter. Below are listed some of the best English works.

In 1911 J. D. Beresford published *The Early History of Jacob Stahl* and followed it in 1912 with *A Candidate for Truth* and in 1915 with *The Invisible Event*. In 1913 D. H. Lawrence published *Sons and Lovers,* Hugh Walpole came out with *Fortitude,* and the first volume of Compton Mackenzie's trilogy appeared—*Youth's Encounter*. In 1914 *Sinister Street* was published and in 1915 W. Somerset Maugham's *Of Human Bondage*. In 1916 appeared *A Portrait of the Artist as a Young Man*, by James Joyce, and *Mendel*, by Gilbert Cannan. *Mary Olivier*, by May Sinclair, was published in 1919.

Writing in 1914, W. L. George pointed to the direction of the effort:

> Dostoievski and M. Romain Rolland had to come to break up the old narrative form, to make a road for Mr. Wells and for the younger men who attempt, not always successfully, to crush within the covers of an octavo volume the whole of the globe spinning round its axis, to express with an attitude the philosophy of life, to preach by gospel rather than by statement.[37]

Elsewhere George expanded his idea. The young men "break away from the old traditions, the tradition of aloofness and the tradition of comment." He continues:

> They do not stand rigidly outside the canvas, as did Flaubert and de Maupassant; nor do they obviously intervene, as did Thackeray. If they look back at all it is to Dostoievski and Stendhal, that is to say, they stand midway between the expression of life and the expression

[37] "Form in the Novel."

of themselves; indeed, they try to express both, to achieve art by "criticizing life"; they attempt to take nature into partnership. Only they do this to a greater or less extent; some do little more than exploit themselves, show the world in relation to their own autobiography; others hold up the mirror to life and interpose between picture and object the veil of their prejudice; and one of them is almost a commentator, for his prejudice is so strong as to become a protagonist in his drama. . . . If *Madame Bovary* were to be written today by a man of thirty, it would not be a good book; it would be a piece of literary archeology.[38]

Writing in 1916 for the *Fortnightly*, Arthur Waugh acclaims the "New Realism of the emotions" as contrasted with "the conventional realism of conditions and environments":

Its interest is not in the material convenience or inconvenience of life, but the spiritual achievement of man, and his ultimate realization of his soul's possibilities. For the artist of the New Realism the Kingdom of Heaven is within the soul of man; for the realist of the last generation it was almost invariably sought from without, in the individual's relation to the rest of the world. . . . The individual emerges, alert and eager, with a wonderfully intensified sense of the value of his own instincts and emotions. He is no longer concerned with the improvement of social conditions, for legislation and trade unionism seems disposed to settle these matters for him without any further effort on his part. Thrown back upon himself, and tormented with the questioning curiosity of youth, he begins to debate his own relationship to his own soul, and in particular is professedly puzzled by emotions which he feels himself impelled to indulge, while he is assured by those in authority that such indulgence is socially and morally reprehensible. . . . The conflict is between man and his fatal incapacity for self-realization.[39]

THE RUSSIAN INFLUENCE

In the eighties Matthew Arnold said, "The Russian novel has now the vogue and deserves to have it." Eight novels of Turgenev were translated into English between 1883 and 1887, seven of Dostoievski from 1881 to 1888, and the com-

---

[38] "Who Is the Man?" *Bookman*, February, 1914. Republished in *Literary Chapters*.
[39] "The New Realism," *Fortnightly Review*, May, 1916.

plete works of Tolstoi by 1888. Yet during the late eighties and early nineties the prevailing foreign influence was that of naturalism. It is true that before 1886 Gissing wrote *Isabel Clarendon* largely under Dostoievski's influence,[40] that Henry James sought to emulate Turgenev, and that, as I later indicate, Galsworthy was a disciple of Turgenev before 1910. Yet before 1910 English emulation of the Russians was by no means considerable. After 1910 and through the early years of the World War the full force of the Russians was felt. The influence synchronized with life-novel tendencies, and it was conducive to what Middleton Murry calls "the break-up of the novel" in England. Mr. Murry has what amounts to a proprietary interest in the Russians, and we need not go the whole way with him when he says of the English novel of, say, 1912: "The Russians had ruined it by revealing its enormous potentialities. The vista was too big; instead of exhilarating, it terrified. Dostoievski and Tolstoi had exploded the novel."[41] There can be no doubt that the Russians, with their concern for states of soul and the drama of feeling, were a powerful though belated influence on English fiction, and that they aided in the orientation toward subjectivism and the inner world of consciousness. The periodicals testify to a progressive twentieth-century English concern with the Russians.

In the first decade of the twentieth century few articles on the Russian novel appeared in the chief English periodicals. In 1901 A. T. Quiller-Couch felt that, aesthetically and morally, the Russian influence was "better" than that of Maupassant and Zola. Of Turgenev and Tolstoi he said:

> They did impressively and in the sight of Europe uphold, vindicate and establish the truth that the concern of fiction is with things spiritual, intimate, deep, not with things material, external, shallow ... that it uses phenomena only as a means to arrive at stability, peace, and law.[42]

[40] Testimony of Madame Fleuroy-Gissing, who owns Gissing's unpublished Journal. Personal interview.
[41] Republished in *Discoveries* (London, Jonathan Cape, Ltd., 1930).
[42] "Novels in the 19th Century," *Pall Mall Magazine,* February, 1901.

In 1905 an article in the *Contemporary* affirmed that

the powerful stream of religious feeling deliberately started by Dostoievski cannot lose itself in the dark abyss of doubt nor sink in the sands of spiritual indifference. ... The reaction against materialism seldom turns to purely Christian ideas, however. In spite of their mystic and religious character they are indifferent and sometimes hostile to religion. In most cases they move toward it by circuitous routes.[43]

But these articles do not seem to have awakened any great amount of interest. Strangely enough, "the Russian novel" still meant to English readers the novels of Dostoievski, Tolstoi, and Turgenev.[44] In 1910, however, we note some concern shown with the younger Russian writers, and, for the first time, a hostile reaction. "Ever since the Crimean War the tendency of what Turgenev aptly called Nihilism has been marked, and continues in Russian literature," writes E. J. Dillon in the *English Review*. He defines Nihilism as "the negation of religious dogma and spiritual truth, a revolt against moral law, a protest against human statutes, a spurning of ideals and a renunciation of hope."

We are interested in Dillon's article not for his valuations but for his diagnosis of the new note that was being sounded not only in Russian but in English literature of the years 1910–15. A probably erroneous statement about the decadence of the new Russian literature is followed by the comment:

The energy that sustained Russian literature in the past ... is spent, and the brilliant efforts of Gorki, Artzybasheff, and Andreyeff may be likened to the last flicker of the candle-end. The dominating idea, the *leit-motiv* of Russian fiction, nay, of Russian art generally, has been it seems to me, a continual struggle to burst the fetters that hampered personality. At first this struggle was unconscious, like that of a bud in the earth shooting upward toward the light and warmth. In time

---

[43] Count S. C. de Soissons, "The New Trend of Russian Thought," May, 1905.

[44] In 1914 the tendency remained much the same. "It is the custom to say in England that Russian literature is contained and ended in the works of Turgenev, Dostoievski, Gogol and Tolstoi." "Modern Russian Fiction," republished in the *Living Age*, June 20, 1914.

it grew more and more deliberate, waxing stronger after each new position it won, and finally it degenerated into an assertion of the all-might of the individual will and the nothingness of social restraints and religious checks. To believe in nothing and to allow oneself everything is the philosophic groundwork for contemporary Russian literature.[45]

Dillon's protest was not echoed by other writers.

In 1911 *Essays on Russian Novelists*, by William Lyon Phelps, was published in England. This had been preceeded in 1910 by Maurice Baring's *Landmarks in Russian Literature*, which, by the way, led Galsworthy to Dostoievski.

During the years 1912–15 Heineman issued Mrs. Edward Garnett's translation of Dostoievski. Says a writer for the *Nineteenth Century*,

Hitherto the greatness of Dostoievski had been apparent in spite of the translations in which he had appeared . . . some of them egregious and intolerable; but now that his novels are appearing, and appearing collectedly, in a translation that is in itself excellent literature, the power of that colossal mind is exerting itself.[46]

In 1912 occurred a memorable event, according to J. Middleton Murry. Arnold Bennett in reviewing Mrs. Garnett's translation of *The Brothers Karamazof* gave evidence of a change in his own standards—a change the more important because it coincided with the prevalent trend of British critical opinion. It seems advisable to quote in some detail:

With his usual honesty, Mr. Bennett, who had painfully formed himself in the school of Flaubert, acknowledged that Dostoievski was a master "impatient of minor perfection," and that this impatience made not the slightest difference in his greatness. The confession that the technical perfection of a Flaubert or a James was, after all, only a "minor perfection" itself marked a minor revolution in the history of modern criticism of the novel. It began to be realized that the method

---

[45] "Nihilism in Contemporary Russian Literature," *English Review*, October, 1910.

[46] Darrel Figgis, "Some Recent Notable Novels," October, 1913. The publication dates of Mrs. Garnett's translations follow: *The Brothers Karamazof*, 1912; *The Idiot*, 1913; *Crime and Punishment*, *The Possessed*, 1914; *The House of the Dead*, *The Insulted and Injured*, 1915.

of saying it was little compared to the significance of the thing said. Tolstoi and Dostoievski had been saying tremendous things, while the novelists of the West had been busy with some private conception of "art." One immediate effect of this shock to accepted critical notions was that Mr. Hardy began to emerge from the comparative obscurity to which criticism had relegated him. After regarding him as an uncouth teller of country tragedies, artistically far less important than James or Meredith, and, of course, not to be mentioned in the same breath with Flaubert, the novelists and critics who had been under the technical spell awoke to discover that he was the only novelist we possessed of sufficient magnitude remotely comparable with that of the Russians. . . . When the commotion had subsided a little, and the attempt began to make an instinctive feeling articulate, it was decided that there were two qualities which distinguish the "great" novelist. He expressed a philosophy of life, and he was formless. . . . The young novelists of the period, imagining that formlessness was in itself a virtue, poured volumes of diluted autobiography into the lap of a patient world. The philosophy of life was rather more difficult. The more enterprising put moral matters on their title pages and hoped for the best. The boldest introduced a little local colour in the shape of perambulatory characters of no fixed abode, who uttered sentiments of Nihilism and world-weariness when nothing else was doing.[47]

Allowing for a certain amount of ax-grinding in Mr. Murry's intention and a certain amount of antipathy toward life-novels in his disposition, we are no less grateful for the dramatic picture he gives us. A change in the conception of the novel was taking place. It amounted almost to a breakup. Experimentation in a novel of spiritual honesty and spiritual intensity was being made. Philosophic views were being aired and the scope of the novel was being extended. A writer for the *Westminster Review* in 1913 stressed the difference between the Russian novelists and the English novelists of the past:

[47] "The Break-Up of the Novel," republished in *Discoveries*. The fact that the Russians gave Bennett a new conception of fiction is proved by his assertion in *The Evening Standard* of March 16, 1927, that the twelve greatest novels of all times were all written by Russians. His list includes four novels by Dostoievski, three by Tolstoi, four by Turgenev, and one by Gogol. In this connection it is interesting to note that Galsworthy chose five Russian novels in his list of the fourteen "greatest"—two by Tolstoi, two by Turgenev, and one by Dostoievski.—"Twelve Books and Why," by John Galsworthy, *Saturday Review of Literature*, December 3, 1927.

The Russians have supplanted English novelists by being more genuine. Unlike the English novelists the Russians never aimed at being masters of laughter and tears. ... Systems of philosophy were brewing in their brains, plans for revolutionary social reformations, the new gospels of universal religions. Antagonism to the present state of civilization is the keynote of all their doctrine.[48]

In the same year a critic for the *Nineteenth Century* pointed to Dostoievski's influence on the younger writers. They invent extravagant situations, he says, in order to display human souls more simply, and more dramatically and more intensely. Walpole has felt the influence of Dostoievski more than anyone; "the same extravagance of characterization is there, though without the same significance; the same crowding of the canvas, without the order and sense of direction." The diffuseness of the writer of trilogies, he suggests, is probably the result of the Russian influence. He would hesitate to deny that Dostoievski was the greatest novelist who had ever written.[49]

Conrad, according to the *Nation* (London) in 1913, has learned the secret of the Russian novelists' high poetic realism.[50]

In 1914 we find the *Times* avowing, "Russia is surely the great literary country of the future."[51]

CONCLUSION

Those who do not hold with Middleton Murry that the Russians, by giving to English novelists conceptions that were vast and staggering, "exploded" the English novel may get some comfort from the statement by Edward Shanks in the *Bookman* that the war instead of the Russians was the disruptive influence:

The novel has never been fully mastered in England. Until quite lately our writers of fiction have been more or less gifted amateurs;

---

[48] Gershon Katz, "Articulate Russia," December, 1913.

[49] Figgis, "Some Recent Notable Novels."

[50] "The Quality of Current Fiction," July, 1913. (The American *Nation* of February 25, 1915, in an article entitled "Russian Novelists and English" was specific: "The influence of Dostoievski on Compton Mackenzie, W. B. Maxwell, J. D. Beresford, Gilbert Cannan and half a dozen others is unmistakable.")

[51] "Modern Russian Fiction," reprinted in the *Living Age,* June 13, 1914.

and the war came at the critical moment when it seemed that some of them might qualify for inclusion in a different class.[52]

Obviously the war was hostile to intellectual tendencies in the novel. A great cry went up in Britain for a novel of diversion, a novel of simple and mixed stimulants. Philosophic questions were postponed, social issues sidetracked. It was not the time to brood over whether the killing of one's father, under certain circumstances, might be an ethical act. The empire called for sustaining illusions, and the development of the British novel was arrested at the moment of transition. A certain amount of work done according to prewar conceptions was completed and the early work of Mrs. Woolf and Mrs. Richardson was written, but the tendency was to neglect artistic considerations. The war, on the whole, acted as the most powerful of setbacks. Says Mr. Shanks, it provided solutions for hundreds of half-completed novels,

It threw separated husbands and wives precipitately into one another's arms or into the arms of other people, it redeemed black sheep, it rescued young men from undesirable entanglements, it removed parental objections to desirable betrothals, it restored broken friendships, it proved the hero a hero, and the villain a villain, a paltroon, by the simplest of all tests, and—the most cynical touch—it restored family businesses which had been on their last legs through many chapters.[53]

The postwar novel would be a novel of fresh beginnings. Yet the very diversity of tendencies had prepared for extensions in all directions. No single tendency other than that of romance had run its course. Tendencies toward objectivity and impersonality and the concentrated impression had reached a high point of perfection in the theories and novels of Henry James and his followers. On the other hand, subjective tendencies had received a fresh impetus from Wells, Butler, Rolland, the Russians, and the British life-novelists. On the

---

[52] "The War and the Novelists," republished in the *Living Age,* November, 1918.
[53] Ibid.

one hand we have the perfection of form; on the other a tendency toward discursiveness and the absence of form. With Galsworthy the critical view of the naturalists underwent a transformation; he showed that within the limits of the objective method social criticism may be carried on "from within" and that delicate shades of a refined sentiment need not be excluded. Elsewhere the critical view had operated in the wide field of institutions and morals, and it extended into the varied fields of industrial development. Naturalism had furnished the impetus, had awakened curiosity, and had established the canon that an artistic production must be a logical one, but Britain had, in the end, refused, "impersonality" and made no objection to the implied expression of the author's view. Finally there had been an awakening to the intensity of the Russian, to his concern with philosophic enigmas and states of soul. On the whole the tendency of the effort was away from the romantic, the picturesque, the sentimental, and the insular.

Since the movement, or combination of movements, in prewar fiction had no chance of crystallizing, we can readily understand that no critic who wrote in 1914 could satisfactorily evaluate the novel of his day. Yet with remarkable clarity the *Athenaeum* commented, "The novel as treated at present by such comparatively young men as Mr. Bennett and Mr. Galsworthy, and such positively young men as Mr. Cannan and Mr. Walpole, has a certain general peculiarity of matter and manner which distinguish it from the English novel of any previous period. Fiction at the present moment exhibits a seriousness of air, a tendency to social criticism, a tentativeness of form, and a confusion of earlier methods which show that it is in a transitional period. . . . Mr. Forster and Mr. Cannan express their conviction that the novel is occupied with the assimilation of wholly new material. . . . The novel's freedom of form and its critical spirit are likely to be permanent since they correspond with the general trend in thought."[54]

[54] April, 1914. Republished in the *Living Age,* May 16, 1914.

❧ XI ❧

THE YEARS 1900–1915

SOCIAL AND LITERARY BACKGROUND

IN the critical comment of the previous chapter we have noted during the years 1900–1915 a preoccupation with both social and individual problems. It was therefore natural that the novel should be something of a narrative and something of a study. Mere entertainment would no longer suffice. There was much more interest in *what* was said than in how the author said it. The aesthetic movement of the past century was dead. The new poets remained only as echoes while the novel gained prestige as the literary medium of a more materialistic generation. According to Amy Cruse its realistic standards were severe: "There must be no Victorian fastidiousness, no glamour of sentiment or imagination, no blindness of hero-worship."[1] Scientific agnosticism and the inquiring spirit were firmly established, and these directed attention to the necessity for change, for revaluation. According to George Dangerfield, "Pre-war reform meant, not tearing the house of English polity down but putting it in order. You admired the firmness of its foundations, its architecture was far from pleasing, the rose gardens were admirable: but how about improving servants' quarters, and putting in a new plumbing system, and letting the public use the park if it promised to tidy up? That was pre-war reform, a passionate

---

[1] *After the Victorians* (London, George Allen & Unwin, Ltd., 1938), 207.

desire to preserve, by improvement, the shape of things as they were."[2]

It is inconvenient to divide the years 1900–1915 by referring to the period 1901–11 as "Edwardian" and the years 1911–15 as "early Georgian." So far as the novel is concerned there was no dividing line. It is true that from 1911 to 1915 the novel turned from the world without to the world within, that it acquired a greater depth and intensity, that it became concerned with the individual problem of fulfillment. Yet this development had its origin in the Edwardian novels of Wells and in Samuel Butler's *Way of All Flesh*, which was published in 1903. In the novels of Wells, Bennett, and Galsworthy there was no change centering around the year 1911.

And yet we cannot well do without the use of the term "Edwardian" since it serves as a convenient label for a state of society which was hopefully breaking with Victorianism even while it maintained a great tradition; which was solving its social problems and advancing to the future with confidence and gusto. Toward its end the pace of living began to be quickened with the use of telephone, telegraph, and automobile, and the hours became enlivened by the gramophone. Well-born people were going into trade unabashed and unashamed. Lowly born and more ambitious men saw romance and adventure in enterprise, as is reflected in Bennett's *The Card*, Wells's *Tono-Bungay*, and W. L. George's *Caliban*. According to John Freeman, "*Tono-Bungay* is as representative of the early bubbling twentieth century as any book of Dickens of the early nineteenth." Moreover, the universal literacy which had followed the Education Acts of 1870, 1891, and 1897 had extended the democratic principle. According to Frank Swinnerton,

Halfpenny newspapers had made the reading of news and views a matter for every breakfast table in the land, a daily feast of excitement, hotter and hotter as competition forced editors and contributors

2 "Review of *The Life and Letters of John Galsworthy* by H. V. Marrot," *Saturday Review*, April 18, 1936.

to ever greater licence. And there was news in those papers, even then, provocative enough to make men thump tables and lose tempers, and to make women argue and lecture and go to prison. Although education had not greatly improved their intelligence, it had without doubt increased group consciousness in these men and women; and popular newspapers were very powerful, not so much in initiating ideas and movements, as in spreading infection far and wide, and in agitating half-developed minds into a state of foaming anger.[3]

The gaiety of the urban nineties persisted in the admiration of cleverness, of smartness. "An Edwardian must be smart, in his dress, in his manner, in his conversation, in all the apurtenances of his daily life. He must live in a smart neighborhood, he must frequent smart society, he must read smart books. . . . The cult of smartness was not confined to dwellers on the summit. . . . Below the Smart Set were the Suburbans."[4] These varied from university educated business and professional men to small shopkeepers. These wanted to be smart and to climb up socially. They bought cheap editions of the classics but never read them, and the only author they really liked was H. G. Wells. The doings of the Smart Set were so much talked about that Eleanor Glyn's *Visits of Elizabeth*, showing an unsophisticated young lady being shocked by the fashionable in London, became a best seller and her sensational *Three Weeks* (1907), the epitome of naughtiness, delighted both Smart Set and public. Said Shane Leslie, "It is typical of the Victorian and post-Victorian ages that up to 1900 everybody pretended they had not read George Moore, while under King Edward all pretended they had." Castigation of the Smart Set was undertaken by "Rita" and Marie Corelli.[5]

Looking back with the perspective of some thirty-five or forty years, we see that the importance of the Smart Set in Edwardian life may easily be overstressed. Yet the Smart Set incarnated the break with Victorian uniformity, regularity, and social certainties. True, they themselves carried on the

[3] *The Georgian Scene* (New York, Farrar & Rinehart, 1934), 6–7.
[4] Cruse, *After the Victorians*, 208 ff.
[5] *Ibid.*

Victorian tradition of great houses and they were but mildly disturbed at the vast disparity between wealth and poverty. Such a picture as that of Sackville-West in *The Edwardians* is certainly more than half true. And, as Douglas Jerrold points out, there was a sharp Victorian distinction between the mondaine and the demimondaine.[6] Yet the Edwardians and the early Georgians were at war with the rigidly righteous, with hypocrisy, with social compulsion, with unimaginative Philistinism, with parental authority and pretension. They were less concerned with art-form in the novel than they were with exploding a fallacy.

Writing in 1927, Joseph Wood Krutch gave a valuable summary:

> Fifteen years ago [1912] it might well have seemed to the casual student of contemporary thought that the world had settled comfortably to a liberal orthodoxy. It had, to be sure, agreed to the existence of many individual disagreements, but since it had accepted variety rather than unity as the most characteristic feature of the aspect under which the universe was to be regarded and had recognized opinion rather than truth as the ultimate possible achievement of the human mind, it was not surprising that opinions should differ. Detailed disagreements notwithstanding, democratic conceptions of the function of government, mechanistic theories of natural science, and relativistic theories of both art and morals had coalesced into a recognizable type of thinking, and whatever voices were raised against it were definitely voices from the past.[7]

PHILOSOPHIC BACKGROUND

The new values which the Edwardians and later prewar writers sought to instill were those which attended the spread of scientific materialism through the ranks of society. From the seventies through the nineties the views of Huxley, Tyndall, Clifford, Bagehot, Morley, and Balfour had been widely circulated, and during the nineties, as we have seen, there was

---

[6] *Georgian Adventure* (London, Collins Sons & Co., Ltd., 1937), 5.
[7] "Wyndham Lewis," *Nation*, April 20, 1927.

a limited public for novels devoid of transcendental values. Not until the later part of the rule of Edward, however, did scientific materialism so pervade the public mind that the mass of new novels was written by and for scientific materialists.

The scientific materialists were interested in substituting human for theocratic values. According to Morley, "It makes all the difference in the world whether we put truth in the first place or in the second," and erroneous belief can have no justification. Huxley suggested, "Teach a child what is wise, that is morality. Teach him what is wise and beautiful, that is religion." Tyndall explained that "nature is seen to do all things spontaneously of herself, without the intermeddling of the gods." Clifford, like Henry James, believed that what is "spirit" in man is but more finely woven flesh. He showed that human concepts of morality originated in ancient tribal necessity, and that conscience is a personal conception of the tribal will. To Bagehot the successful tribe develops a "cake of custom" which has "survival value." Conformity is primitive virtue. Balfour, although attacking the "religion of science," pointed to the futility of man's altruistic aspiration.

Perhaps not a great many Edwardians had read the various expositors of the scientific view, yet the scientific view itself had become common knowledge. It turned attention to new and exciting conceptions of living. Man is a creature of necessity, yet his personal conception of the social will may set him at variance with his fellows. The past is dead; its values were hypocritical, and the institutions men created might be detrimental to human happiness. Since life is short and death is final, man's ethical aim is to avoid unhappiness rather than put up with it.

French naturalism had stressed the fact that individuals are motivated by material considerations generally derived from their environment. Yet even naturalism, in practice, provided an escape from determinism by showing how a person *of a certain temperament* will react under certain circumstances. Prewar English realists stressed variation even while they fol-

lowed the French naturalists in writing novels that are loosely
thematic and filled with the tangible details of human enterprise.[8] Each writer modified the naturalistic technique, and
each was influenced by the critical spirit of social inquiry.
There is no need here to prove the case for naturalistic influence, as was attempted in previous chapters with the view
of determining the beginnings of transition. We are, rather,
concerned with the tenor of change and the particular direction of individual effort. For transition is not merely a matter
of influences. It involves assimilation, alteration, and growth.

On the whole we are impressed with the variety of alteration. Bennett devoted himself to an exciting and impersonal
scrutiny of tangible objects and emotions in industrial towns
of which he had a close knowledge. Galsworthy incorporated
the critical tone of naturalism into a new rendering of the
English family chronicle. May Sinclair, Maugham, Forster,
Cannan, and George all adapted naturalistic techniques and
Wellsian or other ethical concepts to private designs for individual utterance. Their work may loosely be called the "novel
of ideas" and linked with the Edwardian desire to establish
new values.

It is apparent that any novel is, to a certain extent, a "novel
of ideas." Yet the term "novel of ideas" should be used in a
restricted sense just as the "drama of ideas" denotes a tendency
in drama. We speak of the "drama of ideas" when we speak

---

[8] It is readily understandable that English novelists, who never fully accepted determinism, should not try to impose it upon a public hostile to deterministic views.
One may, with Mr. Walter Myers, account for a lack of determinism in English fiction
of the early twentieth century by stating that philosophy itself was undergoing transformation: "By the turn of the century changes had taken place in biological study helping
to break up the determinism that had been important in realistic characterization. This
was due in part to the swing of the philosophic pendulum toward the voluntarism of
Schopenhauer, in part to the origin of biologic metaphysics in the work of Mendal,
Weismann, de Vries, Bateson, and others. These men shifted from a study of survival
values to a study which included individual variations. They wished to know whence
come the characteristics the permanence of which environment tests; to determine, if
possible, why, in the same environment, essentially the same end should be accomplished
by nature in a diversity of species; and to seek for understanding of the more obvious
vagaries in the transmission of characteristics. These purposes centered attention on
individual variation rather than upon selection, and enlarged the conception of heredity
to a roominess which accounts for wide deviations from the type." *The Later Realism,* 29.

of, say, the drama of Ibsen. We mean that Ibsen wrote plays centered about certain conceptions: that women should be individualists, that the sins of the fathers are visited upon the children, that a romantic temperament can create havoc, that enemies of society are often its highly respected citizens. The subjects are handled with almost naturalistic severity; the arrangement of each play is loosely thematic.

The "novel of ideas" is not altogether thematic and it is not universally severe. But it generally has a naturalistic seriousness and its primary purpose is to express a social or ethical conception of the author. Its structure is generally "objective" in the traditional English sense, which implies that the novelist may not personally intervene although he manages to convey his approval of certain ideas and his dislike of others. There is an attempt at naturalistic logicality, but fortuitous association and dramatic stress are not precluded.

Sharply defined differences among the most important novelists of the years 1900–1915 necessitate a separate examination of the method, the field, and the concepts of each.

NOVELISTS OF EDWARDIAN ORIGIN

ARNOLD BENNETT

At the age of twenty-one Arnold Bennett came to London from the dreary pottery manufacturing district of Staffordshire. After working for some years in a lawyer's office, he turned to the most difficult form of journalism—free-lancing. He was not much better pleased. "A free-lance," he writes, "is a tramp touting for odd jobs; a pedlar crying stuff that is usually bought in default of better; a producer endeavoring to supply a market of whose condition he is in ignorance more or less complete."[9] But his journalistic contacts did serve the purpose of stimulating his interest in foreign novels. He continues:

[9] *The Truth About an Author* (London, Methuen and Co., Ltd., 1920), Chapter V.

During all this time I was absorbing French fiction incessantly; in French fiction I include the work of Turgenev, because I read him always in French translations. Turgenev, the brothers de Goncourt, and de Maupassant were my gods. I accepted their canons, and they filled me with a general scorn of English fiction which I have never quite lost.[10]

Many years afterwards he writes:

L'inutile beauté was the first story of de Maupassant I ever read; on its wings I crossed the channel and was transformed from an islander into an awakened and excited citizen of the world.[11]

Bennett next became the assistant editor of a ladies' weekly. Since this position required only one full day and four half-days of his time, he had sufficient leisure for imaginative work. To continue with his own account:

So I sat down to write my first novel under the sweet influences of the de Goncourts, Turgenev, Flaubert, and de Maupassant. It was to be entirely unlike all English novels except those of one author, whose name I shall not mention now, for the reason that I have aforetime made my admiration of that author very public. I clearly remember that the purpose uppermost in my mind was to imitate what I may call the physical characteristics of French novels. There were to be no poetical quotations in my novel, no titles to the chapters; the narrative was to be divided irregularly into sections by Roman numerals only; and it was indispensable that a certain proportion of these sections should begin or end abruptly. . . . So much for the physical characteristics. To come nearer to the soul of it, my novel was to be a mosaic consisting exclusively of Flaubert's *mots justes*—it was to be *mots justes* composed into the famous *écriture artiste* of the de Goncourts. The sentences were to perform the trick of "the rise and fall." The adjectives were to have colour, the verbs were colour, and perhaps it was a *sine qua non* that even the pronouns should be prismatic—I forget. And all these effects were to be obtained without the most trifling sacrifice of truth. There was to be no bowing in the house to the Rimmon of sentimentality. Life being grey, sinister, and melancholy, my novel must be grey, sinister, and melancholy—No startling events

10 *Ibid.*
11 *Things That Have Interested Me* (London, Chatto and Windus, 1921), 194–95.

were to occur in my novel, nor anything out of the way that might bring the blush of shame to the modesty of nature; no ingenious combinations, no dramatic surprises, and above all no coincidences. It was to be the Usual miraculously transformed by Art into the Sublime.[12]

But Bennett did not find the undertaking easy.

Immediately the fundamental brain-work began, I nearly lost all my confidence. With every stroke the illusion grew thinner, more remote. I perceived I could not become Flaubert by taking thought, and this rather obvious truth rushed over me as a surprise. I knew what I wanted to do, and I could not do it. I felt, but I could not express. My sentences would persist in being damnably Mudiesque. The *mots justes* hid themselves exasperatingly behind a cloud. The succession of dots looked merely fatuous. The charm, the poetry, the distinction, the inevitableness, the originality, the force, the invaluable rhythmic contour—these were everywhere save on my page.[13]

There is much truth in Bennett's self-criticism. For one thing, he is temperamentally a rapid writer, almost a carefree writer, and for style there is often mere effusion. It is not that Bennett is incapable of stylistic effects, for in his critical writings especially we have clarity, smoothness, and facile grace. It is merely that the tone is light, even in darker moments; it is that the surface brilliance never varies; it is that the objectivist never permits himself—or his characters—poetry. There is something more, as well. For Bennett the world is made up of *things*—with names to them. *Things* possess us, mold us, give direction to our footsteps. Bennett must overwhelm us with the presence of tangible objects. The names and properties are most often neither euphonious nor poetic.

One would hardly describe Bennett's books as "sinister, grey, and melancholy"—and yet *Riceyman Steps* is darker than these terms suggest. But often the grey and melancholy note is sounded in books which are by no means sinister. Says Follett,

There is no missing Arnold Bennett's vivid and consistent appre-

---

[12] *The Truth About an Author,* Chapter VI.
[13] *Ibid.,* Chapter VII.

ciation of how life tricks and cheats the individual. He leaves his characters pathetically little human dignity, if dignity depends upon self-knowledge and rational hopes. Whatever his people get out of life, they do not get what they are looking for. They remain cooped up in the narrow compartments of their own being, imprisoned by the irony of life in the little cages of materialism and stupidity into which they were born ... his work leaves us with an obstinate and perhaps irrational sense that life is worth living even if it does not give us what we ask for.[14]

To Bennett even more than to Henry James there came from France a vision of evil. The stoic in him will not allow this admission. No, Evil is grotesque and painfully amusing, sometimes pathetic. Bennett closely links it with man's inhumanity to himself. It is the result of man's destruction of the springs of joy. It is often mental frowsiness. Occasionally the author disregards objectivity to speak his mind:

You might walk from one end of the five towns to the other and not see one object that gave you a thrill—unless it was a pair of lovers. And when you went inside the houses you were no better off,—you were worse off because you came at once into contact with an ignoble race of imprisoned serfs driven by narrow-minded women who themselves were serfs with the mentality of serfs and the prodigious conceit of virtue. Talk to Auntie Hamps at home of lawn-tennis or a musical evening, and she would set you down as flighty and shift the conversation on to soaps or chapels. And there were hundreds of houses in the Five Towns into which no ideas save the ideas of Auntie Hamps had ever penetrated, and tens of hundreds of thousands of such homes all over the industrial districts of Staffordshire, Cheshire, Lancashire and Yorkshire,—houses where to keep bits of wood clean and to fulfil the ceremonies of pietism, and to help the poor to help themselves, was the highest good, the sole good. Hilda in her mind saw every house, and shuddered.[15]

But man is also imprisoned. Even the character most sympathetic to the author, Edwin Clayhanger, loads himself with cares:

[14] Helen Thomas Follett and Wilson Follett, *Some Modern Novelists* (New York, Henry Holt and Co., 1919), 219–220.
[15] *These Twain* (Methuen and Co., Ltd., 1920), 102.

Was he ever, in any ideal sense, happy; that is, free from foreboding, from friction, from responsibility, and withal joyous? Was any quarter of an hour of his day absolutely what he would have wished? He ranged over his day and concluded that the best part of it was the very last. ... He got into bed, the candles on the sconce were lit, the gas diminished to a blue speck, and most of the room in darkness; he lay down on his left side, took the marker from the volume in his hand, and began to read; the house was silent and enclosed; the rumbling tramcar—to whose sound he had been accustomed since infancy—did not a bit disturb him; it was in another world; over the edge of his book he could see his wife fast asleep in the other bed, her plaited hair trailing over the pillow; the feel of the sheets to his limbs was exquisite; he read; the book was good; the chill of winter just pleasantly affected the hand that held the book; nothing annoyed; nothing jarred; sleep approached. ... That fifteen minutes, that twenty or thirty minutes, was all that he could show as the result of the tremendous organized machinery of his existence—his house, his work people, his servants, his wife with her child.[16]

Of course, Edwin has more cheerful moods, and so does Bennett. Life, although sinister and grey, is marvelously interesting. The distinctive fact about Bennett's chief characters is that they discover and are excited by their discoveries. Some successes are enjoyed, but for the most part the intelligence plays hop, skip, and jump upon all objects with a maximum of energy and a minimum of mortal bliss. Bennett revels in youth and its hunger for life, yet in his better novels all anticipation is dulled in its realization. In the Clayhanger trilogy the man gets so involved in living that he doesn't make much of a life of it after all; in the *Old Wives' Tale* women growing old become helpless ritualists in the details of household management; in *Riceyman Steps* a man and a woman crush the very life out of themselves by a progressive miserliness.

These are naturalistic themes treated objectively. We note that Bennett takes human beings from one phase of their life to another by certain logical steps. His accomplishment as an artist is that he can make an exciting account out of nearly

[16] *Ibid.,* 400.

nothing. He modifies the naturalistic practice by entering the various characters' minds and accounting for their suspicions, forebodings, jealousies, despairs, and resolutions. And this in a lively manner with gloom relieved by humor.

In his better books, with the exception of *Lord Raingo*, Arnold Bennett gives us a minimum of action with a maximum of mental observations. The procedure, of course, is not new, even for a naturalistic novelist. Maupassant's *Pierre et Jean* immediately comes to mind. But the rapidity of Bennett's style closely resembles that of the later stream-of-consciousness novel, and the quantity of good work no doubt prepared the field for the postwar effort.

Unlike some of the stream-of-consciousness writers, however, Arnold Bennett allows his characters no reflections below the waistline. Neither is there any questioning of God and morality. The order of English life is stodgily wrong, but the institutions of Britannia are generally accepted without question. At first we are inclined to believe that Bennett is the more objective and "scientific" in that he treats the surface. We recall his avowed intention to include nothing "out of the way that might bring the blush of shame to the modesty of nature," and we put this down to a sophistical intention of getting along well with publishers and public. But as Sherman points out in a neatly tabulated series of quotations, Arnold Bennett has convictions about law and order. Bennett believes that "the great principles, spiritual and moral, remain intact," and that "after all the shattering discoveries of science and conclusions of philosophy, mankind has still to live with dignity amid hostile nature." Finally,

What form is to art, conventions are to life. . . . No art that is not planned in form is worth consideration, and no life that is not planned in conventions can ever be satisfactory. . . . The full beauty of an activity is never brought out until it is subjected to discipline and strict ordering and nice balancing. A life without petty artificiality would be the life of a tiger in the forest. . . . Laws and rules, forms and ceremonies are good in themselves, from a purely aesthetic point of view, apart from their social value and necessity.[17]

Now all this is very good writing, and very Victorian. It is Victorian in the best sense, but nevertheless Victorian. The term should bear no opprobrium; it should be merely descriptive. So considered, it is important. It puts Bennett in line as a lineal descendent of Henry James, and it explains, in a way, the particular type of Bennett's modification of naturalism.

It explains, for one thing, that Bennett is at his best as a naturalist when, in *Riceyman Steps*, he makes a patient study of a pair of misers. A good Victorian might well be a critic of miserliness. He might also be a critic of shabbiness in a shabby region of London. But the extent of study is strictly limited and the indictment confined to an aberration in the social scheme of things.

It explains, for another, Bennett's optimism even when he sees the grey and melancholy. For the foundations are not shaken, and despair tinkers with the pen and not the heart. The sense of order and dignity and respect permeates the live brain of the dying Lord Raingo, lending enchantment to his passing:

If he was sick, he was a sick Titan, and from his bed he dominated the country. His bed had majesty. The house was subdued to his bed. The house had been hushed and reorganized about his bed. The house had no life beyond himself. Fighting for breath, he was the source of its life. It functioned solely about his bed. And it functioned with eminent efficiency.—he knew from the smoothness, silence and exactitude with which he was being nursed. There was perfect coordination between the housekeeper's room, the kitchen, the doctor's house, and his bed. It might have been that invisible and impalpable wires ran from his bed along all the corridors and even out into the roads down to the village and even to Clacton. Yes, he was very ill, he was pathetic, he was humiliated and broken, but his illness was marvelous, and in its terror and grandeur it was the most marvelous thing that had ever happened to him.

[17] Quoted in *On Contemporary Literature*, 110–11.

Arnold Bennett's propensity for writing potboilers is well known. Into these, he tells us, he has put "generous quantities of wealth, luxury, feminine beauty, surprise, catastrophe, and genial, incurable optimism."[18] This is a part of Bennett's compromise with the novel-reading public. The public, he says, will not allow the novelist to present life as he sees it, and the professional novelist must strike a compromise:

> In the present state of society, and mechanical conditions of the book market, novelists must remember that their professional existence depends upon the fact that the dullest class in England takes to novels as a refuge from its own dullness. And while it is certain that no novelist of real value really pleases that class, it is equally certain that without its support no novelist could live by his pen.[19]

The English, he holds, have certain temperamental limitations:

> As sure as ever a novelist endeavors to paint a complete picture of life in this honest, hypocritical country of bad restaurants and good women; as sure as he hints that all is not for the best in the best of all possible islands, some witling is bound to come forward and point out with a wise finger that all is not black.[20]

He is inclined to believe that the conservatism of the English "home" is responsible for the restraints under which the English novelist labors:

> Its exclusiveness is equalled only by its dogmatism. In this 'home' there are no doubts, no uncertainties, no 'open questions.' The code, surpassing that of Napoleon, provides for all contingencies. This is right; that is wrong—always has been, always will be. The earth may spin like a fretful midge amid problems, philosophers may tremble with profound hesitations, partisans may fight until the areas are littered with senseless mortality; but the 'home,' wrapt in the discreet calm of its vast conservatism, remains ever stable, a refuge and a seclusion for those who will accept its standards and agree not to create a disturbance.[21]

It is idle to speculate on whether Arnold Bennett wrote for himself or for his public. With Bennett the two are not neces-

---

[18] *The Truth About an Author, Chapter* XII.
[19] *Books and Persons*, 100.

[20] *Ibid.*, 64.
[21] *Ibid.*, 64.

sarily at variance. Indeed, they are strikingly akin. We cannot imagine a closer kinship. Accordingly the works of Arnold Bennett are already dated. His "serious" characters, sustained by the view of their creator, attain no satisfactory resolution, not even a poetic one. They come dangerously near to capitulating to the Victorian compromise—except Lord Raingo. We think of Arnold Bennett as an exceptionally clever evasionist. And Lord Raingo? He is magnificently practical. The locale is a major bureauracy of World War days where the crystal-clear intelligence of Bennett may play with "things" in their more subtle and brilliant and "important" ramifications, materially speaking. *Lord Raingo* is pure conscious intelligence in a world of things, and this is Arnold Bennett at his best.

Arnold Bennett stated in 1917, "The transition of the English novel is by no means complete."²² Was he at this time conscious of what a completed transition would be? Did he see that, eventually, truth-telling according to the lights of scientific materialism would be an accepted procedure? And did he envision the day when the novelist might write with either the abandon of the familiar essayist or the confusion of free association or the formality of Henry James in his middle years?

It is probable that in 1917, at any rate, Arnold Bennett did not see these things. And yet in his own work the transition was materially advanced in certain directions. When his novels of the Five Towns appeared, they were models of simplified form. Individuals were picked up at one stage in their development and conducted by logical steps to the succeeding stage. The novels were vivid, seemingly impersonal, and integrated with a finite milieu. Like the characters in *Madame Bovary*, those of Bennett were "associations of ideas that walk." Event was subordinated to character and social influences, and a revelation of life was, within limits, attempted.

The limitations Arnold Bennett imposed upon himself, perhaps the limitations of his own nature, are responsible for his

²² *Ibid.,* 8.

limited influence on the thought and spirit of subsequent writers. He showed that life is unsatisfactory for a number of reasons and that men do not get altogether what they deserve. As a corrective to Victorian thought this was something. And yet it was not very much.

MAY SINCLAIR

In 1916 William Lyon Phelps referred to May Sinclair as "today the foremost living writer among English-speaking women." The praise was well merited. Miss Sinclair is a novelist with naturalistic vision who is primarily concerned with expressing a revolt against Victorianism. She knows people and their ways, and is none the worse for having read Henry James, for she is not bound by James's Victorian restraints while she follows him in delineating the presence of evil in supposedly nice persons. She presents us with case histories of frustration, of oppression, of useless sacrifice. Even in pre-Freudian days she concentrated upon the vast difference between conscious and unconscious motives, upon delusion, and upon the varieties of what was later to be known as sublimation. Oppression in her novels takes various forms. It is often imposed by unconsciously selfish parents. Often the oppression is the oppression of ideas. Rarely it is circumstance. Everywhere she implies the need of sanity and self-fulfillment.

Let us consider *The Helpmate* (1907) as representative of one of her more complex novels. Here Anne, a religious person, marries Walter Majendie without knowing of his past. During her honeymoon she hears of it. She resolves to stay with her husband and win him to her spiritual level. So she resists the impulse to love in behalf of an impulse to purify. Lady Cayley, once involved in an affair with Walter, casually appears upon the scene and is a further cause for separating Anne and Walter, for Anne demands that Walter keep away from her friends' houses lest, perchance, he see Lady Cayley. Anne's jealousy thus takes the form of oppression even though, consciously, she believes herself to be working for Walter's good. A child, conceived in one of Anne's infrequent moments of softness, is born, but the spiritual Anne is withal cold and unsoftened to Walter while her affection is really concentrated upon a spiritual leader of the church. Walter, still loving his wife, is lead into a liaison with one Maggie. Lady Cayley through malice tells Anne of the attachment, but her resentment changes during the conversation and she tells the frigid wife: "He has kept all his marriage vows except one. You've broken all yours except one." Tragedy is introduced with the death of the child, which Anne blames in a way on Walter. So Walter drinks more than is good for him, sees Lady Cayley again, and has a stroke of apoplexy. Anne relents, nurses Walter through the illness, and enters a state of repentance for her past coldness. She feels that in the new state of self-abnegation she has saved her soul.

Obviously this is not naturalism. In its essentials it is a naturalistic vision of the evils of piety, but the story as told by Miss Sinclair is highly colored by exceptional circumstance. It is really a connected series of dramatic situations arranged to demonstrate the view that religious ideals may be vicious, that they may engender self-deception and become a form of man's inhumanity to man. The effort of the author is, in the word of Wells, "to ventilate the issues" in one situation after another. And the author is not too scrupulous about logicality. The discovery of the husband's fatal past is, of course, an old stage trick. The plot hinges upon an accident—the husband's indirect responsibility for the death of the child. And, finally, there is no particular reason why a mixture of heavy drinking and Lady Cayley should have produced apoplexy. The novelist is revaluing ideals, and so long as motive and character are sound, a certain liberty is demanded in the presentation of incident. The novel still fulfills the naturalistic requirement of being a cosmic commentary—it is perhaps less cosmic than a naturalistic novel, and more of a commentary.

Stripped to their essentials the novels of May Sinclair are

often naturalistic in theme. *Superseded* (1906) is a study of a spinster of forty-five, a teacher, withering away in a loveless life, dominated by an exacting aunt. A flicker of love for a young doctor momentarily stirs her but the aunt's ridicule awakens a feeling of shame. A seemingly unnecessary summons of the doctor produces another outburst from the jealous aunt. Later when symptoms of the same heart ailment occur, she does not call the doctor. She dies. Rannie in *The Combined Maze* (1913) is discouraged by a selfish mother from marrying the girl who has his complete affection. He is encouraged to marry a girl who has less power over him. The marriage ends unhappily but Rannie feels obliged to look after his wife when in her need she turns to him. In *The Cure for Souls* (1924) Miss Lambert, deaconess, is useful to the Canon whom she loves with a half-mystical ardor. The Canon recognizes her as a woman "devoted to the last extremity, a woman with a sacred vocation, a woman who would lift all burdens from his back." He sustains her in her state of exaltation by recommending studies in mysticism. She ends up in a sanitarium, at peace, however, with God.

Yet naturalistic themes are not, in the end, satisfying to Miss Sinclair. Like Wells, whose influence she acknowledges, she would find a way out. Perhaps the way out in *The Life and Death of Harriet Frean* (1922) is not too comforting. Harriet sacrifices her chance for happiness and is compensated by the joy that comes from contemplating her own beautiful act, although the sacrifice is bad for all concerned. Anne in *Anne Severn and the Fieldings* (1922) gives up her husband to the woman he loves because she would hate herself if she did otherwise, and because by giving up her husband in this manner she would really win his love. In a story, "The Cosmopolitan," a girl runs away from an oppressing father in order to find fulfillment with the man she loves.

I have mentioned only a few of May Sinclair's novels. She published twenty-four of them and six volumes of stories between 1897 and 1927. She wrote mostly about the conceptions that people needed to be released from. Her work was largely protest, but sound protest. After getting off to a slow start she became a popular novelist, and her work had a very wide influence.

JOHN GALSWORTHY

Doubtless one of the most impressive of the Edwardians is Galsworthy. Yet, strangely enough, he attained only a moderate popularity in the prewar years. He has said that when *The Man of Property* was published in 1906 he had been writing nearly eleven years "without making a penny or any name to speak of." *The Man of Property* made him known, but by 1914 he had only begun to attain the wide popularity that was later to distinguish his name.[23] Galsworthy had written only one good novel before 1906—*The Island Pharisees* in 1904. His popularity, however, grew steadily with the publication of *The Country House* (1907), *Fraternity* (1909), *The Patrician* (1911), and *The Dark Flower* (1913). During the war his popularity increased with the publication of *The Freelands* (1915), and *Beyond* (1917). But his fame came largely in the postwar years following the publication of *In Chancery* (1920), *To Let* (1921), and *The Forsyte Saga*[24] (1922). Thereafter his position with the public was assured. A poll taken among novel readers in 1925 showed him to be the most popular English novelist, although critics were beginning to forsake him. His post-1922 novels have added little to his reputation.

To account for Galsworthy's popularity is by no means difficult. He began to write social criticisms when the French naturalistic novel had prepared a ready public. He attacked the unimaginative, possessive Englishman of his day, but he was not content with indictment. He suggested an ideal of sympathy, generosity, and liberal values in line with the most

[23] Cruse, *After the Victorians.*
[24] *The Man of Property; In Chancery; To Let;* with two connecting interludes: *The Indian Summer of a Forsyte; Awakening.*

enlightened Edwardian opinion. He suggested an awakening but no precise change or alteration. The situation was by no means hopeless. He was intent and even a little angry; at first he showed no tendency to pull his punches. He was, therefore, to be taken seriously. And yet was he not himself a member of an old Devonshire family, a man educated at Harrow and at Oxford, a polished young clubman living on his income and every whit an Englishman? Here was criticism written "from within"; and it was written clearly, with dramatic insistence, and with no impropriety of language.

Late in life Galsworthy, in a speech to the P. E. N. group in Paris, affirmed that the inspiration of his work had been the fiction of Turgenev and Maupassant. Ford Madox Ford sees in the avowal an act of great candor and one almost of defiance, for naturalism in the early thirties was abomination in the eyes of the French literati. And he credits Galsworthy with a dogged determination throughout his early middle years, and in spite of lukewarm critics, to write serious fiction. For Galsworthy's literary acquaintances, Ford among the rest, persisted in thinking of him as a clubman.

The influence of Turgenev is mildly obvious in Galsworthy's work: the juxtaposition of youth against age, class against class, social philosophy against social philosophy. According to Gerould Gould it is the conflict and not the solution which Galsworthy accepts as final, and he further emphasizes the conflict in Galsworthy's chief novels:

> In *The Island Pharisees* the contrast is between generous impulse and mean respectability; in *The Man of Property,* between the desire for freedom and the instinct of possession; in *The Country House,* between sexual love, and an accepted code of conduct; in *The Patrician* much the same, though there is more complexity and less truth; in *The Dark Flower,* between the violence of passion and the fidelity of affection; in *The Freelands,* between rebellion and tradition; in *In Chancery* and *To Let,* the same, of course, as in *The Man of Property.*[25]

25 "John Galsworthy," *Bookman,* December, 1923.

The sketches in *A Commentary* (1908) suggest Maupassant, but otherwise there is little that recalls him other than the critical view, the clarity, and the even tone of the work. So carefully is juxtaposition handled by Galsworthy, so intent is he on doing justice to both sides, that critics have been puzzled. Grant Overton tried unsuccessfully to get from him his personal philosophy. But in his reply Galsworthy refused to make a commitment:

> The fact is I cannot answer your questions. I must leave my philosophy to my work generally, or rather, to what people can make out of that work. The habit of trying to tabloid one's convictions, or lack of convictions is a rather fatal one; as I have found to my distaste and discredit.[26]

Yet there can be little doubt that he meant for his personal philosophy to emerge. In 1931 he belied the impartiality which early critics were disposed to accord his works,

> It is always comforting to the novelist to know that by the creation of character he contributes to the organic growth of human ethics. If, indeed, a novelist has any use in the world apart from affording entertainment, it is through the revealing power of his created characters.[27]

Elsewhere Galsworthy has been slightly more helpful. Human nature, he has said, "is and ever will be much of a Forsyte, and might, after all, be a much worse animal." Of *The Forsyte Saga*, "This long tale is no scientific study of a period; it is rather an intimate incarnation of the disturbance that Beauty effects in the lives of men. The figure of Irene . . . is a concretion of disturbing Beauty impinging on a possessive world." He states that "he, too, pities Soames," and he does not feel that Irene is necessarily "hard and cruel" but only "wisely realistic."

Early criticism was sympathetic to the Galsworthy aims, sometimes even according him a scientific curiosity. Wrote a critic for the *Westminster Review* in 1909,

> He reminds us of a philatelist. Just as a philatelist pores through

---

26 "Galsworthy's Secret Loyalties," *Bookman*, April 23.
27 "The Creation of Character in Literature," *Bookman*, August, 1931.

the microscope over his treasured stamps, noting almost imperceptible varieties of shades, differences of perforation, and minute "errors," so also Mr. Galsworthy studies the world in which he lives with a close (and it might be added, embittered) observation that no detail, however small, escapes.[28]

In the same year, however, Edward Garnett, writing for an American publication, bases his approval of Galsworthy on the sympathetic spirit with which the social criticism is expressed. Although Galsworthy writes of "the old-fashioned landed gentry's life and the unwritten law of their pursuits, habits, tastes, prejudices and ideas," he "treats sympathetically all the typical characters he introduces," and

he expresses more than any of our other novelists the practical outlook of the modern Englishman, the soft sentimental spot in his soul, if once his feelings are reached, together with his amazing capacity of protecting himself from the inroad of any disturbing ideas.[29]

Similarly a critic for the *Edinburgh Review* approves of Galsworthy because his work is "an elaboration of the British convention itself as it lays hold on life." The British convention

makes no doubt for self-complacency, for an attitude of patronizing aloofness toward the rest of the world, but it makes likewise for what is fine in manners, for an illusion of permanence, a serene perspective, and acquires by the very superiority of its assumptions an exacting decency and sense of duty.

On the other hand, continues the critic, the convention

gives a false air of reality. It wants everything "like life." Its devotees desire that presentation of life that in another art would find its equivalent in the coloured photograph. The fidelity required is thus not to life, but to the appearance of life. The likeness is not to the man as he is, or even to the man as he may be, but to the man as they recognize him.[30]

Little adverse criticism of Galsworthy is to be noted until

[28] M. H. H. Macartney, "The Novels of John Galsworthy," June, 1909.
[29] "English Novels and English Life," *Nation,* March 18, 1909.
[30] "Insular Fiction."

some years after the war. Frank Swinnerton was one of the first to express it, avowing that "the imaginative person is not merely kind," for "burning truth and error struggle in our hearts." The Galsworthy ideal is the person who "hears both sides and then desires a settlement which is balanced in injustice to both parties. He is the embodiment of the committee, a sort of tribunal. When the bloody revolution comes he will be left uttering platitudes about kindness, and will be swept into the gutters by the opposing forces. His ideal is compromise."[31]

D. H. Lawrence, always sparing of praise, took up the cudgel:

> The satire, which in *The Man of Property* really had a certain noble touch, soon fizzles out, and we get that series of Galsworthian "rebels" who are, like all the rest of the modern middleclass rebels, not in rebellion at all. They are really social beings behaving in an anti-social manner. . . . Galsworthy had not enough of the superb courage of his satire. He faltered, and gave in to the Forsytes. It is a thousand pities. He might have been the surgeon the modern soul needs so badly, to cut away the proud flesh of the Forsytes from the living body of men who are fully alive. Instead, he put down the knife and laid on a soft sentimental poultice, and helped to make the corruption worse. . . . What was there *besides* Forsyte in all the wide human world? Mr. Galsworthy looked, and found nothing. Strictly and truly, after his frightened search, he had found nothing. But he came back with Irene and Bosinney, and offered us that. Here! he seems to say. Here is the anti-Forsyte! Here! Here you have it! Love! Pa-assion! PASSION. Irene seems to me a sneaking, creeping, spiteful sort of bitch, and anti-Forsyte, absolutely living off the Forsytes—yes, to the very end; absolutely living off their money and trying to do them dirt.[32]

Swinnerton and Lawrence are representative of left-wing criticism which is not at all temperate. A left-wing historian of the novel follows them in avowing that Galsworthy's characters "are far too much like museum pieces . . . A world

[31] "Mr. Galsworthy's Criticism of Life," Nation (London), November 16, 1920.
[32] *Scrutinies* (by various writers), compiled by Edgell Rickword (London, Wishart and Co., 1931).

which Galsworthy could not understand finally exploded in the war of 1914–1918."[33] We ascribe the criticism to the left wing, yet in making a contemporary estimate we cannot disregard it. Richard Church, sympathetically reviewing volumes 26–29 of the Maniton Edition of Galsworthy's collected works, finds it necessary to mention that

a man's foibles, which he can never keep out of his work, are the quickest elements of his personality to become dated. Unfortunately it is usually on these that the succeeding generation—at least the intelligent and restive generation—seizes. Since the foibles of Galsworthy are toward conservatism, pedigree-faith, and country-house life, it is inevitable that our present-day critics—whose foibles happen to be urbanism, pretence of a cold-blooded economic scansion of aesthetics as well as of life, contempt for pedigree and deification of environmental influence; it is inevitable that our modern monitors of the art of fiction should dismiss Galsworthy as at best a sentimental humanitarian, and at worst as a mere subscribing-library author.[34]

Late in life (1927) Galsworthy compiled a list of the twelve greatest novels and explained why he had selected them. The comment is valuable as revealing Galsworthy's admiration for characters so typical that they are emblematic:

in the greatest fiction the characters, or some of them, should sum up and symbolize whole streaks of human nature in a way that our friends, however well known to us, do not. . . . Within their belts are cinctured not only individuals but sections of mankind. . . . Within the corset of Irina is bound up all fascination. Within Bazarov we have the very kernel of modernity, its brutal frankness, its passion for life stripped, its denial, its unquenchable curiosity, and its native energy.

After paying tribute to "that supple and complete cat Becky" he continues,

All boyhood is in Tom and Huck; all parade in Porthos; all girlhood in Natasha; all scheming subtlety in Aramis; all starved virginity in Betsy Trotwood; all gambling optimism in Micawber, and so forth and so on.

[33] Philip Henderson, *The Novel Today* (John Lane The Bodley Head, 1936), 107.
[34] "Afterthoughts on Galsworthy," *London Mercury*, September, 1935.

In this manner, fiction becomes richer than life. "Selection, conscious and unconscious, is the secret of art."

But characters, continues Galsworthy, are not everything. Novels should be easy reading and of a "springy" texture. They should be characterized by a "familiar spirit"—the reader will live, while reading, in the same houses, the same streets and towns and countries, as the people in these books.[35]

It is hard to resist a comparison of the extended Forsyte narratives to one of the books Galsworthy most admired—*Vanity Fair*. In both accounts we have primarily a story, or series of stories. Character is carefully built up and developed, and the author's social views and criticisms are obvious though by no means deep. In neither account is there a theme. The primary interest is centered on the interplay of character.

And yet there is a studied sobriety in Galsworthy's method, an avoidance of Victorian claptrap even though the author uses some Victorian devices, a relentless determination to give social observations. In his problem plays and in his short stories we find Galsworthy very much of a naturalist. When he is dealing with Forsyte, however, the author relegates intellectual power to a decided second place. Heart throbs and yearnings are rather poetically treated. The treatment is here far different from that in "Loyalties," in which typical strikers and typical capitalists are presented, and from that in "Quality," in which a conscientious bootmaker upholds the standards of his craft even though it leads to death from undernourishment. Forsyte is more complicated, and Galsworthy in his presentation of the highly complex was unable to think his way out. Something was drastically wrong with Forsyte, yet when the author posed the question of uprooting Forsyte

[35] "Twelve Books—and Why," *Saturday Review of Literature*, December 3, 1927. The list of twelve best novels (or series of novels) follows: *Don Quixote*, by Cervantes; *War and Peace* and *Anna Karenina*, by Tolstoi; *Pickwick Papers* and *David Copperfield*, by Dickens; *Fathers and Sons* and *Smoke*, by Turgenev; "The Musketeer" series and "The Reine Margot" series, by Dumas (but only when read in their native French); *The Brothers Karamazof*, by Dostoievski; *Tom Sawyer* and *Huckleberry Finn*, by Mark Twain; *Vanity Fair*, by Thackeray.

and replacing it by something else, his imagination failed him. He temporized: human nature "is and ever will be much of a Forsyte, and might, after all, be a much worse animal." This is perhaps wise and mature, but it is insufficient of an illusion for an artist. In the days of his initial critical urge, Galsworthy had created his métier and his people. He had seen the older Forsytes as a tough, unbreakable lot. But in his later vision the younger generation was softened and altered. Galsworthy knew them well and he contented himself with fashioning stories about them.

E. M. Forster

In *Aspects of the Novel* (1927) Mr. Forster writes suavely and simply of novelists of all time, comparing novels that have appeared centuries apart to establish criteria of excellence. He would seem to deny the effect of the time-spirit upon fiction, and to believe that the technique of construction has not been materially altered by the passage of years.

In his own novels Mr. Forster employs a technique that belongs in part to previous generations. He has no hesitance in employing a plot which depends upon an irrational mistake, an accident, or a fortuitous event. Harriet in *Where Angels Fear to Tread* (1905) accidentally kills her dead sister's baby by dropping it, thus making way for the revelations that follow. There is a sacrificial death and a rescue in *The Longest Journey* (1907) and much of the action depends upon a dark secret of concealed parentage. A death is produced in *Howards End* (1910) by the attempt to transform a man's values. Miss Quested in *A Passage to India* (1924) is positive of the identification of the native who attacked her, but after the major events of the story have transpired, she rather weakly confesses that she was mistaken. The technique is dramatic in sometimes the worst sense.

Yet in spirit there are few authors more influenced than Mr. Forster by the ideas of his day, and few whose impress upon current ideas has been stronger. He closely follows Wells in the feeling that civilization is out of joint, and everywhere he suggests the development of a new understanding, new values, a new man. Says Howard N. Doughty, Jr., in his excellent analysis,

Mr. Forster starts with the common observation that modern civilization distorts and deforms the life of the individual in all its range. Industrialism, by driving man from the soil, has spoiled his capacity for the naive life of the body that flourishes in contact with the earth, and the regimentation of democracy has substituted in him a set of automatic responses for the idiosyncrasies of real personality. Pledged as he is to archaic individualism, Mr. Forster displays, as one might expect, a profound distrust of the machine and of all forms of organization. . . . As for the life of the spirit, as I have said, Mr. Forster disallows it if it involves a rejection of the life of the body. Furthermore it is not genuine if it is based on any retreat from reality, a shutting of the eyes, a shrugging of the shoulders. The pursuit of culture as an end in itself, for instance, is for him one of the worst of perversions. Finally, as a real "inner" life, it postulates an "outer" life, that is, a world of action, a society of which it must not only be aware but in which it must have some stake, from which, to be healthy, it must not feel itself totally cut off.[36]

Obviously much of this bears a close relationship to the doctrine of D. H. Lawrence, and it is not illogical to suppose that Forster was the chief influence upon Lawrence's fiction. There is, to be sure, only one instance in which Lawrence has borrowed a situation: *The Lost Girl*, like *Where Angels Fear to Tread*, shows an English girl marrying and living in Italy with a sexually attractive, irresponsible Italian who is unworthy according to English standards. But the similarity between Forster and Lawrence goes even further than Mr. Doughty has suggested. Both writers give us characters who are protagonists of certain divergent views; they give us action that is symbolic. And both give us at least one crude, back-to-nature type—Stephan in *The Longest Journey* like the lodgekeeper in *Lady Chatterley's Lover*—who is a rough gran-

[36] "The Novels of E. M. Forster," *Bookman,* October, 1932.

ite figure, expressive of the author's insistence that simple emotional values are of primary importance.

Mr. Forster's rough granite Stephan is no very likeable person. A bastard, he is contrasted with the febrile Pembrokes, into whose family Rickie Elliot marries. Stephan is a drunkard, uncouth and bitter, a realist and an atheistic materialist. He scorns false and sentimental values and advocates whatever is natural, physical, and direct. Against him the Elliots and the Pembrokes turn because he represents the antithesis of their values. Only Rickie, exiled from the two families because he resents their treatment of Stephan, is sympathetic to the outcast. He saves Stephan's life but sacrifices his own in the attempt. The events have a symbolic meaning: what is worth saving is saved. It is as if the judgment pronounced by Rickie's mother in a dream foreshadows the death of Rickie and the eventual elimination of all the Elliots and Pembrokes. She is, as Mr. Doughty points out, the earth-mother. "Come away—never mind—let them die out—let them die out," she has muttered; and in so doing she had "expressed her choice for the basic type that shall replace the tainted Elliots and inherit the world from which they sprang."

Howards End carries a similar condemnation. This time the author condemns the Wilcoxes, who are enemies of the elemental because of their preoccupation with business and practicality, which renders them insensitive to the inner life. Margaret, who is poetically responsive, marries a Wilcox, but with the passage of years comes to reject him. Meanwhile the husband goes from bad to worse under a confusion of ideas, his own and his wife's, which he is unable to harmonize. Margaret goes with her child to the old Wilcox country home, which is untainted by the influence of the last generation and where the earth-mother spirit of old Mrs. Wilcox presides. Here the simplicities of country life can be counted on to restore the strain of Wilcoxes to its former basic nature. Yet Margaret cannot be sure; corruptive influences are everywhere. "London's creeping," she says, "and London is only a part of something else. I'm afraid. Life's going to be melted down, all over the world." On the other hand, "Because a thing is going strong now, it need not go strong for ever. All the signs are against it now but I can't help hoping, and very early in the morning in the garden I feel that our house is the future as well as the past."

All of Mr. Forster's novels have an intellectual element. In his first novel, *Where Angels Fear to Tread*, the author in dealing with Philip's development exposes two false attitudes —aestheticism and indifference. *A Room With a View* deals with the emancipation of women. It preceded Wells's *Ann Veronica* by a year. In *A Passage to India* Forster is a critic of British imperialism. His sympathy here is with the rumbling discontent of the natives on whom the customs of a crude Western civilization are imposed. East is East and West is West, and never the twain shall meet. Said Fielding to the native Dr. Aziz, "Why can't we be friends? . . . It's what I want. It's what you want." But the friendly clasp of the two riders was broken. Comments the author,

> But the horses didn't want it—they swerved apart; the earth didn't want it, sending up rocks through which the riders must pass single file; the temples, the tank, the jail, the palace, the birds, the carrion, the Guest House, that came into view as they issued from the gap and saw the Mau beneath: they didn't want it, they said in their hundred voices, 'No, not yet,' and the sky said, 'No, not there.'

Finally, in *The Eternal Moment* (1928), the author looks far into the future and paints a horrible picture of the civilization which will result from present mechanical and devitalizing trends. In the land of the future all problems are solved, every wish gratified. People live without work in underground cells, breathing artificial air, listening to music or being entertained by television programs. One has only to punch a button for food and another for a television conversation with a friend. One's time is supposed to be spent in contemplation and in originating ideas. Yet a young man becomes vaguely troubled.

He goes through forbidden passages to an opening from which he can see the beauty of the Devon hills. Thereupon he starts a revolution which brings to an end, amid explosions, the sterile, nonhuman world of the mechanists.

GILBERT CANNAN

One of the men whom Wells stirred into activity was Gilbert Cannan. Everywhere in his writings are intelligent young men, rebels from the established order, who make adventures of living and learning, and who seek for new realities and a new revelation through experience. They are undisciplined, often incoherent, but they never cease to desire a better world than the one they were born into. Says one of them, who has grown older, "Do you want the young to be more helpless in the world than we have been, to find no life, to collapse of disappointment in the middle years? . . . I will have things true and full, or not at all. If all I could have on these terms was misery, very well then, I would have misery . . . we must bridge the failure of our generation and the collapse of the next."[37]

Unlike Wells, Cannan has no social program. He sees a civilization which is devitalized and insincere, a state of being in which all capacity for enjoyment, all sensibility to art and emotion is dead or dying of starvation. Salvation is an individual matter, and one can only learn what is delectable by seeking it. Yet how "without adventure, without mistakes, folly, suffering, is the discovery to be made?" The promised land is rarely discovered by Cannan's characters. They wander through Europe, America, the near East, and all of Africa searching for it. Yet they find something, some surety, some satisfaction, some hint that the way to further discovery has been opened. At times it seems Cannan would suggest that an unadorned pagan joy is sufficient; that this is at least an escape from the soul's imprisonment by society. But the author is not

[37] *Annette and Bennett* (New York, Thomas Seltzer, 1923).

satisfied with the suggestion. René does not achieve any permanent happiness when he turns taxicab driver and lives with the factory worker whom he has picked up. His "animal life, free of deliberate purpose" gives him happiness for only a short time. When the girl becomes pregnant he cries out, "I will not cloak brute creation with a seeming joy distilled by mind and time and custom. That which I have done with the spirit not awakened in me is done and no longer a part of me. That which the spirit does in me lives on forever and ever."[38]

What the author seems intent upon saying is that the creation through joy of a vital and abundant nature is the major purpose of living. Social responsibility need not be a hindrance; the soul may select its own society and then shut the door. It is the soul's duty to seek its own harmonious expansion. Suggestions of this are everywhere in Cannan's work but only in *Annette and Bennett* (1922), a comparatively late work, does the author express his full conviction. Jamie goes on a solitary walk over the Lake hills,

> Lonely? Good God! What needs a man to be lonely when he has eyes in his head and a heart to feel? What if excess of feeling does drive away men and women? There are still trees and clouds and birds ... there was always happiness in the world, too much ... there was nothing this heavenly world could not yield if it were wooed aright; no need that it could not satisfy.

In addition to the influence of Wells, that of Rolland is everywhere present in Cannan's work. Almost everything Cannan wrote was spiritual biography, or autobiography. So *Peter Homunculus* (1909) is a study of childhood and youth, ending with the publication of Peter's first book. Serge Folyot in *Round the Corner* (1913) is a youth yearning for the larger life who flees incompetent parents to the ends of the earth. David Brockman in *Devious Ways* (1910) seeks a way of life in the colonies and America when the oppression of his stepmother becomes too severe. In these early books happiness is always "around the corner," or it comes "in devious ways."

[38] *Young Earnest* (New York, Martin Secker, 1915).

More ambitious studies were attempted in *Little Brother* (1912), *Young Earnest* (1915), and *Mendel*[39] (1916), in which he treats the development of genius—no doubt inspired by *Jean Christophe;* but in expressing the selfishness that genius necessitates, Cannan gives the theme a different turn. *Old Mole* (1914) is a delightful comedy, showing the awakening in middle life of a frosty teacher of dramatics who is catapulted into the lower social orders of London. "Old Mole" learns life at first hand—and likes it. *Pink Roses* (1916) shows a returned soldier in danger of being reduced to "frozen insensible imbecility" by reflections on the life of the trenches. He has a liaison with the Lady of Roses and is restored to himself.

In a critical study of Samuel Butler written in 1915, Cannan remarked, "The French technique is too rigorous, the Russian too large for our insular temper. . . . Our own writers are either too near their emotions or too near their facts." Cannan himself is detached from his facts; suggestions of egotism are nowhere present in his study of young men's development. Except in *Devious Ways* he sticks to naturalistic logicality, but the logicality is often one of strange temperaments. Yet the characters are convincing, partly because of their imperfections. The author refuses to bind them with the limitations of naturalism since they are to express his ideas upon art, literature, drama, civilization, convention, and the enigma of existence. There is something Russian in the hypersensitive philosophizing of his men, in the formlessness of his account, and in occasional transformations of thought and habit, such as that of René, but the deep intensity of Dostoievski is generally lacking. Cannan is concerned with normal human possibilities.

W. Somerset Maugham

Few English writers were so influenced by the grim intensity of the French naturalists as Maugham. Lighter modes, it is true, prevail in some of his writings. As successful man of

---

[39] For further consideration of *Mendel,* see Chapter XIII.

letters he has written much magazine fiction, much light drama. Yet few English novelists have been more hostile to facile sentiment, more on guard against life, more bent upon dissecting the affections with surgical care. His middle years extended through the problem-conscious era of the Edwardians and through the period of postwar disillusionment. Yet Maugham has held aloof from social problems and from the subjective tendencies of postwar days. He has remained stolidly opposed to those novelists who "held that the novel was a suitable vehicle for ventilating every sort of view and advocating any kind of theory." Writing to a young novelist, he confesses, "I certainly find in myself no urge to reform, admonish, or instruct my fellow men, and if I desire information about town planning or the Montessori system I shall not look for it in the pages of a novel." Although he used his experience with the Intelligence Service to write magazine fiction, the feelings and interests which concern him in his best fiction are timeless; and yet they belong essentially to the twentieth-century revolt against accepted patterns of life that do not lead to mortal happiness.

More than anything his reaction is against man's enslavement to his chivalric notions and, in special, against his generosity to women, with whose frailty the author is entirely out of sympathy. For social codes and customs the author would substitute common sense and natural inclination. He would proscribe maudlin sentiment. In *The Merry-Go-Round* (1904), the barrister-lawyer has married a barmaid to save her honor and succeeded only in making the two of them miserable. When Jenny commits suicide he voices his own, and Maugham's, sound conviction,

"For God's sake let us be free. Let us do this and that because we want to, and because we must, not because other people think we ought. If I'd acted like a blackguard and let Jennie go to the dogs, I should have remained happy and contented and prosperous, and she, I daresay, wouldn't have died. It's because I tried to do my duty that all this misery came about."

In *Of Human Bondage* (1915), the author has no sympathy for Fanny Price, who hanged herself because of frustrated ambition and frustrated love—the fruition of ill-considered desires. If Fanny had once subjected herself to realistic self-inventory she might have realized that she had little talent and less personal attraction. And what of Mildred? The indictment is here more pointed, for the author has made Mildred an incarnation of feminine malice, self-will, and instability.[40] In *The Moon and Sixpence* (1919) we must, of course, be guarded against attributing to Maugham the opinion of the demoniac painter, Strickland. Yet the dramatic purpose of the author is to show that genius may take no account of a certain type of woman, and Strickland's view at least reflects Maugham's opinion in this regard. Says Strickland,

"I know lust; that's normal and healthy. Love is a disease. Women are the instruments of my pleasure. I have no patience with their claim to be helpmates, partners, companions. ... The soul of man wanders through the uttermost regions of the universe and she [woman] seeks to imprison it in the circle of her account book. ... Life has no value. Blanche Strove didn't commit suicide because I left her, but because she was a foolish and unbalanced woman. ... She was an entirely unimportant person."

Strickland is the remorseless, egocentric seeker for beauty, and he has Maugham's qualified sympathy. The author wished to show that genius makes its own terms. The episode of Blanche Strove accentuates the grandeur and infamy of Strickland's soul. Maugham is hardly concerned with the justice of Strickland's view.

To be sure, Maugham can give us admirable women. Perhaps he is most sympathetic with Rosie in *Cake and Ale* (1930). Here there is natural physical harmony, unpretentious kindliness, and a gentle flame of charm. Rosie fulfills herself through love affairs, avoids all complexes, and makes life pleasant. As mother and as lover she finds life good, and at the age of seventy she has a vital concern with what is happening, her natural

---

[40] For further consideration of *Of Human Bondage*, see Chapter XIII.

force no whit abated. In *The Painted Veil* (1925), another comparatively late work, he portrays the transformation of Kitty's soul. For her, physical love is not the way. When she is virtually forced into the fight against cholera in a Chinese district, her sexual concerns are quieted, and she finds a new life through unselfish effort. Maugham permits her to express one of the few idealistic sentiments in his work with which he may be held, in part, to sympathize. Says Kitty, after her transformation,

"I see in front of me the glorious fun of the world, people and music and dancing, and I see its beauty, the sea and the palm-trees, the sunrise and the sunset and the starry night. It's all confused, but vaguely I discern a pattern, and I see before me an inexcusable rich-ness, the mystery and the strangeness of everything, compassion and charity, the way and the wayfarer, and perhaps at the end—God."

It is needless to say that Kitty and Rosie are in the minority. Maugham's critical view of women is but one instance of his attack upon idealisms. He is ruthless in dealing with human error, and he has little belief in mankind. He sees little hope in nature, which is indifferent to man's welfare. He sets high value on the tangible and on what is civilized and delectable. There are few perfected men in his novels. The imperfect Philip is doubtless the one nearest to him. But Alex Mackenzie in *The Explorer* (1907) is closest to his ideal—a person of nat-ural strength and sincerity, one who sees the possibilities of life for greatness and beauty.

W. L. George

During the nineties, advocates of change in fiction did much to destroy the Victorian conception of woman. By way of reaction some of them introduced the drab and the pros-titute. Others gave critical treatment to women of varied so-cial station, but they were incomplete in their portrayals. George Moore at best could portray types—often non-native types. Gissing stressed brutal and incompetent types, on the

one hand, and on the other, ideal women. Shaw's New Woman reverberated with ideas rather than emotions, and Bennett's was a provincial lady seen through a mildly Victorian
haze. Henry James gave reticent treatment to the affairs of
shrewd continentals and Americans on the loose. May Sinclair
and Maugham wrote of real women, but they risked no run-in
with the censor. The conceptions they wished to emphasize
did not necessitate the portrayal of intimacies.

With W. L. George the case is different. His specialty is
women. And with women he associates a preoccupation with
sex:

> The English, particularly English women, speak a great deal
> about sex and, as they are certainly shy of the subject, they must devote
> to it a great deal of thought that they never put into words. If anyone
> doubts this ... let him discreetly ascertain the topics young women
> discuss when no men are present. ... Conversation is oversexed, the
> novel is undersexed, therefore untrue, therefore insincere. ... It is a
> cruel position for the English novel. The novelist may discuss any-
> thing but the main preoccupation of life. ... No character in a modern
> novel has been fully developed. ... A hundred kisses do not make one
> kiss, and there is more truth in one page of *Madame Bovary* than in
> the shackled works of Mr. Hardy. ... There should be as many scenes
> in the bedroom as in the drawing-room, probably more, given that
> human beings spend more time in the former than in the latter apart-
> ment. ... In England the public of the novel is almost exclusively
> feminine. Few man read novels, and a great many nothing at all except
> the newspaper.[41]

George's first novel was in line with his convictions. Fear
of prosecution made many publishers reject *A Bed of Roses*
(1911). The book was finally issued with seventy pages de-
leted, and even then was banned by all libraries. But it achieved
"a moderate measure of scandalous success" and the author
ascertained the limits he could go. Thereafter he went about
as far as the policeman and the publisher would let him, protesting, meanwhile, that novelists "must cast over sex a thick
veil of ellipse and metaphor."

[41] *Literary Chapters,* 128–34.

Since George's early influence was Zola we may presume that his desire was to expose motives rather than to scandalize. And yet he was personally fascinated by the emotional simplicity of women—even feminists. He shows himself a partisan of Wells in saying, "A novelist will not merely record; he must expound, preach and denounce." And he avowed that it was his right, nay, his duty as a novelist to expose cant, denounce hypocrisy, question authority, and accentuate the importance of sex. As to method of presentation, he felt that the novelist must show life as it is, "and to make it so vivid that it will become interesting."[42]

Vividness is a feature of *A Bed of Roses*. To concentrate our attention on the problems that single women without friends face in London, George has created as heroine a woman who at length decides to war against society. Society gives Victoria rough treatment. When she comes, a capable but inexperienced woman, to London from India, where her husband has died, she finds employment only as waitress in a cheap restaurant. She works there until varicose veins in her legs force her to quit. Then and then only does she decide to become the mistress of a rich and retired army officer whom she met on the boat. Major Cairns buys her a house and furniture, prides himself on her youth and beauty, and teaches her to love luxury. Then the major dies and Victoria is alone again. But she has come to hate society and she resolves to prey upon it, maintaining her integrity though not her chastity and abiding by the rules of the game. As a buccaneer she enters the glittering dining room of the Hotel Vesuvius. . . . Her successful career is completed by the time she is thirty, and with money in the bank she retires to the peace of a country home.

In *The Second Blooming* (1915) George is less startling, more general in his sympathies. Here he has the problem of three women in their early thirties who, having been married six or seven years, become aware that they feel restless

[42] "Unpleasant Fiction," *Bookman* (London), April, 1925.

and uneasy. To each he grants fruition: Clara is triumphantly active and political, Mary has a number of children which serve her as a drug against the call of life, and Grace follows the call of love which, in no uncertain terms, the author glorifies. Grace has "loved and piled up memories that would inflame her life, irradiate the future." She philosophizes in the author's vein:

If men have beaten us it's because they're finer. They could do things better and they could stand them better; what we've got to do is to do them and to stand them as well, and then women will be big serene people too, and they won't be afraid. They won't be afraid because they'll know that the whole of life is a thing to be taken bravely, as a sort of store of memories that are going to make one still bigger and still serener.

Here we have George in his typical role as feminist.

Ursula Trent (1921) is the story of a manicurist who knows her way around and manages to find a good bit of interest in life. Says Ursula, "A woman can scratch up a living but not a future, and the only job she's really fit for is to be a man's keep, legal or illegal, permanent or temporary." *Children of the Morning* (1927) is a careful study of the origin of language and customs. A shipload of children, refugees from a South American earthquake, are cast ashore, without an adult to direct them, on an uninhabited tropical island. *Caliban* (1920) is of particular interest to Americans as furnishing a possible antecedent for *Babbitt*. Yet Richard Bulmer is a far more purposeful creature than George F. Babbitt. His attainments as the owner of a London press syndicate are considerable, and he is spared those moments of true illumination in which Babbitt realizes that his life is not altogether perfect. Bulmer's only failure is his effort to capture the socialite Eleanor, who would supply to his establishment the tone which he as a person of low origin lacks. His compensation for the failure is his possession of an upholsteress with a sullen, sensuous beauty, a person always ready to smile and listen when he talks. *Gifts of Sheba* (1926) is a study of marital difficulty. Isabel, who became a business woman during the war, finds herself unhappy with a strong husband and even less contented with a weak one. She finally turns to the philosophical Angus because he understands the pattern of feminine emotions.

Among the novelists here discussed, the view of life was critical and severe. We find, as one might expect, Victorian values are attacked and new conceptions suggested. Women are found to be as faulty as men; neither good intentions nor the church are accorded any special favors, and often the parson is an egotist suffering from a mixture of delusions; the aristocracy is generally neglected, but if Lord Blake is introduced there is certain to be something the matter with him, and Lady Constance may be casually pleased with a liaison; unconventional sexual affairs bring no necessary retribution; there is no tendency to glorify imperialism and few occasions in which there is any marked pride in England and things English; some attempt is made to show man in relation to his physical background, but no stress is placed on determinism; spiritual values which are considered important are those which are conducive to individual fulfillment; there is a general absence of transcendental values. We see here that the sharp difference in philosophical and ethical and social ideas which once separated the English novel from the French naturalistic novel is no more. The difference which continues to exist is that English writers steer away from brutality and that they "throw over sex a thick veil of ellipse and metaphor."

In matters of technique, likewise, an evident change has occurred since Victorian days. The structure of the novel has been simplified and the number of characters reduced. The interest in plot has been largely replaced by an interest in people who are representative of social groups or certain fairly typical attitudes toward life. In either case a careful attention is given to social background. Accidental and fortuitous events are looked upon with disfavor. Although the novel continued to be somewhat dramatic, there was a pronounced tendency to stress the interior conflict rather than the external event. And the ending if not tragic was at least not happy; the author worked out some fair compromise between the two. But in any event the ending was not too neatly conclusive.

⊷§ XII §⊷

THREE SPECIAL INFLUENCES

1910–1915

H. G. WELLS, SAMUEL BUTLER

ROMAIN ROLLAND

WELLS'S importance as a social philosopher lay not in the fact that his views were accepted but that they were read. In the early 1900's a person less well known who expressed the same views as Wells expressed would have been looked upon as an eccentric. But the man who at forty-two had published more books on more subjects than any other man in England was a public figure. Actually he had published thirty volumes. And no one who had read his novels could be convinced that Wells was other than human and altogether sane. So a reviewer for the *Quarterly* after dubbing him "a revolutionary fanatic with a doctrinaire cast of mind" must confess that he sees also in him "a child of nature, as little concerned as Charles Dickens" with sciences and sermons, a person "enticed to the warm green earth by the sounds, the stir, the hues and the fullness of life."[1]

Wells's social conceptions, however, were often taken quite seriously. A writer for the *Contemporary Review* in 1906, after reading *A Modern Utopia*, avowed that

Mr. Wells possesses one of the boldest, freest, best-informed minds of our age, and I know of no book which would, in the hands of a capable master, serve better as a textbook of general politics among per-

[1] "The Ideas of Mr. H. G. Wells."

sons capable of free thinking and really solicitous to understand the large and tangled issue of modern progress.[2]

So Wells's influence as a novelist is partly to be associated with his influence as a public figure. And the influence of Wells was, as everybody knows, to establish the right of the novelist to prove his point through the action and speeches of his characters. Although the themes he employs are often naturalistic and the details of human enterprise are crowded in, the novels as a whole are by no means objective or impersonal. The central characters are dynamic creatures who would be no more content than Wells to leave the world as they found it. They live in revolt, but it is a glorious revolt. The objectives are no whit less important for not having been attained. And if the clutches of passion serve to obstruct the attainment of a worthy human aim, the world and not the passion is at fault, for joy is a stimulant to generous and noble deeds.

If the author could not use the novel to tell us these things and give us his view of society and the social order, he would not have written fiction. It is therefore idle to inquire why he disdained objectivity at a time when objectivity had been established as a primal canon of art in fiction. The fact is, he simply didn't like it and wasn't going to put up with it.

Wells's friendship for Gissing, and his familiarity with Gissing's writings, may have been responsible for the turn he gave realistic expression. On the one hand, he found Gissing's discursive conversations the model for the argumentative discourses so necessary for his purpose. On the other hand, he disagreed violently with Gissing's defeatism. As to Gissing's social conceptions, he said, plainly, that Gissing didn't know what he was talking about. It is quite probable that Wells wrote in the spirit of reaction.

We have every reason to believe that Wells had a very thorough knowledge of the canons of naturalistic art. His article on "The Contemporary Novel," published in the *Fort-*

[2] "The New Aristocracy of Mr. H. G. Wells."

nightly for November, 1911, contains much that any of the naturalists might have written:

> We are going to deal with political questions and religious questions and social questions. We cannot present people unless we have this free hand, this unrestricted field. What is the good of telling stories about people's lives if one may not deal freely with the religious beliefs and organizations that have controlled or failed to control them? What is the good of pretending to write about love, and the loyalties and treacheries and quarrels of men and women, if one must not glance at those varieties of physical temperament and organic quality, those deeply passionate needs and distresses, from which half the storms of human life are brewed? We mean to deal with all these things, and it will need very much more than the disapproval of provincial librarians, the hostility of a few influential people in London, the scurrility of one paper, and the deep and obstinate silence of another, to stop the incoming tide of aggressive novel-writing.

Elsewhere in the article he says:

> The conflict of authority against criticism is one of the eternal conflicts of humanity ... and today while we live in a period of tightening and extending social organization, we live also in a period of adventurous and insurgent thought, in an intellectual spring unprecedented in the worlds' history.

Naturally Wells took issue with Henry James, who was not particularly interested in "adventurous and insurgent thought" and was most particularly interested in technique. To Henry James, The Novel was a very high and important achievement. "He thought of it as an Art Form and of novelists as artists of a very special and exalted type." To him the duty of the novelist was to render a series of impressions. Says Wells: "He had no idea of the possible use of the novel as a help to conduct. . . . But I was disposed to regard a novel as about as much art as a market place or boulevard."

Wells tells us that *Tono-Bungay* was as near a deliberate attempt at The Novel, according to the James conception, as he ever came. But

even *Tono-Bungay* was not much of a concession to Henry James and

his conception of an intensified rendering of feeling and characterization as the proper business of the novelist. It was an indisputable
Novel, but it was extensive rather than intensive. That is to say it
presented characters only as part of a *scene*. It was planned as a social
panorama in the vein of Balzac. That vein has produced some physi-
cally and mentally great books, and it continues in this day to produce evidences of the nervous endurance of ambitious writers, vast
canvasses, too often crude or conventional in interpretation, superficial in motivation and smeary and wholesale in treatment. . . . Next
to *Tono-Bungay, Mr. Britling Sees It Through* and *Joan and Peter*
come as near to being full-dress novels as anything I have written.[3]

We gather that Wells regrets his inability in those days
to insist, in arguments with James, upon an art-form that was
his very own. He had not yet formulated clearly his own conception. Today he would take issue:

It is beyond the power of man to "create" individuals absolutely.
If we do not write from models, then we compile and fabricate. Every
living character in a novel is drawn, frankly or furtively, from life—
is filched from biography whole or in scraps, a portrait or patch-up,
and its actions are reflections upon moral conduct. . . . That is the conclusion I am coming to now, but I did not have it ready at that time.
I allowed it to be taken for granted that there is such a thing as The
Novel, a great and stately addendum to reality, a sort of super-reality,
with "created" persons in it, and by implication I admitted that my
so-called novels were artless self-revelatory stuff, falling far away from
the stately ideal by which they had to be judged.[4]

Wells is by no means disdainful of his early efforts. He sees
fiction, now as then, to be a convenient medium for the con-
veying of one's social impressions.

I was feeling my way to something outside the established form for
the novel altogether. In the established novel, objective through and
through, the characteristic exterior reactions of the character were
everything and the change of ideas within his brain were ignored. But
I was becoming more and more interested in the interior conflict, its
controversial matter stewing and fermenting in all our brains, and its
ventilation in action.[5]

[3] *Experiment in Autobiography*, 423.　　　[4] *Ibid.*, 415.　　　[5] *Ibid.*, 418.

So the uncongenial limitations of The Novel resulted in what Wells calls the Dialogue Novel. It was a novel with a purpose, but so were the novels of Dickens—the difference being, as Wells tells us, that the novels of Dickens never dealt with any inner confusion, any conflicts of opinion within the individual character, any subjective essential change. To Wells the novel is properly concerned with a discussion of relationships and may well have for its theme a dislocation and an adjustment.

With his characteristic glance into the future, Wells is inclined to hope and expect that fiction will be replaced by searching and outspoken biography and autobiography. The freedom allowed the biographer today forecasts this happy result.

The world of H. G. Wells is sufficiently well known to us. The author is in revolt against dinginess and sloth and meekness and conformity. He likes a man who chooses "to run dangers and be singed and tormented and destroyed." Each central character of the more serious novels could pray with Wells: "Break me, O God, disgrace me, destroy me as you will, but save me from self-complacency and little interests and little successes and the life that passes like the shadow of a dream."

His central character is not to have his ardor dimmed by continence. A great good love is a great good love, anytime, anywhere. A social aim may be frustrated, but for the individual whose life is a flame, it is sufficient that the fire shed its illumination. The triumph may be one of the spirit; "So long as your courage endures you shall conquer . . ."

No less carefully than the French naturalists, Wells presents us with studies: studies of shopkeeping, of advertising, of marriage, of politics, of education. The conclusions are mostly naturalistic. But what is distinctive of Wells is the illumination of the issues, the ideal of cosmic progress which is always foremost in the mind of at least one character, the breadth of his moral judgments or implications.

Accordingly, what he has presented to us is not a group

of separate segments of life, but rather a commentary on the whole of it. In this respect his work resembles that of Romain Rolland in *Jean Christophe*. Indeed, it is remarkable that critical interpretations of *Jean Christophe* are applicable to the total effort of Wells. According to Stefan Zweig the attempt is "to write a book that is encyclopedic, not merely narrative. . . . It is the portrait of an entire generation. . . ." It is not merely a cross section of our society "but it is likewise the religious confession of its author. . . . It is critical, but at the same time productive; at once criticism of reality, and a creative analysis of the unconscious . . . a fresco of contemporary ideas . . . an Eroica of the great European fellowship . . . it is as comprehensive as humanity."[6]

SAMUEL BUTLER : THE WAY OF ALL FLESH

One may differ from Sherman in ascribing to Wells the change of an entire generation of novelists and readers. *Jean Christophe* is of almost equal importance. And what of sly, wry old Samuel Butler?

It would be a hopeless task to disentangle the influences which created the English life-novel. Rolland's influence on Wells is one complication. The chances are that the success of *Jean Christophe* suggested emulation on the part of English writers (the translated volumes of *Jean Christophe* were published between 1910 and 1913). Yet the vogue of the life-novel did not begin in England until 1911, whereas *The Way of All Flesh* was published as early as 1903. Again it is likely that *Jean Christophe* proved difficult to imitate and so turned English writers to the subject matter and ideas of Butler's semi-autobiographical account. Furthermore there is little doubt that the vigor and breadth of Wells's views had permeated the minds of all English writers of the time, and had suggested the value of a subjective treatment of life. But the matter of individual influences is not highly important. The three influ-

---

[6] Stefan Zweig, *Romain Rolland* (New York, Thomas Seltzer, 1921), 166–68.

ences worked jointly to extend the range of fictional expression in England.

We are indebted to Chavelley for the information (1925) that "not a year has passed since 1908 without a new and large edition of this book [*The Way of All Flesh*], the reprinting of which was uninterrupted even during the war."[7] Chavelley further states that between 1915 and 1918 he had counted four popular editions of the old *Erewhon*, which was first published in 1872.

We recall Shaw's indebtedness, of course, and we have ourselves witnessed the revival of interest in all that Butler has written. Having once read *The Way of All Flesh* we will not soon forget the pain and resentment of the book, the loneliness and suffering, the diligent plodding to find a way of life; we will not forget the idiocies of educational and religious training, the parental inflexibility, the domestic discords, the attack on "romantic" relations between the sexes, the dealing with prostitutes; nor will we forget the emancipation from "duty," the discovery of pleasure as the motive of life, and the progress toward a view of life which is hard headed and sensible, without much hope and without regrets.

The influence of *The Way of All Flesh* is strong in Maugham and Beresford and Wells, as well as in the early works of Cannan. But I shall not risk being tedious by summarizing the well-known affairs of the Pontifex family. Readers need only recall Butler's horse sense in a section where Ernest is speaking:

"What care I about being what is called a gentleman? ... What has being a gentleman ever done for me but make me less able to prey and more easy to be preyed upon? It has changed the manner of my being swindled, that is all. ... Will being a gentleman bring me money at the last, and will anything bring me as much peace at the last as money will? They say that those who have riches enter hardly into the kingdom of heaven. By Jove, they do; ... They live and live and live and are happy for many a long year after they would have entered

[7] Abel Chavelley, *Le roman anglais de notre temps* (Oxford, Humphrey, Milford, 1921), 87.

the kingdom of Heaven if they had been poor. I want to live long and raise my children, if they would be happier for the raising. ... Being a gentleman is a luxury which I cannot afford, therefore I do not want it. Let me go back to my shop again and do things for people that they want done and will pay me for doing for them. They know what they want and what is good for them better than I can tell them."[8]

Romain Rolland : jean christophe

Jean Christophe appeared serially between 1904 and 1912 in a little-known French periodical, *Cahiers de la Quinzaine.* For several years following the appearance of the first part of the story it attracted casual attention. Then suddenly the literary world awoke to its significance and beauty, and it was acclaimed throughout Europe as the first great book of the twentieth century. It was crowned by the French Academy, and in 1915 its author was awarded the Nobel Prize for Literature for the two years 1914 and 1915. In England the work appeared between the years 1910 and 1913. By April, 1912, three of the four volumes had been published in English.

The life-novel, of course, was no new literary form. Rolland doubtless had read *L'Education sentimentale* and *Wilhelm Meister;* he had profited from Huysmans' intensity and discursiveness, but more from Huysmans' theories of fiction.

The English reader of *Jean Christophe* is struck not so much by new material and a new technique as by a new intensity. Rolland's vivid treatment lighted up the years of infancy. The reader's attention is focused upon the painful family situation, the early discouragement and hate. He feels the presence of poverty and the embarrassment caused by it, the humiliation. He remembers the tears and the uncompromising purpose of Christophe. And then he witnesses the treatment of adolescent love, fumbling liaisons and passion— presented with an unconventional detail of half-satisfactions so lacking in the English novel. He sees Christophe not altered

[8] Modern Library Edition, 365.

by his emotional disturbances but storming through life, elated by friendships and possessed by everlasting hates, taking part in brawls, expatriated, his aims frustrated but his spirit never weakened. The reader sees that Christophe came to understanding not through books but through the tragedies of his personal experience, that despair clutched his soul only at moments when dark death seized his loved ones, that through the chastening influence of death and perfected love a great soul was born.

Christophe's own summary is permeated with that overflow of emotions which Englishmen would look for only in poetry:

As a succession of stages he looked back over the whole of his life: the immense effort of his youth to win self-possession, his desperate struggle to exact from others the bare right to live, to wrest himself from the demons of his race. And even after the victory, the forced unending vigil over the fruits of conquest, to defend them against victory itself. The sweetness, the tribulation of friendship opening up the great human family through conflict to the isolated heart. The fullness of art, the zenith of life. His proud dominion over his conquered spirit. His belief that he had mastered his destiny. And, then, suddenly at the turn of the road, his meeting with the knights of the Apocalypse, Grief, Passion, Shame, the vanguard of the Lord. Then laid low, trampled under foot by the horses, dragging himself bleeding to the heights, where, in the midst of the clouds, flames the wild purifying fire. His meeting face to face with God. His wrestling with Him, like Jacob with the Angel. His issue, broken from the fight. His adoration of his defeat, his understanding of his limitations, his striving to fulfill the will of the Lord, in the domain assigned to him. Finally, when the labors of seed-time and harvest, the splendid hard work, were at an end, having won the right to rest at the feet of the sunlit mountains.

Perhaps our discussion of the book should end with these words. And yet the broad sweep of the novel as interpreted by critics is well worth our attention: Rolland "does not merely depict the history of his generation but discusses the cultural history of his age, exhibiting the radiations of the time spirit, concerning himself with poetry and with socialism, with music and the fine arts, with the woman question and with race problems. Jean Christophe the man is the whole man, and *Jean Christophe* the book embraces all that is human in the spiritual cosmos. This novel ignores no questions; it seeks to overcome all obstacles; it has a universal life, beyond the frontiers of nations, occupations and creeds.[9] ... The book furnishes an outlook on the universe, thus becoming a philosophic, a religious novel. The struggle for the totality of life signifies for Rolland the struggle to understand its significance and origin, the struggle for God, for one's own personal God. The rhythm of the individual existence is in search of an ultimate harmony between itself and the rhythm of the universal existence."[10]

The English adaptation, for the most part, lacks the broad sweep of Rolland's narrative. The tendency was to a more personal account. But without the intense spaciousness of *Jean Christophe* to serve as an example, English writers would not have permitted themselves a slow inquiry into the stages of formative experience. With *Jean Christophe* supplementing the writings of Wells, they would not have felt that fiction was the proper medium for the exposition of their own philosophy of existence, and the steps in its discovery.

We will recall that the twentieth century dawned with the canons of naturalistic fiction established in England. Naturalism was, of course, an intensified effort in the direction of objectivity and depersonalization. Whether or not England liked undiluted naturalism, the importance of its corrective influence was recognized. We may seriously doubt whether, despite Wells, the shackles of "objectivity" would have been soon lifted without the world-wide popularity of *Jean Christophe*. The book signified to English writers that a new day had dawned, and that fiction might be poetry, autobiography, a discussion of ideas, or anything else so long as it was honest and interesting.

[9] Zweig, *Romain Rolland*, 169. (Author's note: I have taken the liberty of changing "poesy" to "poetry" and "romance" to "novel" in the English translation by Eden and Cedar Paul.)

[10] *Ibid.*, 170.

❧ XIII ❧

THE LIFE-NOVEL IN ENGLAND

1910–1917

THE tendency to write life-novels was in England a special movement or impulse which lasted only a few years. Certain writers—Lawrence, Mackenzie, Beresford, and Joyce—substantially began their careers as novelists by writing life-novels;[1] and subjective tendencies are prevalent largely in their later work. But others—Maugham, Cannan, Walpole, and George—had previously written objective novels and later reverted to objective tendencies. The current of the life-novel was arrested by the war, but its tendency to subjective expression made possible the concern with "private worlds," which was the dominant tendency in postwar fiction.

The life-novel is identified by the fact that it begins with the birth of the central character and traces his early influences and education. There was little attempt in England, further than this, to stick to *Jean Christophe* as a model. For *Jean Christophe* treats a genius and, aside from *A Portrait of the Artist as a Young Man* and *Mendel* the English life-novel was concerned with men of rather average mold.

The vogue of *Jean Christophe* awakened English writers to the possibilities of a less restrained fiction, a fiction which might deal candidly with the theme of youth and its struggles with itself and the world. A distinctive feature was a central character sympathetic to the reader and at the same time one

---

[1] Mackenzie had written a novel concerned with the graces of eighteenth-century life; Beresford had written a fantasy in the manner of H. G. Wells.

who was not too representative of the established social virtues. In this way it provided for a troubled study of living, of living in England, of confronting difficulties as they present themselves to the young, of experiencing love and passion as it presents itself to a man, and of finding an honest philosophy of life which, if not altogether satisfactory, would enable one to meet the world and accept what fate has to offer.

The element of groping and discovery had been noticeably absent from English fiction in the years preceding the twentieth century. There had, of course, been novels about people who struggled with religious doubts. There had been many novels about young people and their difficulties. But the very air breathed was heavy with certainties. In any case a man ought to be, or try to become, a Gentleman, and that was that.

The matter is important, for to be or become a gentleman one must indorse a certain attitude toward life and toward society. One becomes involved with the details of the ritual. So English fiction had shown a certain tendency to deal with tragedy and heart throbs among the subgentleman species. Otherwise a gentleman betook himself to adventure or to conversations and decisions which give one a better sense of fine distinctions but reveal little of the knowledge of life that comes through suffering over false values.

We will remember that one of George Moore's best characters, Mike Fletcher, did not wish to be considered a gentleman. The idea was startling at the time. But with the writers of life-novels the emancipation of their young men from the social ideal of Gentleman was a necessary step in the acquisition of a philosophy, just as it was necessary for Christophe Kraft to escape from German idealism. We remember the strength of his protest:

Idealism! That meant that they were afraid of looking at life squarely, were incapable of seeing things as a man, as they are. . . . Everywhere the same timidity, the same lack of manly frankness. Everywhere the same chilly enthusiasm, the same pompous lying solemnity, in their patriotism, in their drinking, in their religion.

Perhaps Beresford expresses the protest against the English social ideal more strongly than the rest. In *House-Mates* he tells us,

I was, I still am, a plastic, adaptable creature, and I had sedulously modelled and enthroned the one idea that had always been put before me. The profession of becoming a gentleman had been the idol that I was taught to worship, and none had ever suggested to me that my idol lacked comprehensiveness. Good form, the esteem of my contemporaries, a little fame and position, and the getting of as much money as I could honestly acquire, these were the sole objects of social life. Behind them lay the necessity of ensuring peace through eternity by the careful observation of certain ritual formalities. No one had ever gone deeper than that with me; no one had ever talked to me of a beauty that was not stereotyped.

As a resident of a rooming house in a low district the character awakes to self-realization and a feeling for the vitality of human experience:

My sudden enlargement had been brought about by intense nervous excitement, and a new sight of life—life unrestrained, passionate, elemental. I had been ready and the freedom of my loneliness had helped to release me.

Perhaps the underlying cause for dissatisfaction with the world's valuations came from a realization that scientific materialism had disrupted old values but had failed to substitute anything new. Life in the light of the new revelation was uncharted, and wide regions of uncertainty provided the impulse to explore. The central character in one of Gilbert Cannan's novels ponders the difficulty:

there seemed no security in existence; civilization was no longer an achievement, but a fluid stream flowing over a varied bed—rock, mud, pebbles, sand; society was no establishment, but a precarious, tottering thing, a tower of silted sands with an oozy base, blocking the river, squeezing it into a narrow and precarious channel. In the nature of things and its law the river would one day gather unto itself great waters and bear the sands away. . . . Meanwhile men strove to make the sand-heap habitable, for they were born on it, lived and died on it, and never looked beyond. Their whole lives were filled with the dread of its crumbling, their whole energies devoted to building up against it, and against the action of wind and rain and sun. They built themselves in and looked not out, and made their laws by no authority, but only by expediency, and the young men, in their vitality too great for such confinement, knew that somewhere there must be firm ground, and were determined to excavate and explore.

The young men whose lives are traced by English life-novelists must grope their way through a maze of social customs and traditions. They do not possess themselves of their deamon and flee to France for the attainment of a supernal goal, as did Christophe. Except with Wells they do not wrestle with God on the heights. Rather they divest themselves of pretense and fraud, and, through pain and suffering, through liaisons and books and conversations, they get some tangible understanding of what life is. Whatever they discover, the novelist marks it down as a net gain, an acquirement, for the past has bequeathed only confusion and empty hopes.

J. D. Beresford

The earliest and most prosaic of the life-novels is Beresford's trilogy—*The Early History of Jacob Stahl* (1911), *A Candidate For Truth* (1912), *The Invisible Event* (1915). And yet it is a doggedly honest document with Jacob Stahl sinking lower and lower until he strikes firm ground, and then, as a writer, rising slowly and persistently to a modest distinction. Both his fall and his rise come from feminine influences. Lola, vain and ignorant and extravagant and religious, causes him needlessly to expend his capital in the fruitless attempt to succeed as an architect without connections. Reduced to poverty and want he takes to book-reviewing and is lonely. Denied a divorce by Lola, he tries to persuade a well-connected young boardinghouse keeper, Betty, to live with him unmarried. He succeeds in persuading her. Betty encourages him, and he gets an autobiographical novel published.

This is a meager story for three volumes. Beresford's interests are so constricted that even his impersonation must write autobiographical novels, and the taint of egotism, so dangerous to the life-novel, is accentuated. Moreover Jacob has no dynamic purpose, no significant enthusiasms, little learning, and a very casual concern with the arts. He is, like Beresford, a rather unwary plodder.

The pages are lightened by two love affairs which are, like everything else that Beresford writes, genuine. The indiscretions of youthful passion with the aristocratic Madelaine are handled discreetly but rather expertly. The solace provided by Betty is portrayed with mildly critical tenderness.

Obviously the chief influence is that of Samuel Butler. Christianity is the villain of the show. Narrow-minded and selfish women revel in its justifications. Christian charity is everywhere in Beresford's writings, except with the Christians. Many people are kind to Jacob. Moreover the extramarital relationship with Betty is imposed on society, which, after all, is more influenced by the fear of the Christians' criticism than by any religious principle of its own. Perhaps society's acceptance of the comman-law wife symbolizes the author's belief that rugged honesty will win out in the end.

These not-too-effusive remarks having been made, one may say a word of appreciation. It is good for English fiction that Beresford's trilogy was written. The book is sober and real and painful. It suggests that English fiction writers do not have to be entertaining if they are honest. It performed for the life-novel the service that *Germinie Lacerteux* performed for naturalism.

W. Somerset Maugham : of human bondage

The first of Mr. Maugham's novels, *Liza of Lambeth*, was discussed in Chapter VI, and the general implication of Mr. Maugham's novels was treated in Chapter XI. Only Maugham's life-novel will be dealt with here.

Of Human Bondage is a story of wrecked ambitions. Philip first had dreams of living abundantly, of living in art. He found that he had little talent and took up the study of medicine for a career. But all the time he dreamed of travel and the wonderful corners of the world. He dissipated his fortune in helping others, was obsessed by a humiliating love, finally came to terms with life by accepting a simple life and a simple love:

What did he care of Spain and its cities, Cordova, Toledo, Leon; what to him were the pagodas of Burma and the lagoons of South Sea Islands? America was here and now. It seemed to him that all his life he had followed the ideals that other people, by their words or their writings, had instilled in him, and never the desires of his own heart. Always his course had been swayed by what he thought he should do and never what he wanted with his whole soul to do. He put all that aside now with a gesture of impatience. He had lived always in the future, and the present always, always had slipped through his fingers. His ideals? He thought of his desire to make a design, intricate and beautiful, out of the myriad, meaningless facts of life: had he not seen also that the simplest pattern, that in which a man was born, worked, married, had children, and died, was likewise the most perfect? It might be that to surrender to happiness was to accept defeat, but it was a defeat better than many victories.

This is certainly not Rolland or Wells speaking. Is it nearer the conclusion of Samuel Butler?

We remember Philip's revolt, his hatred for his uncle, the intellectual awakening in Paris. We remember the tragedies of Fanny Price and of Mildred. We remember Philip's friends and his failings; we remember the symbolic club foot. We remember Philip's poverty and his wish for his uncle's death. We remember the various atmospheres and environments, always portrayed with strict veracity. We remember the varieties of love, and again the painstaking veracity.

There are no more painful chapters in the language than those dealing with Philip's entanglement with Mildred. They broke every tradition in English love-making. That a well-born man should be deeply and sentimentally in love with a waitress who disliked him, that he should come to dislike her utterly and still love her, that he should permit her to ruin him financially even while he hated her—these harsh facts do not belong to the English tradition.

He did not think her pretty; he hated the thinness of her, only that evening he had noticed how the bones of her chest stood out in evening dress; he went over her features one by one; he did not like her mouth, and the unhealthiness of her color vaguely repelled him. She was common. Her phrases, so bald and few, constantly repeated, showed the emptiness of her mind; he recalled her vulgar little laugh at the jokes of the musical comedy; and he remembered the little finger carefully extended when she held her glass to her mouth; her manners, like her conversation, were odiously genteel. He remembered her insolence; sometimes he had felt inclined to box her ears; and suddenly, he knew not why, perhaps it was the thought of hitting her or the recollection of her tiny, beautiful ears, he was siezed with an uprush of emotion. He yearned for her. He thought of taking her in his arms, the thin, fragile body, and kissing her greenish cheeks. He wanted her. . . . He had thought of love as a rapture which seized one so that all the world seemed spring-like, he had looked forward to an ecstatic happiness; but this was not happiness; it was a hunger of the soul, it was a painful yearning, it was bitter anguish. . . .

He tries to think his way out, but

he did not act with a part of himself but altogether. The power that possessed him seemed to have nothing to do with reason; all that reason did was to point out the methods of obtaining what his whole soul was striving for.

Mildred comes back to him for help, and Philip plans to break up a very happy liaison. He thinks it out while talking to Norah:

She was worth ten of Mildred; she amused him much more and was jollier to talk to; she was clever, and she had a much nicer nature. She was a good, brave, honest little woman; and Mildred, he thought bitterly, deserved none of these epithets. If he had any sense he would stick to Norah. . . . After all she loved him. . . . But when all was said the important thing was to love rather than be loved; and he yearned for Mildred with his whole soul. He would sooner have

ten minutes with her than a whole afternoon with Norah, he prized
one kiss of her cold lips more than all Norah could give him. . . . He
did not care if she was heartless, vicious and vulgar, stupid and grasp-
ing, he loved her. He would rather have misery with the one than
happiness with the other.

Equally candid is Maugham's treatment of Philip's progressive philosophical discoveries:

> Society stood on one side, an organism with its own laws of growth
> and self-preservation, while the individual stood on the other. The ac-
> tions that were to the advantage of society it termed virtuous and those
> which were not it termed vicious. Good and evil meant nothing more
> than that. Sin was a prejudice from which the free man should free
> himself. . . . The free man can do no wrong. He does everything he
> likes—if he can. His power is the only measure of his mortality. . . .

> Philip exulted, as he had exulted in his boyhood when the weight
> of a belief in God was lifted from his shoulders: it seemed to him that
> the last burden of responsibility was taken from him; for, if life was
> meaningless, the world was robbed of its cruelty. What he did or left
> undone did not matter. Failure was unimportant and success amount-
> ed to nothing. He was the most inconsiderate creature in that swarm-
> ing mass of mankind that for a brief space occupied the surface of the
> earth; and he was almighty because he had wrenched from chaos the
> secret of its nothingness. . . .

> Philip thought of the countless millions to whom life is no more
> than unending labor, neither beautiful nor ugly, but just to be accepted
> in the same spirit as one accepts the changes in the seasons. Fury seized
> him because it all seemed useless. He could not reconcile himself to
> the belief that life had no meaning and yet everything he saw, all his
> thoughts, added to the force of his conviction. But though fury seized
> him it was a joyful fury. Life was not so horrible if it was meaningless,
> and he faced it with a strange sense of power.

JAMES JOYCE : A PORTRAIT OF THE ARTIST
AS A YOUNG MAN

A primal requisite for the life-novel is that it must be
painful. Generally the anguish is that of the soul and, except

in *Of Human Bondage* and Beresford's works, the physical pangs of poverty do not enter. The individual is trying to adjust himself to the world, and he finds that the ways of thinking and of feeling which he early acquires are in opposition both to dim urges of his nature and to the broader world that he later encounters. The resolution which the character generally attains is a form of liberation. He fastens upon a living truth and relegates his former complexities to limbo—not always, of course, for Lawrence's Paul Morel continues in life with an Oedipus complex.

A Portrait of the Artist as a Young Man harks back to more remote origins than those discussed in the previous chapter. The primary influence is Huysmans, and Joyce had read Moore —both *A Mere Accident* and *The Lake*. But Stephen, unlike Durtal, does not come to Catholicism through satiety. His early rearing has instilled a certain religious acceptance. Sin and a good hot sermon on Hell turn him to piety.

The redemption of Stephen from piety is, of course, the theme of the book. Yet the author tells us little of the influences which produced the change. Stephen feels an upwelling of soul that urges him to seek wisdom in the world, and that links him unalterably with God and creation.

Joyce's power is his poetry—each successive stage of Stephen's experience is portrayed with the certainty of a powerful personal experience. He has given to the life-novel in England its greatest intensity.

The point, perhaps, deserves to be stressed since the life-novel, as we shall later see, gave to the contemporary English novel its flavor of experienced emotion.

Stephen in his 'teens has erotic urges:

He turned to appease the fierce longings of his heart before which everything else was idle and alien. He cared little that he was in mortal sin, that his life had grown to be a tissue of subterfuge and falsehood. Beside the savage desire within him to realize the enormities which he brooded on nothing was sacred. He bore cynically with the shameful details of his secret riots in which he exulted to defile with patience whatever image had attracted his eyes. . . . His blood was in revolt. He wandered up and down the dark slimy streets peering into the gloom of lanes and doorways, listening eagerly for any sound. He moaned to himself like some baffled prowling beast. He wanted to sin with another of his kind, to force another being to sin with him and to exult with her in sin. He felt some dark presence moving irresistibly upon him from the darkness, a presence subtle and murmurous as a flood filling him wholly with itself.[2]

Stephen sinned, and the sermon brings him to repentance:

Against his sin, foul and secret, the whole wrath of God was aimed. The preacher's knife had probed deeply into his disclosed conscience and he felt now that his soul was festering in sin. Yes, the preacher was right. God's turn had come. . . . The wind of the last day blew through his mind; his sins, the jewel-eyed harlotries of his imagination, fled before the hurricane, squeaking like mice in their terror and huddled under a mane of hair.

He goes to confessional and becomes a convert to piety:

His life seemed to have drawn near to eternity, every thought, word and deed, every instance of consciousness could be made to revibrate radiantly in heaven. . . . The world for its solid substance and complexity no longer existed for his soul save as a theorem of divine power and love and universality.

But the final revelation was yet to come; it was entirely apart from "the inhuman voice that had called him to the pale service of the altar":

His soul was soaring in an air beyond the world and the body he knew was purified in a breath and delivered of incertitude and made radiant and commingled with the element of the spirit. . . . His throat ached with a desire to cry aloud, the cry of a hawk or eagle on high, to cry piercingly of his deliverance to the winds. This was the call of life to his soul not the dull gross voice of the world of duties and despair, not the inhuman voice that had called him to the pale service of the altar. An instant of wild flight had delivered him and the cry of triumph which his lips withheld cleft his brain. . . . His soul had risen from the grave of boyhood, spurning her grave clothes. Yes! Yes!

[2] From *A Portrait of the Artist as a Young Man,* by James Joyce. Copyright 1916 by B. W. Huebsch. By permission of The Viking Press, Inc., New York.

Yes! He would create proudly out of the freedom and power of his soul, as the great artificer whose name he bore, a living thing, new and soaring and beautiful, impalpable, imperishable. A wild angel had appeared before him, the angel of mortal youth and beauty, an envoy from the fair courts of life, to throw open before him in an instant of ecstasy the gates of all the ways of error and glory. On and on and on and on!

Certainly the lyrical powers of Rolland have awakened a worthy response here.

Stephen shows up later in *Ulysses* (1922), which is treated in Chapter XIV.

GILBERT CANNAN : MENDEL

Mr. Cannan's work as a novelist was treated at some length in Chapter XI. In the section which follows only the life-novel *Mendel* will be discussed.

As is to be expected, the life-novel written by Rolland's English translator is more similar to *Jean Christophe* than any other English life-novel.

Mendel is the story of a young Jewish painter's struggles —with poverty, with art, and with himself. Cannan doubtless makes a Jew his hero, much as Rolland did a German, in order to treat the development of genius as a subject outside the range of national traditions, social judgments, and conventional valuations. The novel is essentially about Art and Life; it is an exposition of the possibilities of life in its more intense aspects, where despair and hope and failure and exhilaration alternate from page to page.

Thus conceived, the life-novel does much to deepen the channels of fiction. The artist's search is for sincerity in life and experience as a prerequisite to art, for there can be no art without sincerity. So fiction becomes a study of the possibilities of life as viewed from the vantage ground of lofty vision or attainment. The young Mendel perhaps overstresses the point:

"I tell you," cried Mendel in a fury—"I tell you I know what art is better than anybody. It touches life at one point, at one point only, and there it gives a great light. If life is too mean and beastly to reach that point, so much the worse for life. It does not affect art, which is another world, where everything is beautiful and true. I know it; I have always known it. I have lived in that world. I live in it, and I detest everything that drags me away from it and makes me live in the world of filth and thieves and scoundrels."

Like Christophe, Mendel is experimental, and the affairs similarly leave him untouched. His young companion tries to understand him by reading *Jean Christophe*, which he admired:

When she found that Mendel was becoming a fixed idea, to escape from it she took up the second volume, and was enthralled by the tale of Christophe's love for Ada, thrilled by the sudden scene of his assault on the peasant girl in the field, and with a growing sense of illumination followed his life as it passed from woman to woman, finding consolation with one, relief with another, comradeship with yet another, and the physical relationship slipped into its place and was never dominant. And Christophe, too, had had women of passage because his vitality was so abundant that it could not be contained in his being. It must always be flowing out into art or into life, taking from life more and more power to give to art.

One must avoid stressing any ethical quality of Cannan's novel. Mendel is essentially a story of art and the passion of the artist. It is also a story about Jews, for the solid Jewish racial quality pervades Mendel's paintings when he would free himself from his race. The young Mendel grows to love the city of his adoption, he is well treated by Londoners, and he is successful in his art so long as his mind is integrated with his race and his work within the traditions of a school. It is when his mind is perplexed by his groping and his heart torn by those whom he loves that he drifts to despair. A new integration eventually is attained, but he knows that it is temporary. For the artist there is no settled peace:

"You must not expect me to be happy. I cannot be happy. I will swing up to it as high as ever you like, but I must swing back again.

... I know that when I swing from happiness, from good to bad, from light to dark, then a force comes into my soul and I can move up to art, and beyond art, and into that place where it can be free."

H. G. WELLS : JOAN AND PETER

Although the subjective tendencies in Mr. Wells's fiction have been indicated in the preceding chapter, it seems advisable to show in this section his handling of the life-novel.

Joan and Peter begins with the birth of a child and carries him well past his formative years, but it differs rather remarkably from *Jean Christophe*. Indeed, except for the concluding chapters on God, there is only a surface resemblance. Neither Peter nor Joan is a genius, and, of course, the life history is about two people instead of one. It is really about three people. We pick up Oswald, the guardian, at about the age we leave Peter, and we witness his progressive attainment of understanding. So the discovery of life is really complete, but Wells divides it into segments.

We would hardly expect Wells to follow a ready-made pattern. And so for the wild and poetical will of Christophe is substituted the dogged determinism of Oswald who, as a modified and quiet empire builder, is bent upon doing a decent job in the rearing of his wards. Furthermore the form of the "educational novel" prescribed limits by which Wells could not abide, for he felt that education was a social problem and therefore a subject for much rumination. A full illumination of the subject would have been hampered by considering it alone from Peter's point of view. But through Oswald the author could speak in his own person.

Joan is introduced to complete the picture. The author would not leave out the education of women. And, the opportunity being thus given, he pictures an ideal marriage based upon companionship.

Peter does not suffer through his liaisons. They are unimportant incidents in his life. His sufferings, like those of Oswald,

are caused by shot and shell; each suffers for the empire, but
also for civilization. Each attains a consciousness of the possibilities of a better world order and a determination to struggle
to that end. And this, to Wells, is the attainment of understanding.

According to Wells, the education of the very young can
best be carried on by deliberately determining not to do too
much:

> Artificiality is the last resort. Instinct is our basis. For the larger
> part the boy has just to grow. But we watch his growth. Education is
> really watching—keeping the course. The human error is to do too
> much, to overteach, over-legislate, over-manage, over-decorate. . . ."

Oswald objects to formal education in preparatory schools:
"It's like trying to graft mummy-steak on living flesh. It's like
boiling fossils for soup." Mr. McKinder explains that the cur-
riculum is determined by the parents and the universities. There
is resistance to constructive change. Teachers are ill-paid. He
does what he can.

Education at Cambridge was little better:

> There was a smattering of Latin, a thinner smattering of Greek, a
> little patch of Mediterranean history and literature detached from past
> and future—but then he would have considered any history fragmen-
> tary that did not begin with the geological record and end with a clear
> tracing of every traceable consequence of the "period" in human af-
> fairs; there were mathematical specializations that did not so much
> broaden the mind as take it into a gully, modern and medieval lan-
> guage specializations, philosophical studies that were not really philo-
> sophical studies at all but partial examinations of remote and irrelevant
> systems.

So Oswald took Peter to visit foreign countries, studying
civilizations.

The tragedy, as Oswald saw it, was that individuals who
had grown up without any clear aims or any definite sense of
obligations, knowing themselves and the world so little, should
have been brought face to face with a war.

But Oswald had underrated the disposition of youth to think for itself.

Wells has written many spiritual biographies. Perhaps our selection should have been *The New Machiavelli* (1911). Perhaps it should have been *The Undying Fire* (1919), or *The World of William Clissold* (1926). The central effect of Wells has been to emphasize life-novel tendencies.

OTHERS

Obviously the life-novel is the vehicle for thought and philosophy. If a writer has not found some meaning or significance in life, or if he has not completely satisfied himself that life has no meaning or significance, we would assume that he would choose another mode of narration. Similarly we would assume that the author who is fond of decoration and romantic associations would hesitate to use the life-novel form. Such assumptions, however, are not in accord with fact. Several Englishmen wrote life-novels which, though recognizable as such, seem rather forced, "literary," and insincere.

One of these was Compton Mackenzie. He may be called the virtuoso of the life-novel. The form pleased him. He wrote at least three different life-novels, two of which extended through several volumes. He writes with verve, éclat, and precision. He is one of the most engaging writers of fiction that England has produced and one of the most inconsequential. The surface brilliance of his volumes is everywhere evident; but he rarely gives us anything more than a surface brilliance.

Youth's Encounter (1913) and *Sinister Street* (1914) tell vividly of the youth, awakening, and early experiences of Michael Fane. The chapters on Oxford are the best ever written about the place. Michael is drawn to the Church just as Sylvia is drawn to it in a later book. Huysmans' influence both in this and in the recurrent philosophical reflections is pronounced. But the reader is not at all convinced about Michael's living in the slums in order to find Sylvia, nor does he feel that Michael is otherwise actuated by a comprehensible motive. The leaning toward the Church seems literary.

In *The Early History of Sylvia Scarlett* (1918) and *Sylvia and Michael* (1919) the motivation is even worse. Sylvia undergoes an amazing series of self-mortifications and right-about turns. Moreover, the author introduces the accidental, the coincidental, and the fortuitous with utter disregard for the reader's credulity. We may note a sample:

Sylvia, a chaste entertainer at a Bucharest cabaret, takes a cocotte under her wing to protect her from the influences of the world. By doing so she precipitates a brawl and is fired. The two women then go to a near-by town but find the cabaret there closed and no employment available. Worst of all, Sylvia finds that she has lost the five hundred franc note which represents the savings of herself and friend. She returns to Bucharest to borrow money from her former husband, who had arrived there on government business lately. But the husband had suddenly died a day or so before Sylvia returns; so she goes again to the little town resolved to sell her body. The gentleman to whom she offers it, however, is more interested in her young friend, and declines. Fortunately he lost a ten franc piece out of his trousers pocket, so Sylvia takes the money and returns to Bucharest. All this time she had forgotten that she could sell her gold bag; so she now sells it. Flush with money she returns to the small town, but her friend has run off with a man. Feeling rather carefree she pops into the cabaret where a wealthy old gentleman wishes to drink champagne with her. They drink until 4:00 A.M. and the old gentleman leaves her well off—without, however, having touched her. She leaves for England through Bulgaria, but Bulgaria enters the war as her train is passing through, etc.

It is the incredible which ruins much good writing in Mackenzie's works. Sometimes an incongruous note is struck. Sylvia makes most of her money by persuading men to pop champagne corks, yet her musings are generally in the Huysmans vein. There is no necessary contradiction, of course, but the reader cannot readily mix pep and piety:

Sylvia, however, wanted a hundred and fifty francs for herself, and invoking the little red devil she showed a way of breaking a bottle in half by filling it with hot water, saturating a string in mentholated spirits, tying the string around the bottle, setting light to it, and afterwards tapping the bottle lightly with a knife until it broke. The Count was delighted with this trick but thought, as Sylvia hoped that he would think, that the trick would be better if practiced on an unopened bottle of champagne. In this way twenty-six bottles were broken in childish rage by the Count. . . .

In all her readings she had never paid proper attention to the doctrines of Christianity, and she longed to know if some of these dim facts after which she was now groping were not there set forth with transparent brightness and undeniable clarity. Good or evil must present themselves to every soul in a different way and it was surely improbable that the accumulated experience of the human mind gathered together in Christian writings would not contain a parallel by which she might be led toward the truth, or at least be granted the vision of another lonely soul seeking for itself salvation.

Fortitude (1914), by Hugh Walpole (whose other work is discussed in Chapter XV), has a certain affinity to the Victorian novel. There are stock characters (the village philosopher, the village fool, the schoolteacher, etc.), coincidences, picturesque settings, a sentimental sympathy for the rustic, and unlimited enthusiasm for sterling qualities of character. A rough philosophy suffices for all problems: "'Tisn't life that matters! 'Tis the courage you bring to it."

The reader soon finds out that Walpole's work strikes the highest point of giddiness in English spiritual biography. He lacks sensibility, horizons, cynicism, profundity. The liveliness of his pages is generally the result of the old art of puppetry. Sometimes he is plainly sophomoric: Jerrard, the school's best bowler, is exposed just before the big game.

The Making of An Englishman (1914), by W. L. George (treated in Chapter XI), is probably not spiritual biography at all. A young Frenchman grows up in England, learns English ways, becomes in time an Englishman. He is misunderstood, particularly in his love affairs, but he accepts his defeats, determining to become more socially acceptable, more English. There is much genial analysis, much praise of England.

D. H. Lawrence's *Sons and Lovers* (1913), an authentic life-novel, cannot well be detached from the main body of Lawrence's work. It is discussed in Chapter XIV.

❦ XIV ❧

THE POSTWAR NOVEL

1919–1929

IMPRESSIONISTS AND FREUDIANS

AN EXPLORATION OF THE PERIODICAL COMMENT

IT is significant of the postwar state of mind that a critic for the *Quarterly Review* of October, 1921, listed as best sellers for the year,

The Master of Man, by Hall Caine

The Mountebank, by W. J. Locke

Her Father's Daughter, by Gene Stratton-Porter

We need not expect too much of best sellers, but the above list suggests rather pointedly that the English novel had suffered a backset. "Mediocrity continues to rule, with the standard of excellence decreasing," moaned the critic.

Those of us who remember the postwar letdown do not find it hard to understand the English public's attitude. We ourselves in those years enjoyed easy reading and the most elemental of stimulants. For a time we permitted ourselves the luxury of sentiment. Then the war consciousness reclaimed us. We reacted from an overdose of sentiment and looked for reading matter that was properly frigid and skeptical.

No doubt in the immediate postwar years Englishmen did more than relax to light reading. No doubt there was an attempt to catch up on one's Galsworthy and Conrad, and to keep up with one's Wells. But inevitably the war consciousness originated a fiction peculiar to itself. According to Mr. Philip Henderson the direction of the impulse was toward a concern with "private worlds":

If we compare the important novelists of the post-war period with the tradition of Bennett, Wells, and Galsworthy, a progressive withdrawal from the external world to the world of fantasy is clearly perceptible. Overwhelmed with a sense of the collapse of their world, the later writers have retired further and further into private worlds detached from social reality, their characters attempting to live entirely in an intense emotional, passional plane as with Lawrence, or on the plane of aesthetic abstraction and contemplative withdrawal from all significant activity whatsoever, as in the case of Joyce and Virginia Woolf.[1]

We should admit the truth of Mr. Henderson's generalizations were it not for the fact that he here leaves out of account an active, almost militant, phase of the reaction. I refer to the progressive extension of the critical spirit of scientific agnosticism. We have seen that scientific materialism was the basis of naturalistic thought and that it pervaded Edwardian and prewar Georgian fiction, leading to a criticism of man's inhumanity and focusing attention upon the desire to alter the shape of things to come. In the postwar years scientific materialism induced a state of mind that was not merely critical but skeptical. Science had failed as an instrument of human betterment. Men were sadder even though wiser, and science had provided no checks for the unlimited powers of destruction it had made available. To a skeptical generation, scientific knowledge was alone acceptable, but faith in science as a means of obtaining general human happiness was lacking. According to Professor Lovett, "The loss of faith in knowledge emphasizes the already felt inadequacy of naturalism as an aesthetic creed. In consequence, the pursuit of reality takes the only other possible road, that of exploration of consciousness."[2]

[1] *The Novel Today,* 103.
[2] R. S. Lovett and Helen S. Hughes, *The History of the Novel in England* (Boston, Houghton Mifflin Co., 1932), 414.

The exploration of consciousness was not, perhaps, the main direction of English fiction for the years 1919–29, for during the middle years of the decade "sophistication"—a more direct offshoot of scientific skepticism and despair—was the vogue. Yet the recent revelations of psychoanalysis were novel and stimulating. Writers could speak of complexes, unfulfilled desires, compensations, frustrations, and wish-fulfillments with the expectation that the terms would seem neither strange nor barbarous to their readers. Furthermore the conclusions of psychoanalysis, its ethic of sexual normality and its fear of psychoses, were tacitly assumed by writers who would avoid the appellation "Victorian." Stream of consciousness and "free association" fundamentally affected the techniques of several important writers. And yet few books were written in which the psychology of sex was given more than a surface treatment, and there was no novelist, with the exception of Lawrence, to whom the conclusions of the new psychology seemed so fundamental as to be a necessary part of all that he wrote.

Considering the attention given to psychology in English fiction from the time of George Eliot, it seems rather curious that the remarkable twentieth-century progress in the understanding of motivation has so little affected English novelists of the postwar period. With the concern of the postwar novelists in a factual universe, with the intensity of their search for what is genuine, with iconoclasm noised abroad and the basic ideas of Freud virtually accepted, we might well expect a fiction of painful and unconventional analysis. What resulted was stream-of-consciousness technique (in Richardson and Woolf influenced by Henry James), a concern with subconscious and preconscious volition, a few sporadic case histories, and whatever is permanent in *Ulysses* and the novels of Lawrence. What remains is an interest in the ethical conclusions of psychoanalysis and in conversations about it—but no interest in a psychoanalytic novel.

It seems necessary in treating the novelists markedly influenced by psychoanalysis to distinguish between those who used stream of consciousness as a technique and those so far influenced by Freud and his followers that they concern themselves chiefly with complexes, neuroses, and the phantoms of the unconscious. On the one hand we have a group (the Impressionists) who give objective, detailed, and often breathless and colorful accounts of tangible phenomena; on the other we have the Freudians who may or may not use stream of consciousness in dealing with problems of volition, frustration, and fulfillment. English critics have drawn a rather strict line of demarcation between the two groups.

THE IMPRESSIONISTS

Under this title English critics seem disposed to treat Frank Swinnerton, Dorothy Richardson, Virginia Woolf, and Katherine Mansfield. Obviously stream of consciousness is not present in all the works of these writers. Only Dorothy Richardson used it throughout her long series of twelve volumes; Virginia Woolf had already published two novels and a volume of short stories when she adopted the technique in 1922. What is common to the group is a tendency to render the "intense moment," to exhaust the dramatic possibilities of the minute and the fragmentary. There is a strenuous avoidance of retrospect and exposition, a concern only with what is immediate in consciousness. Social significances are shunned. The view, whether it is of temperament or scene, is sharply focused and crystal clear.

Henry James comes to mind as a major influence. Katharine Fullerton Gerould even makes James responsible for stream of consciousness:

Before Dorothy Richardson was Conrad; and before Conrad was Henry James. Henry James, rather than anyone else, may be said to have introduced the method [stream of consciousness] in English fiction. . . . That Henry James began the method in English fiction is proved, I think, by the very basis of the old adoration of his prose. Those of us who adored Henry James in the days when such adoration existed, adored him chiefly because he seemed to us the only person who ever recorded the things that go on in the mind *exactly as they go on in the mind.* Only for that could anyone adore the later work— *The Spoils of Poynton,* let us say, down to and including *The Golden Bowl.* The people who really loved Conrad—by which I mean the people who loved him early before the critics had told them to—were usually Jacobites, people who already adored Henry James. Conrad applied the Jamesean method to exotic new material; and that made a very enticing combination. They were different, the two of them, from all their contemporaries in that they used mental rhythms instead of rhetorical ones—especially Henry James, who, indeed, became so intent on the accuracy of his mental rhythms that he neglected rhetoric entirely, forsaking the forum for the laboratory. That is the whole secret of his "later manner," and his debâcle—for rhetoric is merely the art of communicating ideas to an audience, and while no man is rhetorical in solitude, every man is rhetorical as soon as he is with someone else. In "The Finer Grain" and *The Ivory Tower* James adopted even the syntax of solitary reflection; the stumbling, elliptical, parenthetical, almost unparsable complex of our thoughts. No one, of course, could read them. The Master had gone too far into the jungle. But if you really want "stream of consciousness" there it is.[3]

It was probably Wells who gave the term "impression-ism" its current literary meaning; and, incidentally, it was Wells who said the first funny things about Miss Richardson. In the preface to Mr. Swinnerton's *Nocturne* (1918) Wells avowed,

> Mr. Swinnerton sees life and renders it with a detachment and pa-tience quite foreign to my nature. He has no underlying motive. He sees and tells. His aim is the beauty which comes with exquisite pre-sentation. Seen through his art, life is seen as one sees things through a crystal lens—more intensely, more completely, and with less tur-bidity. . . . He is not alone in this clear, detached objectivity. Dorothy Richardson probably carried impressionism to its fullest limits. In *Pointed Roofs* and *Honeycomb,* for example, her story is a series of

---

[3] "Stream of Consciousness," *Saturday Review of Literature,* October 22, 1927. See also Lovett and Hughes, *The History of the Novel in England,* 448: "Miss Richardson's method is an extension of that at which Henry James arrived in his later work. . . . Un-doubtedly her *Pilgrimage* [a general title for her long series of novels] has an unmis-takable relation to the work of Marcel Proust, *A la Recherche du Temps Perdu,* which was appearing in parts simultaneously with her own."

dabs of intense superficial impression. Her heroine is not a mentality but a mirror. She goes about over her facts like one of those insects that run over water sustained by surface tension. But Mr. Swinnerton, like Mr. James Joyce, does not repudiate the depths for the sake of the surface. His people are not splashes of appearance, but living minds.

Impressionism is closely paralleled by developments in American imagist poetry. Here the tendency to "imagism"—to vivid and impersonal treatment, to the use of the exact word for giving a concrete impression—became so strong for a time that the expression in poetry of a natural emotional impulse was a barbarism. The parallel is further evident in that both imagism and impressionism were presided over by women and were featured by qualities that might be looked upon as "feminine"—mental agility, a passion for the minute and the fragmentary, a love of color and preciosity, and a feeling for the atmosphere of exaltation. Conversely (and Joyce is not an impressionist) the product of both schools lacked a cosmic, philosophical view—a sense of social values.

Unlike imagism, impressionism made its way without agents and manifestoes. It was not until December, 1923, that Virginia Woolf published an article entitled "Mr. Bennett and Mrs. Brown," which is nearer to a manifesto than anything the impressionists issued. Mrs. Woolf takes as her text a statement of Arnold Bennett that the aim of fiction is the creation of character. She proceeds to show that the Edwardians—Wells, Galsworthy, and Bennett—were too much interested in a social view to portray character, and that the "capturing of Mrs. Brown," the imaginative grasp of a character in its totality, is the foundation of good fiction. In the writings of the Edwardians,

every sort of town is represented; we see factories, prisons, workhouses, law courts, Houses of Parliament; a general clamour, a voice of aspiration, indignation, effort and industry rises from the whole; but in all this vast conglomeration of printed pages, in all this congeries of streets and houses, there is not a single man or woman whom we know.

The Victorians, unlike the Russians, gave us characters that are simple and crude because "the features are so few and so prominent." A keyword serves to recall them instantly. With the Russians the portrayal of character is truly complex:

> What keyword could be supplied to Raskolnikov, Mishkin, Stavrogan or Alyosha? We go down into them as we descend into some enormous cavern. Lights swing about; we hear the boom of the sea; it is dark, terrible and uncharted.

Mrs. Woolf observes that the Edwardian novelists "give us a vast sense of things in general" but "a vague one of things in particular." The pursuit of Mrs. Brown is the proper endeavor of the novelist, but Mrs. Brown is elusive. Once you are on her trail she becomes "a will-o'-the-wisp, a dancing shadow."[4]

The pursuit of Mrs. Brown was not the central aim of the impressionists, or even that of Mrs. Woolf. But the complexity of consciousness which Mrs. Woolf mentions and her interest in individual rather than social consciousness allies her closely with the group.

The effort so far made in this chapter has been to clarify the purposes of a clique which extended the range of the English novel by providing a new emphasis. The freshness and clarity of the impressionists' view was to have a wide but superficial influence on the writers of the following decade. They had no important imitators or even followers. Perhaps the adverse periodical comment on their writings had something to do with the matter.

In 1919 the *Nation* launched forth against the absence of philosophy in fiction. If a man took the role of life's interpreter, he had no right to shrink from the formidable title of philosopher, "for to hold a philosophy, in its broad and practical sense, merely means that a man does accept some principle of value or definitely he believes in the futility of all belief." A man should be unprejudiced, certainly, but he cannot be disinterested.

---

[4] Virginia Woolf, *Nation* (London), December 1, 1923.

Without philosophy

fiction is as dead as the autumn leaves blown hither and thither by the winds of opportunity. It is sometimes thought that definite beliefs tend to make a man narrow and therefore destroy the truth of his picture of life. But life can never be pictured without selection and unification, and thus art can never live without philosophy. Emphasis may be a means of falsification, but without it we can only say everything in a monotone, which is the same thing as saying nothing at all. It is the lack of coherence which is the main weakness of modern fiction. . . . It is plain that specialization upon details of dull lives is stale beyond endurance and that the immense psychological picaresque has had its day. Analysis is played out, whether it is analysis of passion or of boredom or of Leicester Square; when, at about page four hundred, our heroine looks into her soul and finds there is nothing there, it is time to call a halt. For analysis is born of conceit, the idea being that we are all most exceptional people and worthy of infinite study.[5]

In 1920 W. L. George expressed his fear that

the modern novel is becoming a painter's literature. . . . The painters have imposed themselves upon the novelists, have made them feel that intellectual influence is a smudge upon art. . . . When paint does not coat their work it coats their intellect. So deliberate an attempt to avoid expressing ideas can be traced only to paint, because paint cannot express ideas, and as the novelist may have no other gods but paint, he must deal not with ideas, but with impressions. . . . Miss Richardson gives herself to any and all details. . . . The result is mental chaos.

George disapproved of "impression without conception" because thus "all impressions have the same value." Although Virginia Woolf had not yet taken up stream of consciousness —she had published only *The Voyage Out* (1915) and *Night and Day* (1919)—George found her view restricted:

her interest is so-far confined to love in cultured society. Only the tip of her wing touches social impulses and intellectual movements in the masses of mankind. Here again, excessive prominence is given to minor emotions, while no space at all is accorded to social stirrings.[6]

In 1921 the *London Mercury* was inclined to be critical of

5 "Philosophy in Fiction," *Nation* (London), November 29, 1919.
6 "A Painter's Literature," *English Review*, March, 1920.

Miss Richardson's "five or six" volumes of Miriam Henderson's adventures:

> their merit is their absolute, immediately convincing fidelity to fact. Their demerit is their lack of interest. The incidents that happen to Miriam are not exciting, and her capacity for finding humor in life is not great.[7]

In the next year Rebecca West showed anxiety over the nature of women's work in fiction. The trouble is, she concluded, that a feminine writer is herself "news" and that she is fearful of personal criticism. Hence she avoids the controversial.[8]

In 1923 Mrs. Woolf issued the manifesto "Mr. Bennett and Mrs. Brown." Beresford promptly defended Wells, Galsworthy, and Bennett: "their characters are, like themselves, composite, full of irresolutions, often self-conscious and apt to change their minds."[9] I find no other response. Are we to gather that the public was not vitally interested?

By 1925 Aldous Huxley was not at all convinced that the portrayal of mysterious, thrilling details—such as he found in Katherine Mansfield's work—is really good fiction. There are two ways of looking at characters, he says. One is the traveler's-eye view and the other is the god's-eye view. Conrad has the traveler's-eye view and we feel the mysterious thrilling charm of his characters. "But it is foolish to admire mystery too much. The characters of the greatest novelists, like Dostoievski and Tolstoi, are not mysterious." He continues,

> Katherine Mansfield likes the traveler's-eye view. She sees her characters from a distance, as though at another table in a cafe; she overhears snatches of their conversations—about their aunts at Battersea, their stamp collections, their souls,—and she finds them extraordinary, charming, beyond all real and knowable people, odd, immensely exciting. She feels that they are life itself,—lovely, fantastic Life. . . . She

---

[7] Edward Shanks, "Reflections on the Recent English Novel," *London Mercury,* June, 1921.

[8] "Notes on Novels," *New Statesman,* December 2, 1922.

[9] "The Successors of Charles Dickens," *Nation* (London), December 29, 1923.

rarely makes herself at home in their everyday lives. She invents suitable lives for the fantastic creatures glimpsed at the cafe. And how thrilling those fancied lives always are! Thrilling, but for that reason not very convincing. One sees them for a moment, haloed with significances.... Then one passes. They disappear. Each of Miss Mansfield's stories is a window in a lighted room. The glimpse of the inhabitants sipping their tea and punch is enormously exciting. But one knows nothing, when one has passed, of what they are really like. That is why, however thrilling at first reading, her stories do not wear. Chekhov's do; but then he has lived with his people as well as looked through the window.[10]

Comment on Mrs. Woolf seems to have been reserved largely for the years 1926–30. Even during these years I find only one full-length article and occasional paragraphs scattered here and there. Since Mrs. Woolf is not treated elsewhere in this volume,[11] it may be advisable to give the full-length article in some detail. Dudley Carew in the *London Mercury* deals with Mrs. Woolf's pursuit of Mrs. Brown in a rollicking mood, inappropriate to the consideration of an author who enjoyed any critical support:

If *The Voyage Out* [1915] had something of the staidness and dignity of the stage-coach, *Jacob's Room* resembles a kind of mental airplane from which her passengers can look down on the life spread out beneath them. Everything is quite orderly and clear, but no one part of the landscape has any kind of connection with any other part. It is too arid, too remote, even too unreal, to shelter Mrs. Brown. Something else must be done, so Mrs. Dalloway is built, a motor car without steering wheel or brakes, but with a powerful engine. If Mrs. Brown is to be found at all, this will find her. Brakes and steering

---

[10] *Along the Road* (New York, George H. Doran Company, 1925), 40–42.

[11] The view I am taking is that the influence of impressionistic technique is important —more so than the accomplishments of the individual impressionists. Those who wish a careful analysis of Virginia Woolf's fiction may see *The Novel and the Modern World,* by David Daiches (Chicago, University of Chicago Press, 1939). Philip Henderson, in *The Novel Today,* is rather hard on Mrs. Woolf: "After all, says Mrs. Woolf, are we not all just sitting in a railway carriage, rushing towards our final destination in time, and all we can hope to do is to gaze about us, bewildered by the world and the complexity and confusion of our own emotions. Know anything? Make decisions? Act? How can we?— not, at least, till our dividends begin to drop off. All we can really know is the suffering of our lonely souls. Far better identify one's outlook with a literary lap-dog!"—27. See also 87–91.

wheel are unnecessary. There is more chance of running Mrs. Brown down if one doesn't know where one is going.

The critic then relinquishes the image of the chase of Mrs. Brown, and he wonders at Mrs. Woolf's real intention. Surely these strange men and women of hers, who are not obedient to the workings of the ordinary laws dictated by common experience, are meant to be considered as important. What else could the author be intending? He looks up "Mr. Bennett and Mrs. Brown" again. This time there can be no doubt. Mrs. Woolf meant to draw full-sized, normal, responsive creatures, "not the curious, closed-in little vehicles they so much resemble, through which a never-ending roll of impressions can flow and flow." Mrs. Woolf has been unfair to herself because

she has made her great fort, that of imaginative description, play second fiddle to an inferior one, that of creating character. Indeed, the richness of that gift, the keenness of that sense of restless, abundant, exhilarating life, has completely ruined whatever success she might have gained in the work she most values, for her characters, far from moving in worlds half realized, move, half realized themselves, in worlds of bright, hard outlines and curious checkered colors.

So her people seem like dangling puppets designed to show off the author's skill of painting on the dark cloth of background. But this is not all. There is an overstrained effort to represent the events of life as isolated, independent, unforeseeable, and unmeaning:

Jacob is alive but each picture of him is separate and distinct. He is shown with his mouth open, but no word ever comes, with his foot raised as he walks, but it never descends to the pavement. He falls in love, but he is incapable of the continued stress and strain that love demands.

A day passes in Jacob's life, but it is "an isolated thing, a bubble full of the most radiant color while it lasts, but going out and leaving no mark upon the untroubled air."[12]

[12] Dudley Carew, "Virginia Woolf," *London Mercury,* May, 1926.

Three years later (1929) an equally damaging criticism appeared in the *Quarterly Review:*

So exquisite is her sensibility, so rapid her reactions, that a cloud cannot pass over the sun but the face of the world is rapidly changed for her. At the same time, so unimportant do the objects of cognition appear in comparison with the process of cognition itself, that only after exacting labours is one able to deduce the celestial phenomena from the presentation of the psychological. . . . She is so self-bound that her imagination never escapes from the upper middle-class. Her sweetest and strongest passages are punctuated with the clinks of silver teaspoons against delicate china.

With Katherine Mansfield the critic is even less sympathetic:

Though Chekhov gave to Mansfield's lips the kiss of futility, Miss Mansfield—and she is not an Englishwoman—won more praise than power. Already her work is regarded by the young as rather "old game."

The critic similarly finds that the day of Dorothy Richardson has passed:

The perversity and complexity of her style called attention to the content. If she had nothing to say, she said it so confusedly that it was noticed. For a period she was applauded. If today she be forgotten, yesterday she was called an innovator. Her experiment was an interesting one.[13]

It is to be noted that critics pay tribute to Virginia Woolf's sensibility and her gift for imaginative description, her "ecstatic sense of emotion," the "enchantment of ecstasy" in her delineations, even while they call attention to the thinness of her stories and her poor pretense to character portrayal. This view of her work has persisted. V. Sackville-West has put it in definitive form:

It is all very well for Mrs. Woolf to say that we must at all costs hold on to the skirts of Mrs. Brown. Mrs. Woolf herself does no such thing. She will chase a butterfly or look out of a window at a starling on the

[13] H. C. Harwood, "Some Tendencies in Modern Fiction," *Quarterly Review*, April, 1929.

lawn, but Mrs. Brown herself (for all her clean little boots and mended gloves) will remain but a shell resounding with thoughts and with an imagery conceivable only by her creator. Mrs. Woolf pretends to be interested in Mrs. Brown, but she is really not interested; she is interested only in the idea that Mrs. Brown starts up in her. Mrs. Brown (if ever Mrs. Woolf writes a novel about her) will find herself twisted into an unrecognizable repository. . . . She will not be "true to life." The reader who has fetched her from the library will not be reminded of his Aunt Emily. Disconcerted, his conventions upset, he will find his judgment called upon for an aesthetic, not a practical, appraisement, as though he were reading poetry.[14]

In this study of movements and tendencies the effort is made to treat novels as they reflect the time-spirit. We are concerned, as I previously remarked, with a progressively sincere attempt at a revelation of life in the spirit of scientific materialism. In accord with this intention, changes in technique are examined—but not too precisely.

To trace the development of impressionist technique from Henry James through Conrad and Swinnerton, and to see it merging with stream of consciousness in the work of Dorothy Richardson and Virginia Woolf and Ford Madox Ford, would be a study of a highly specialized, and probably unreadable, nature.

I make this explanation to indicate why I am not presenting separate sections on Miss Richardson, Mrs. Woolf, and Mr. Swinnerton. Their technique, it is true, has had a minor general influence on much subsequent fiction (although stream of consciousness has long since played out). But the substance of their revelation was not very important. The true apostles of psychoanalytic faith are those whom we here call the Freudians.

THE FREUDIANS

The critic who expects to find treatment of the abnormal in English novels will locate few case histories to reward his search. J. D. Beresford in the *Mercure de France* gave, perhaps,

[14] "The Future of the Novel," *Bookman*, December, 1930.

the best explanation. It is that the public will not tolerate investigations of the morbid. According to Mr. Beresford, by the year 1926 English tolerance had gone a long way. There was no longer any objection to seductions and adulteries if the details were not too precisely mentioned—even though the guilty escape punishment. But

the public will not tolerate any study of morbid psychology, any suggestion of what might pass for an unnatural act, or even mention of sexual proclivities which are not readily understood, and hence abnormal.

The Oedipus complex, he continues, was tolerated so long as there was no suggestion of anything sexual, and a mention of abnormalities coming from sexual repression was likewise accepted. But for the most part the critics were cold or they took the attitude of being bored. It was not merely prudery but something akin to aversion. The critics had not objected to non-Freudian accounts which were scandalous if not downright immoral (W. L. George's *A Bed of Roses*, for example); but *The Rainbow*, by Lawrence, was persecuted because of its Freudian implications. Only people of extraordinary talent like Miss Sinclair could overcome the obstacles.

Mr. Beresford concludes with a statement of his own psychoanalytic bias and the expression of his fears. We can no longer treat human conduct with the ignorance of Charles Dickens. If the novel is to remain naturalistic, it must take account of psychoanalysis. But a romantic current threatens the realistic novel. And, a more serious difficulty, psychoanalysis in concerning itself with the exceptional and the remote does not readily lend itself to artistic interpretation. Many of its revelations are humanly incredible. Mr. Beresford himself is skeptical about the interpretation of dreams.

Mr. Beresford feels that a novel is truly psychoanalytic only when it reveals a case of repression producing a complex. He finds that this limitation excludes all but three English novels:

1. His own *God's Counterpoint,* which shows a recovery from perversion. The book was recommended by doctors.
2. *Return of the Soldier,* by Rebecca West. Here a shell-shocked soldier was cured by a psychoanalyst.
3. *The Romantic,* by May Sinclair. The causes of an inferiority complex are given in the clinical exposure of the last chapter.

Dangerous Ages, by Rose Macaulay, is excluded because the visit to a psychoanalyst is satirized. Huxley's story of a split personality, "The Farcical History of Richard Greenow" (from *Limbo*), is not a complete novel. Even Lawrence's *Sons and Lovers,* he says, was written when Lawrence "had never heard of Freud or his theories." Dorothy Richardson studied psychoanalysis "but there is little of it in her work. Her autobiography reveals an influence not greater than the influence of psychoanalysis on Marcel Proust." There is "only the subconscious influence" in *The Regiment of Women,* by Clemence Dane; only a trace in *Legend*.[15]

We must disagree in a measure with Mr. Beresford. The exploration of the subconscious by Joyce and Lawrence, and their insistence upon sex as a dominant motive, will serve to class them as Freudians. And we cannot exclude several other novels of Miss Sinclair and Miss West. As Walter Myers points out, not merely the emphasis upon sex in *The Three Sisters* but "the submerged quality of much of the thinking" classes the book as the product of the new psychology. The "vampirish maternal self-assertion" in *Mary Olivier* has sexual implications, and *Anne Severn and the Fieldings* is not only a study in sublimation but an instance of a physical cure brought about by exposing the causes of an aversion. *The Judge,* by Rebecca West, is a case of the Oedipus complex.[16] It need hardly be said that a new approach and a new jargon has been added to fiction.

[15] Mr. Beresford's delimitation is severe but it serves as a corrective to such generalizations as that contained in "Sex Psychology in Modern Fiction" appearing in an American publication, the *Independent,* of December 11, 1926: "If the twentieth century has contributed anything whatever to the advance of the novel, or to its decline, we must look for it in the influence of Havelock Ellis, Freud, Jung, and other investigators of the sex life of man. . . . They have succeeded somehow, in making the abnormal, if not palatable, at least popular."
[16] *The Later Realism,* Chapter II.

In English drama there has been little Freudian interest. A critic for the *New Statesman* wrote in 1929, "I know of no good play whose theme is psychoanalysis, although the operation of all plays lends itself to the operation of psychoanalysis."[17]

The new psychology would have been important if it had given us only *Ulysses* and the work of Lawrence. Yet it exerted a wide general influence over the understanding of motives. We have seen that the French naturalists believed "tout comprendre est tout pardonner." As one of them expressed it, "The cannibal who eats his fellow-man is as innocent as the child who sucks his lollypop." The tendency of the psychoanalytic view was to extend tolerance to deviations formerly considered inexcusable.

H. C. Harwood genially satirized the extension of the new tolerance. He gave the hypothetical case of a villain, Jasper, who sewed a heroine in a sack. The Victorian audience would have been concerned with the heroine. Not so nowadays.

Jasper must be explained. Perhaps his mother was a sadist—blessed word—who drowned kittens in the presence of her children, and Jasper wishes to prolong the experimentation. Perhaps Jasper has a morbid love of sacks. Or perhaps Jasper was a kindly, decent chap, one of ourselves, who was insensibly led into committing a brutal murder.[18]

In the late twenties the position of Lawrence as the focal point of controversy was in many ways similar to that of Joyce in the early twenties. Critical comment tended to be unfavorable. Not much was written about *Ulysses*, since the book was banned. Yet the literati read it and talked for a time of little else. Criticism of Lawrence was more analytical and more expository. Many good and revealing comments were made, yet the non-English quality of Lawrence's writing did not, during his lifetime, win over critics for the leading periodicals.

[17] J. B. W., "The Eater of Dreams," November 23, 1929.
[18] "Some Tendencies in Modern Fiction."

I find no full-length articles on Joyce other than two appearing in the *English Review* (which was edited by Ford Madox Ford). The first one is by Richard Aldington and may be taken as representative of the average view. Says Mr. Aldington of *Ulysses,*

> The achievement, I am convinced, is remarkable; its influence, I fear, may be deplorable. . . . Mr. Joyce is a modern Naturaliste possessing a greater knowledge of intimate psychology, but without the Naturalists' preoccupation with *l'écriture artiste. Ulysses* is a tremendous libel on humanity which I at least am not clever enough to refute, but which I am convinced is a libel.

Mr. Aldington recalls that Pound dubbed Joyce "a modern Tertullian." But, he continues, "I can find nothing of Tertullian which shows such repugnance of humanity, which teaches such abhorrence of the human body and particularly of sexual relations, as I find in *Ulysses.*"[19]

Ford Madox Ford was evidently not satisfied with Mr. Aldington's article. After waiting a year and three-quarters he published one of his own. We may read between the lines that Ford would like to say more than he does. But what he says is favorable:

> For the first time in literature on an extended scale a writer has attempted to treat man as the complex creature that man—every man! —is. . . . England has formerly not contributed to the literary expression of the complexity of mixed motives. . . . Gradually across our literature there will spread the Ulyssean complexion.[20]

The foreigner looks with some surprise on the fact that English periodicals neglected Lawrence during his life and expressed disapproval of his intent on the occasion of his death. There is one notable exception. Writing for the *Outlook* (London) in 1927, H. C. Harwood included *Women in Love* in a selection of the three best books which appeared during the years 1918–26. He commented, "Mr. Lawrence's *Women in*

---

[19] "The Influence of Mr. James Joyce," *English Review,* April, 1921.
[20] *"Ulysses* and the Handling of Indecencies," *English Review,* December, 1922.

Love, and all his subsequent novels, display an imagination brighter and more powerful than anyone's since Blake."[21] A later article by Mr. Harwood is less sympathetic to Lawrence. We may, perhaps, guess the causes. For one thing, the postwar intensity and its search for a new revelation were dying out. For another, Mr. Harwood was writing for the *Quarterly Review*.

Mr. D. H. Lawrence, that smoky volcano, does not repudiate sex; he worships it; like so many half-educated persons he confuses power with truth; and because the dark flame of sexual desire is universally potent, he would build upon its strong secret manifestations a whole philosophy. A great poet—perhaps the greatest of living poets—he has been able to impose upon the young his lurid, though imperfectly synthesized thought, and to induce them to read by lightening flashes a script of blood. Yet he does not convince.[22]

Mr. Harwood's statement that Lawrence "does not convince" expresses what for many years amounted to a qualified popular rejection. Until Lawrence's death in March, 1930, only one full-length article appeared in an important British periodical—"Love and Mr. Lawrence," by Roger Chance, *Fortnightly*, October, 1929. This one article, excellent in its analysis of Lawrence's qualities, concludes with the judgment that Lawrence stresses too much the animal level of consciousness, that he neglects the "higher" forms of human consciousness. Mr. Chance's remarks show a progressive English frankness:

Sex is a delicate subject; but fortunately the times are past when the discussion of sex in public was considered indelicate. We all know, or we ought to know, that sex is of fundamental importance in our lives and that it is important to find out as much as we can about sex. Psychoanalysis, and the question of birth control, have raised sex into a position which attracts as much attention as does religion; and perhaps it is natural that this should be so, because sex and religion are intimately connected.

21 "The Post-War Novel in England," May 7, 1927. In spite of his liberalism, Mr. Harwood calls *Ulysses* "an abominable book."
22 "Some Tendencies in Modern Fiction."

An article for the *Nineteenth Century,* probably written in anticipation of Lawrence's death, and published the month following it, shows a rather imperfect sympathy:

> He had an intense, almost medieval, vision of the body and soul at war. The dead poet in him, seeing in what hellish shapes the soul had cast the world, championed the body. "Back into the beast," he cried, because in the beast there were the grave perfections of unself-conscious life—life as it was before all that aimless thinking marred it.[23]

Another article written under the same circumstances for the *Fortnightly* was even less sympathetic: "Since the war even more than before that dividing period he was the leader of revolt. The man's whole nature was insurgent, up in arms against restriction or limitation." Though the critic granted Lawrence a seriousness of purpose, he thought Lawrence's concern with sex rather unbecoming.[24]

D. H. LAWRENCE

Lawrence aspired to cosmic range in the manner of a major apostle. Yet as a poet he lacked a gusto of epic proportions and his lyrics are fragmentary, unfelicitous. The vast reaches of his composite view were reserved for his novels.

In a letter written in 1914 he came nearest to expressing his special view of fiction:

> Somehow, that which is psychic—non-human—in humanity is more interesting to me than the old-fashioned human element, which causes one to conceive a character in a certain moral scheme and make him consistent. . . . You mustn't look in my novel for the old stable ego of the character. There is another ego, according to whose action the individual is unrecognizable, and passes through, as it were, allotropic states . . . . which . . . . are states of the same radically unchanged element.[25]

---

[23] Humbert Wolfe, "Lawrence and the Post-War Generation," April, 1930.
[24] Stephen Gwynn, "Ebb and Flow," *Fortnightly Review,* April, 1930.
[25] To Edward Garnett, June 5, 1914.

An apostle of the older school would have said, "We are nothing but the Light is all." The nonhuman exerts its force through mankind and spurs each person in his own way to a response. Generally the response is unworthy. Social ideals and religious codes serve to deflect or deny its strength. The intended harmony is lacking, and men in following the ideals of the world go their separate ways toward corruption. How then is the harmony to be attained, what new vitality experienced in its attainment? Lawrence's own life was the search and his findings went into his novels.

Lawrence did not pursue his search unaided. The central ideas of Whitman dominated his consciousness. For Lawrence also hated those with low aims or no aims at all, the money-grubbers, the fops. He believed it is as great to be a woman as a man, and he yearned for a race of deep-bosomed individualists. He wore his hat as he pleased, indoors or out. He found no sweeter fat than stuck to his own bones. He was resolved not to participate in war. He was unconcerned with the blurt about virtue and about vice, choosing rather to moisten the roots of action and contribute to growth. He would launch all men into the unknown and bid them be bold swimmers. He believed that life should flow through us, that we should be Answerers. He was acutely aware of the voice of the night and the stars, of the slumbering and liquid trees, the procreant urge of the world, the mystery that lurks in all things. He might well have said with Whitman,

Through me forbidden voices;
Voice of sexes and lusts—voices veil'd, and I remove the veil;
Voices indecent, by me clarified and transfigured . . .
I believe in the flesh and the appetites;
Seeing, hearing, feeling, are miracles, and each part and tag of me is
    a miracle.
Divine I am inside and out, and I make holy whatever I touch or am
    touched from.

Where Lawrence differed sharply from Whitman was in his scorn for the doctrine of universal love. Lawrence was sharply critical of mankind, sharply critical of his contemporaries. Whitman's robust affirmations were too general, too indiscriminate for Lawrence. And in Whitman's general acclaim of sex there was also something too indiscriminate. Lawrence was early convinced that his own fulfillment would come through sex, and yet early experiences, as recorded in *Sons and Lovers* (1913), showed him that relationships must be perfected in order to be significant, and that even then sex is a part of something else, something greater—"a consummation in darkness preparatory to a new journey towards consummation in spirit." Lawrence's intense treatment took account of aversions and felicities outside the general range of Whitman's power.

In his study of Lawrence, Stephen Potter has traced the route of Lawrence's inquiry and discovery. First came the prison-like, intense love of Miriam, a denier of the body, who approached love in the spirit of sacrifice. Next came Helena, who saw love only in terms of what she had read. In *The Rainbow* (1915), a new emphasis on "centrality"—a subconscious self beneath the ego—begins to emerge, and in his poems of this time he suggests that the "perfect meeting," in marriage, involves complete isolation and a mutual exchange of revelation. In *Women in Love* (1920), two ways of corruption are envisaged: sensuality, as personified by Gudrun, and the "blond, Northern" way as typified by Gerald. In contrast Lawrence, speaking through Birkin, suggests a love that is "polarized," like two stars, an intensification of the bond dependent upon isolation and differences:

> Why, there is a final me which is stark and impersonal and beyond responsibility: so there is a final you. And it is there that I would meet you . . . not a mingling, but an equilibrium, a pure balance of two simple beings.

Sex is not an end in itself but a spur to activity, not instrumental but inspirational: "and there can be no successful sex union unless the greater hope of purposive, constructive activity fires the soul of man all the time." So in *Aaron's Rod* (1922) the failure of friendship as an end is suggested and in *Kangaroo* (1923) the failure of leadership. Lawrence's impersonation in each book loses interest. What then? The revelation comes in *The Plumed Serpent* (1926). Kate, in a Mexican setting, frees herself from old European associations and lets in the Dark God, an impersonation of Lawrence named Cipriano. Conscious of her own fulfillment, Kate is resolved "not to get caught up in the world's cog-wheels any more." She knows that "ye must be born again. . . . Out of the fight with the octopus of life, the dragon of degenerate or incomplete existence, one must win this soft bloom of being."[26]

So a rebirth, a renewal, a surrender to the forces of life is the end. No doubt Lawrence had hoped for something more tangible, the "purposive, constructive activity" which was to fire the soul. What he discovered were "passional" modes of being which seemed to give, in part at least, the answer to his search. He could both criticize and affirm. So *The Lost Girl* (1920) was both an indictment of dreary middle-class English life and the record of a girl's attachment to a colorful, indolent Italian, who brings her an intensification of life even if it leads to keeping house in a dirt-floored cabin in remote Italian mountains. *St. Mawr* (1925) is partly an exposure of the enervated upper class into which Lou marries. Lou contrasts them with the man-killing stallion, St. Mawr: "Most men have a deadness in them that frightens me. . . . . Why can't men get their lives straight, like St. Mawr, and then think? . . . It's the animal in them that has gone perverse, or cringing, or humble, or domesticated, like dogs. I don't know one single man who is a proud living animal. I know they've left off really thinking, when the last bit of animal dies in them." But the book is more than an indictment. Rather than let the splendid St. Mawr be destroyed for his latest crime, Lou takes him to Arizona and wakes the wild beauty of the desert. "There's something else that loves me and wants me. . . . It's a spirit. And it's here

26 Stephen Potter, *D. H. Lawrence* (London, Jonathan Cape, Ltd., 1930).

on this ranch. . . . It's something more real to me than men are
. . . a wild spirit wants me, a wild spirit more than men." In
Lady Chatterley's Lover the advantages of wealth and position
are as nothing compared with the rebirth through sex, involving here an intensification through a meeting of opposites.

It is perhaps needless to criticize the bad free verse of the
chants and prayers to the Aztec gods in *The Plumed Serpent*
or to point to Lawrence's habit of letting his books trail off
into nothingness at the end. Lawrence's influence has been wide
and we are properly concerned with those phases of his effort
which have been continued by other writers.

Lawrence's strange vocabulary of "centrality," "other-
ness," "blood-consciousness," "polarity," "separateness," and
like words, has gone out of use, along with his search for a
new religion. What remains is his emphasis upon the subconscious and a new sensitiveness to emotional states. The surface
manifestations amount to little; what is significant is the emotional undercurrent, the dimly sensed psychic flow of personality, the vitality of organic substance. Lawrence is, as Stuart
Sherman affirms, the true "priest of the wonder and bloom
of the world":

he responds as if there were no barrier between him and the life that
pulses in beasts, birds, flowers, clouds, the sea and the spumy star clus-
ters of the Milky Way. . . . It is a question of life discovered afresh
by a sixth sense—life magically rendered, rippling and quivering under the impulse of the *élan vital*.[27]

His "special and characteristic gift," as Aldous Huxley points
out, "was an extraordinary sensitiveness to what Wordsworth
called 'unknown modes of being.' "[28] With Lawrence the range
of the novelist's perception extended beyond the tangible
and the finite. Drama was no longer a conflict between good
and evil but one between symbolic presences who felt strange

[27] *Critical Woodcuts,* 24.
[28] Introduction to *The Letters of D. H. Lawrence* (New York, The Viking Press,
1932), xi.

powers. The flow of response took the place of action—became action, in fact. Lawrence's challenge was to a deeper receptiveness, a quiet contemplation of the fundamental poetry of living.

JAMES JOYCE : ULYSSES

In *Ulysses* more than elsewhere the postwar interests are presented as intensifications. Here free association is more involved, subconscious sexual prepossessions more frankly exposed, and the attack on shams more virulent—but Joyce's very intensity precludes the possibility of classing him as a sophisticate.

Ulysses (1922), in spite of censorship, was the most talked of book in the postwar world. To an amazing degree it expressed the note of postwar bitterness and conveyed the feeling that all preconceived values were forever dead. It exposed the subconscious in its more profound, as well as sensational, ramifications. The frequent brutality of its language was in keeping with its remorseless intent, and the broken pattern of its revelation suggested to writers of the novel further experimentation with form.

The book is, of course, a protest at man's lot. The author would blast the sorry scheme of things entire. The novel, says Knight,

derides every thought, every aspiration, every ideal, every custom and aspiration that man has held dear; it is full of loathing for everything connected with the human body; it has a mock for motherhood, a filthy jest for Christianity.[29]

Joyce, says Swinnerton,

rarely soars above the base; but the base is known to him without mercy. He can lay his hand upon its heart and feel the very beat of it, so that the reader of what he writes may feel that this at this moment is the whole of life.[30]

[29] Grant C. Knight, *The Novel in English* (New York, Richard R. Smith, Inc., 1931), 356.
[30] *The Georgian Scene*, 416.

Stephen Daedalus from *A Portrait of the Artist as a Young Man*
is still with us and may be taken to represent Joyce. But Joyce
knows the values which Stephen represents have broken down
and he has no others with which to replace them. Doubtless
the Christian upbringing of Joyce and Stephen has much to
do with the presentation of the body's vileness. Yet Joyce is
really fascinated with the sexuality that he castigates. He can
no longer live on the spiritual plane and turns to life, yet what
he finds fills him with loathing. So Joyce expresses what Lawrence could not stand, "deliberate dirty-mindedness."

There is, of course, malice in Joyce's exposure. Much of
the malice, however, is directed against shams and deceits and
evasions and half-lies. In a manuscript notebook which Joyce
kept in Paris during 1903 appears this sentence: "The music-
hall, not poetry, is a criticism of life." In the very heartlessness
of *Ulysses* the postwar generation saw the deification of truth-
telling. And in his use of obnoxious words they saw an em-
phatic protest against cant. The lyrical conclusion emphasized
the indictment by pointing to the beauty of simple and natural
things:

> I love flowers I'd love to have the whole place swimming in roses
> God of heaven theres nothing like nature the wild mountains then
> the sea and the waves rushing then the beautiful country with fields
> of oat and wheat and all kinds of things and all the fine cattle going
> about that would do your heart good to see rivers and lakes and flowers
> all sorts of shapes and smells springing up even out of the ditches prim-
> roses and violets nature it is.[31]

Joyce is an important figure in the transition of the English
novel as a representative of naturalistic truth-telling tendencies.
In his first volume, *Dubliners* (1912), he is a belated follower
of Maupassant in the rendering of episodes. As we have seen
in the preceding chapter, he is a "spiritualistic naturalist" in
the manner of Moore and Huysmans as well as Rolland—the
attempt being to go beyond naturalistic veracity in giving a

[31] *Ulysses* (Paris, Shakespeare & Co., 1922), 731.

natural history of the soul's development. *Ulysses* is an intensification of realistic urges in that the attempt is to render what is unconscious and half-conscious as well as conscious; and while *A Portrait of the Artist* concluded with the feeling that truth was to be found, *Ulysses* takes pains to expose the wide range of man's illusions. To give the full range of his nihilistic view, it is necessary that the various levels of consciousness be exposed with infinite speed, that mutations of emotions be juxtaposed, and that figments of the brain be treated as realities. And so we have the swirling of currents, the backwash of eddies, the overtones of waves. Often the reader cannot follow Joyce, who becomes at times willfully dadaistic.

XV

THE POSTWAR NOVEL
1919–1929
SOPHISTICATES AND OTHERS

AN INTERPRETATION OF PERIODICAL COMMENT

THERE were few strictly Freudian novels because there were comparatively few people entirely sympathetic with Freud. On the other hand, impressionism attracted wide popular interest. It failed as a movement because it had nothing to say at a time when people were inquisitive. It reflected the war consciousness only in that it dealt with nonobjectionable subjects in a nonobjectionable manner. Its impersonality was congenial to the postwar attitude of nonparticipation in traditional sentiments and sentimentalities. The essential element of the war consciousness was revolt, and at best a feeble interest would be taken in the fragmentary and minute. Sophistry would demand a colorful substance. Inevitably postwar fiction would be linked with the feelings of the propaganda-conscious soldier—a suspicion of all accepted ways of thought, the approval of tangible and pleasant realities, a contempt for bourgeois ideals and for most traditional values and standards. In all countries the impact of the returning soldier was felt. Agnes C. Hansen, a student of postwar European fiction, best summarizes the rise of the insurgent spirit. For the first years of the war, according to Miss Hansen, a hierarchy saw to it that the soldier was sustained by ideals of heroism, valor, partiotism, and honor,

But the war got beyond the control of its instigators and leaders, and the great body of common men as they saw their common sacrifices, their common suffering, their common idealism reaping no reward, became critical, more subjective. A new type of novel began making its appearance. That "conflict between the generations," which has been one of the phenomena of post-war life most frequently reflected in the novel, began in the trenches. Youth began to realize its dilemma and the ironic disparity in point of view of the man at the front and the man directing operations on a vast scale in the rear, and envisaging the contending armies not as so much human flesh and blood and sentiences, but as so much cannon fodder, or as so many pins in certain areas on the map. This was the view of things which began to creep into fiction toward the end of the war. And when the tragic holocaust was over and the youth that was spared returned to civil life, they came, both victorious and defeated, minus their respect for the older generation and shorn of most of their ideals and illusions, with a whole new set of concepts concerning life and their place in the universe, concepts which were to influence world fiction for almost a dozen years.[1]

It is hardly strange that the writers who were young in 1910–15 did not in the postwar years give expression to the insurgent spirit. None of the significant ones were active combatants. Said J. D. Beresford in 1930, "In the years immediately following the war I often felt that for such non-combatants as myself there was little left to write about." Furthermore the tendency in the immediate prewar years to the autobiographical, to the search for a way of life, the tendency toward synthesis, was out of keeping with the postwar disintegration. Continues Beresford,

> Our themes were horribly restricted; the whole of modern life had been sharply divided into the two incompatible periods of "before" and "after" the great event, and it was exceedingly difficult to bridge them and still preserve the nice sense of continuity that was essential to the life-story of hero or heroine.[2]

For any number of reasons the war produced a break, or

---

[1] *Twentieth Century Forces in European Fiction* (Chicago, American Library Association, 1934), 33–34.

[2] "The Tendency of Recent Fiction," *Bookman* (London), May, 1930.

at least a sharp deviation. Of the older writers, Conrad was not affected. Wells and Bennett by constant modification seemed forever new. Galsworthy lost ground with the critics and gained ground with the public, who were just catching up with him. But elsewhere interest in the prewar hopefuls was declining. Said J. B. Priestley in 1925,

> The real difference between the situation twelve years ago [1913] and the situation today is that there were a number of young novelists who carried with them an air of great promise, and that now most of these writers, though they have all the ear of the reading public, have not entirely fulfilled that promise. To be brutally frank, we must say that they have not only not improved, but they have quite definitely deteriorated. They promised us great novels but they have given us "potboilers." Most of them have written too much and too easily. . . . I do not hesitate to say that a list of younger novelists who have not fulfilled their early promise would include Compton Mackenzie, Oliver Onions, J. D. Beresford, Frank Swinnerton, Gilbert Cannan and Hugh Walpole.[3]

Mr. Swinnerton tries to explain the matter by saying that the prewar young had views of life which were different from those of the postwar years; "the young of 1914, however false their expectations might have been, could contemplate a stable future."[4]

Perhaps it is as difficult for a novelist to change his social and philosophical conceptions as it is for him to change his technique. Prewar fiction was first of all "problem" fiction, and later it grappled with the deeper theme of self-realization. But to those who had witnessed mass slaughter, the prewar social problems were insignificant and the prewar search for self-realization hopelessly academic. Those possessed of the war consciousness felt primarily a sense of the incongruous, of staid valuations out of keeping with a blood-and-thunder

[3] "The Younger Novelists," *English Journal*, June, 1925. In *The Nineteen Hundreds* (London, George Allen and Unwin, Ltd., 1922), Reginald Auberton had a different list of authors who started off with a good book but "of their subsequent output —well, the less said about it the better." His list consisted of Gilbert Frankau, W. L. George, Stephen McKenna, W. B. Maxwell, Temple Thurston, and Hugh Walpole.
[4] *The Georgian Scene*, 435.

world. The age of "sophistication" arrived and Aldous Huxley was its prophet.

"We live today," wrote Huxley, "in a world that is socially and morally wrecked. Between them the war and the new psychology have smashed most of the institutions, traditions, creeds, and spiritual values that have supported us in the past. Dadaism represents in the field of art this complete disintegration of values. Dada denies everything; even art itself, that last idol we tried so pathetically hard to keep standing when everything else—the soul, morality, patriotism, religion—had been laid low, even art itself was assaulted by Dada and smashed. . . . Dada was an exhilarating spectacle when it appeared on the scenes. One enjoyed it as one enjoys the sight of crockery being smashed by the music hall comedian; it gratified the childish love of destruction that lurks in the heart of all of us. But after a time this crockery smashing grew tedious. It was time to pick up the bits and make something new. What is the new artistic synthesis going to be? It is too early to be able to answer definitely. But we can guess. The work of the Sitwells and a few others in England, of Cocteau, Morand, Aragon, MacOrlan and the rest of them in France helps me to make that guess. The new synthesis that will reassemble in an artistic whole the shattered relics of the postwar world, the synthesis that will reflect the disintegration in an artistic unity, will surely be a comic synthesis. The social tragedy of these last few years has gone too far and its nature and origin is too profoundly stupid to be represented tragically. And the same is true of the equally complicated and devastating mental tragedy of the breakup of old traditions and values. The only possible synthesis is the enormous farcical buffoonery of a Rabelais or an Aristophanes,—a buffoonery which, it is important to note, is capable of being as beautiful and as grandiose as tragedy."

Possibly because of the crockery smashing, the postwar years were years of great vitality. Like the eighteen-nineties they were years of ethical unrest, of experimentation, of moral insouciance, but they possessed an intensity which the nineties lacked. In the nineties revolt had an amateur, a dilettante, quality. It was smart to revolt; to go life-tasting was an adventure. Many of the more daring spirits of the nineties were so terrified by their enormities that they became Catholics—which, after all, was a fashionable procedure in an age of French influences. But in the postwar years revolt was not daring; it was chronic. And the postwar writers spent much energy insisting that nothing but the truth was now to be told, that a clear-sighted generation would forge its own chains if chains were to be forged, and that something pretty good would have to be offered to take the place of cynicism. The New World would be built on solid foundations. But there was no hurry about building it and some doubt about the advisability of constructing anything. Meanwhile there were diversions. For one thing, sex offered possibilities. It had never been properly written up. A prosaic commentator on the twenties provides us with the social background:

> The popularization of motor-cars and motor-cycles, coinciding with the decay of authority in churches and families, gave to many thousands for the first time in the nineteen-twenties that freedom of movement which is necessary for experimental unsanctioned relations between the sexes. There followed a widespread change of attitude in regard to marriage. Contraceptive devices removed the fear impulse which, combined with irresistible sexual curiosity, has often led to disastrous marriages.[5]

He gravely interprets the philosophy of the experimentalists:

> They deplore the dualism (trialism, rather) which still strives to departmentalize body, mind, and spirit. They desire to substitute a monism (or holism) which would bring all three into a single harmony to express the whole-power of man and woman. . . . The New Amoralists regard the culminating emotion of physical love as a flame which can burn with clear and cleansing intensity only when *all* the faculties of the lovers are actively and completely adjusted.[6]

[5] A. C. Ward, *The Nineteen Twenties* (London, Methuen and Co., Ltd., 1930), 14.
[6] *Ibid.,* 203–204.

On its sentimental side, sophistication found expression in the Lady of the Green Hat, in whose person the topsy-turvy values of war consciousness were incarnated. As we look back upon *The Green Hat* from the year 1941, the book may seem melodramatic and a trifle *salé*, but to the war generation it expressed an insubordinate contempt for the older generation, the generation of lies. The returned soldier loved Iris from the moment that she calmly sauntered into a man's apartment and, without fuss or stew, began to act naturally. Her erotic affairs showed her to be honest with herself and the world. But those possessed of the war consciousness liked more than anything the grand gesture of her revolt, ennobled by casual and fine phrases. There was no sympathy for an unborn child. Better not for it to be born than to give further pain to souls already sufficiently troubled. Syphilis itself symbolized the mortal agony that one must feel in order to be purified with the greater purity of pity and contempt. Iris bore a symbol of the current sorrow.

However prevalent the mode of sophistication, it enjoyed scant critical support. A full-length article by Claude C. Washburn attacked it unmercifully:

To be sophisticated you must be *blasé,* you must be witty; you must not take anything, especially vice, very hard; you must be gay and casual about problems that unsophisticated people are earnest about, though you may (here you are reaching rarefied heights of sophistication) be as earnest as you like about things that average people consider trivial. You must show familiarity with the world of High Society, but also amused disdain for it. . . . We all admire sophistication in real life and we admire it still more in novels. We love Iris Storm fastidiously and consider Silvia Tietjens' complicated vices with tolerant weariness. We, too, are of the *haut monde* and are very offhand about it. We, too, have loved very, very hard and exhausted everything and have come to look with mellow amusement upon all intensities. It is delightful. . . . You must know, and prove that you know, everything about ordering a dinner at such places as Ciro's (Monte Carlo), the Ritz (Paris), and the Café de Paris (Biarritz). You must also be able to let fall—now and then, very carelessly, merely because you cannot at the moment think of the English word—a French or an Italian or even a German word or phrase; but it is not excessively important that you should do this correctly or appropriately; the effect will be the same anyway. Among contemporary writers Carl Van Vechten and Ronald Firbank are sophisticated; and so is Michael Arlen, and so is Ford Madox Ford (né Hueffer).[7]

Ivor Brown was not surprised that the dramatized version of *The Green Hat* delighted Chicago, for, he says,

If anything could be relied upon to make England look ridiculous, it is surely the introduction of this outlandish portrait of our landed gentry. The great families to whose domestic interiors Mr. Arlen is our guide consist of fools and cads.

Of Mr. Arlen's style he is contemptuous, "The odor of hair-oil hangs to Mr. Arlen's descriptive prose."[8]

The *Adelphi* mixed tolerance with incredulity, "Mr. Arlen's works are so full of incredible people doing incredible things that one feels it quite impossible not to believe everything he tells us."[9]

The *Contemporary* made some attempt to be fair to Rose Macaulay, who "reproduces the tragic futility and chaos of the post-war world." For her elderly young people "truth, the sharp and abstract," is a jewel for which they, as quizzical spectators of life, will barter their souls. Yet her very young investigators lack a sense of proportion. They are never thankful for "the chocolates and universities and congenial literary posts with which Providence and industrialism have endowed them."[10]

In an exceptionally liberal article written for the *Outlook* (London), H. C. Harwood was impressed by Miss Romer Wilson's *Death of Society* (as well as Forster's *Passage to India* and Lawrence's *Women in Love*). "One or the other of these books deserves to be called the best book of the 1918–

---

[7] "Sophistication," *Nineteenth Century and After*, October, 1925.

[8] "The Theatre," *Saturday Review*, September, 1924.

[9] John Shand, "An Explorer in Mayfair," *Adelphi*, March, 1926.

[10] Doris N. Daglish, "Some Contemporary Women Novelists," *Contemporary Review*, January, 1925.

1926 period," he avows. Miss Wilson has performed the "double feat of suggesting Fairyland without destroying the Land of Every Day." Yet Mr. Harwood issues warnings to enthusiastic sophisticates. They must get rid of certain illusions:

1. That in 1918–19 novelists became daring. It is true that Mr. Arlen mentioned syphilis. Mr. Arlen was really dealing in sentimental melodrama.
2. That the modern young woman is something uniquely potent.
3. That the form of the novel has substantially changed.
4. That the mention of Black Bottom and Cocktails makes a writer up to date.
5. That the younger generation is better than the old.

He concludes with the observation: "There is in contemporary fiction a detachment from accepted standards of morality, and from all political activities that has never been known before."[11]

Critical opinion in England is notoriously hesitant at the prospect of change. It thus seems strange that the genius of Aldous Huxley made its way against all odds, and that he eventually won the day for his own particular brand of sophistication. Perhaps the reason, as Mr. Swinnerton suggests, was that Huxley wrote first-class satire of first-class people. Success was not late in coming. As early as February, 1926, Edwin Muir in the *Nation* (London) marveled at his popularity:

Within the five years since Mr. Huxley became known to the public he has written eight books comprising novels, short stories, a poem, and two volumes of essays. Production such as this is unusual, but as remarkable as Mr. Huxley's industry has been his popularity. Most of his books have run into a third impression; even his essays and poems have been popular. No other writer of our time has built up a reputation so rapidly and so surely; compared to his rise to acceptance that of Mr. Lawrence and Mr. Eliot has been gradual, almost painful. Mr. Huxley's public capitulated almost at the first stroke of his pen, and they have been docile ever since. ... There is no philosophy, no at-

[11] "The Post-War Novel in England."

tempt to account for the world in general, neither is there any psychology. And, curiously enough, it is this that makes him such a perfect representative of one current of feeling of the age. The crash of an order which was preparing before the war, and which the war precipitated does seem to have left a generation who in their universal uncertainty doubt even such terms as the world and the mind, are skeptical of any conclusions that may be drawn from these things, and are prepared only to accept the sensations they feel and the deceptions practiced by everybody to conceal them. ... To be so completely of the period, to say what nine out of ten literate people wish to be said, finally to say it gracefully and wittily—this is in a sense its own reward.[12]

Chaotic and divergent as was the postwar novel of the twenties, we may yet see in all of its divergence and through its various trends certain composite factors. On the whole the novel tended to be, in spirit, subjective. The tendency was still realistic, or naturalistic in a very specialized sense. The naturalism of determinism, the concern with a dominating social environment—the naturalism of Zola, the Goncourts, and to a certain extent the naturalism of Flaubert—was well-nigh forgotten. Likewise was gone the naturalistic impulse to social investigation and the posing of social questions. What remained of naturalism was its cosmic consciousness, its will to truth at any price, its aversion to facile idealisms, its detachment from the local and the insular, and its insistent demand that all phases of emotion be freely handled by the novelist. This does not mean, of course, that the cosmic consciousness of naturalism was present in all English novels; it affected the leading spirits of the decade and its influence was felt by many writers. The "experimental novel" was gone but the novelist was more and more influenced by natural science.

Ten years is too short a time for changes in fiction to be completed. Yet a number of new tendencies were dominant during the years 1919–29. The novel of these years was still the novel of ideas, but it was a different novel of ideas. It was

[12] "Contemporary Writers," February 27, 1926.

a novel of disturbing ideas, a novel of disturbing values. It was not political minded and it cared little for reform. Like the life-novel it was concerned with the inner man and his failure to achieve fulfillment, but unlike the life-novel it was not concerned with the early life of the central character and his early influences. The new novel was concerned with revaluation. It was concerned with the forces and circumstances which are at variance with individual and pagan happiness. Of course, this was the concern of the life-novelists as well, but the life-novelists were merely questioners of the established order and none too sure of themselves in their break with society. They felt their way to something better than communal happiness. But the novelists of the twenties had no doubts. They gave the world up as a bad job and made war on its claims upon them. The individual was sure of himself and the value of tangible pleasure. He was sure of little else. With the individual's search for happiness there was associated a Rousseauistic concern for the rights of other individuals to happiness, and consequently a generous and humanitarian treatment of those whom the world has wronged. "One thing is certain," said H. C. Harwood in 1929, "if the moderns come back to life they will do so with a skin too few, as the Great Victorians approached it with one too many."[13]

The writers of the twenties chose to probe the human consciousness, to be intensely realistic in temper. At the same time they disdained subjects most generally congenial to the realistic temper—political novels and novels of social reform. Thus each novelist found the necessity of creating a private world of his own, a world in which his essential vision could be more readily reflected. So we have the "worlds" of Romer Wilson and Joyce and Arlen and T. F. Powys and Wyndham Lewis and Huxley and Lawrence. Wyndham Lewis proclaimed his view that the written story should not be an adventure into the objective world but

[13] "Some Tendencies in Modern Fiction."

a stimulation of your own private world, with all its oddities: blind spots, omissions, colour-blindness (if present), astigmatic distortions, and the rest of it; all physical singularities, doubled with all the mental singularities, too.[14]

A critic for the *New Statesman* in 1926 found subjective tendencies everywhere:

In some cases the author parades his "heart" in a series of open disquisitions: in others he so far impregnates the thoughts of his characters with his own attitude and sensibilities, that every passage in the book which appears at first sight to be the thought of a character is in reality the writer's thoughts.[15]

So the novelist cared little that his writing was true *to* life so long as it was true *of* life.[16] Said Mr. Harwood in 1929,

At no time has the mind of man, the mind of the novelist, swung so far from the usual concerns of humanity. . . . The novel is not describing the modern world. . . . There is in contemporary fiction a detachment from accepted standards of morality, and from all political activities, that never has been known before.[17]

The "usual concerns of humanity," however, were not completely neglected by the fiction writers of the twenties. Readers who had made an adjustment with life demanded fiction other than the fiction of discontent. Moreover, many persons with settled minds would not turn readily to the Russians in spite of Galsworthy's statement that five of the twelve best novels were Russian and Bennett's dramatic declaration that all twelve were Russian.[18] So a goodly number

---

[14] "Detachment and the Fictionist," *Quarterly Review,* April, 1929.

[15] Arthur Waley, "The Quartette," January 2, 1926.

[16] Storm Jameson, "The Decline of Fiction," *Nation and Athenaeum,* August 3, 1929.

[17] "Some Tendencies in Modern Fiction."

[18] Galsworthy's list appeared in *The Saturday Review of Literature,* December 3, 1927. It appears in a footnote at the conclusion of the section on Galsworthy. Bennett's list as it appeared in the *Evening Standard* of March 17, 1927, follows: *The Brothers Karamazof, The Idiot, The House of the Dead, Crime and Punishment,* by Dostoievski; *Anna Karenina, War and Peace, Resurrection,* by Tolstoi; *Spring Floods, Virgin Soil, On the Eve, Fathers and Children,* by Turgenev; *Dead Souls,* by Gogol.

of the cultivated became interested in regional novels which, with certain exceptions, were not at all disturbing. Sheila Kaye-Smith was writing of Sussex, Quiller-Couch of Cornwall, Walpole of the Lake District, John Hamson of the Midlands. The settled minds enjoyed the aristocratic discriminations of V. Sackville-West, the beauty and suavity of Francis Brett Young, the nature worship of Mary Webb, and the dignity and tragedy of simple lives in the work of Constance Holme. A reaction against rebellion made the regional novel of increasing importance.

The satiric intensity of the twenties tended to obsolescence as the war receded into the past. The growing popularity of detective novels signified that a less thoughtful hedonism was taking the place of an insistent paganism. Sentiment was becoming interesting again, and the publication in the late twenties of war-novels suggested that the recollection of the war was no longer painful. Finally the spontaneous Priestley boom testified to the return of humor and gusto, and hence normality.

The word "sophisticate" may cover any number of attitudes. In general we may say that it was a lighthearted, intellectual, and pagan revolt against all ideologies. Douglas took delight in learned chatter which proved the extent of human idiocy even among the cultivated. Romer Wilson wanted a woman's sex life to be unrestrained even by marriage. Rose Macaulay sympathetically presented a "lost generation" which could hold on to intellectual honesty when it had nothing else to hold to. Aldous Huxley ridiculed the attempts of even the best of scientific intellectuals to be happy. Gerhardi wrote of a disintegrated postwar world where the most absurd things occur. Arlen wrote about the sophisticates themselves who have just and discriminate ideas about things. Wyndham Lewis pictured a world devoid of dignity, sense, and generosity. The writers themselves shunned any attempt at definition. Perhaps they held (1) in a mad world beware of madness, and (2) in a region of total darkness any light is a good one.

SOPHISTICATES

NORMAN DOUGLAS

has been popularly cited as the man from whom the sophisticates got their inspiration. The statement is largely true. Douglas, older than the postwar writers, is a "modern spirit" so broad in his humanity, so liberal in his values, and withal so logical and sound that writers of various temperaments could be nourished by him. According to Frank Swinnerton, "Rightly to apprehend Norman Douglas one should be a Scotsman, a student of antiquity, an epicure, a wit, a naturalist, and an amoral philosopher." Douglas, he continues, "has loved life, women, boys, food, drink and knowledge."[19]

South Wind (1917) influenced the postwar generation in spirit, subject matter, and technique. Although the "dialogue novel" is at least as old as Peacock, Douglas revived the form and made it the vehicle for learned and often profound chatter. He popularized heathen and egoistical philosophies and took a conscious delight in human idiocy. *South Wind*, moreover, set the fashion for artificial gatherings of people who could be counted on to provide entertainment for one another and to "ventilate" issues. The events which bring the people together and any incidents which may occur are not, therefore, necessarily logical. The link with naturalism is that a goodly number of the intellectuals express naturalistic views.

We will recall that the novel of ideas explores the issues in a single social or individual problem. The dialogue novel differs from it in exploring any and all issues. One critic would call *South Wind* a "ventriloquial book" since "the author gives his puppets his opinions to play with, and then turn inside out." Needless to say, such a book is subjective since the author will, in the end, impose the results of his own thinking. Nevertheless the thread of a story is necessary. Says H. M. Tomlinson of *South Wind:*

[19] *The Georgian Scene,* 162–63.

As to plot, it seems to me a plot intricate enough to put a kindly, learned, and orthodox Anglican Bishop into a warm south wind, among hedonists, drunkards, wantons, remittance men, blackmailers, sceptical philosophers, and men of such skill and learning that they can easily impose imitations of ancient art upon the specialists, allow him there to suffer joyful attacks upon his faith, threatening its foundations, and a murder, and a volcanic eruption, and scenes which would make the liveliest London night-club seem as demure as a curate's sewing circle; and on the last page leave him, delighted with two moons, yet with our respect for the man heightened, for he has withstood, with little change except a few opinions, an attack upon his soul which would have ruined anyone but a bishop; though it may have ruined him as a bishop.[20]

A noteworthy point in Douglas' technique is that he employs rather easily distinguished types, or characters—composite personalities. It is not surprising, therefore, that he castigates Lawrence "and other modern novelists" for being too lazy or too stupid to create a character of their own. He continues:

An entire school has grown up which thrives on writing up other people in books and newspapers. . . . Now this personality-mongering is a nuisance. . . . It is not only bad literature but bad breeding. You can hardly pick up any volume by a member of this school without finding caricatures therein of some acquaintances—all unfavorably drawn, and derided not with frank wit or invective or mockery or Rabelaisian laughter, but with the squeaky suburban chuckle which is characteristic of an age of eunuchs.

For the "dialogue" or "ventriloquial" novel, as written by Douglas, the thread of a story suffices. And, although much charming banter is expended upon the various characters, the reader need not remember the details. It suffices to keep in mind a few essential qualities. Mr. Heard is a broad-minded bishop not unfavorably impressed with the African savages among whom he has lived. Mr. Eames is a pedantic antiquarian. Denis is a young man of nineteen, possessing the idealism of

[20] *Norman Douglas* (New York, Harper & Bros., 1931), 64.

youth and English universities. Mr. Parker is a social person and something of a rascal. Miss Wilberforce is a tippler; the Duchess a *grande dame* and something of a fraud. But Mr. Keith, the encyclopedic realist, is the author's chosen puppet. He provided the model for the best of the Huxley self-impersonations and he expressed opinions about the body and about individualism which Lawrence later developed. To the scientific-minded sophisticates he provided the perfect model of the thoughtful hedonist.

Keith was a pertinaceous and omnivorous student; he sought knowledge not for a set purpose but because nothing was without interest for him. He took all learning to his province. He read for the pleasure of knowing what he did not know before; his mind was unusually receptive because, he said, he respected the laws that governed his body. Facts were his prey. He threw himself into them with a kind of piratical ardour; took them by the throat, wallowed in them, worried them like a terrier, and finally assimilated them. They gave him food for what he liked best on earth: "disinterested thought." They "formed a rich loam." He has an encyclopaedic turn of mind; his head, as someone once remarked, was a lumber-room of useless information. . . . He had lately attacked, in Corsair fashion, the Greek philosophers and had disembowelled Plato, Aristotle and the rest of them, to his complete satisfaction, in a couple of months; at present he was up to the ears in psychology, and his talk bristled with phrases about the "function of the real," about reactions, reflexes, adjustments and stimuli . . .

. . . "Believe me, this hankering after purity, this hypersensitiveness as to what is morbid or immoral, is by no means a good sign. A healthy man refuses to be hampered by preconceived notions of what is wrong or ugly. . . . I could give you a long list of celebrated statesmen, princes, philosophers and prelates of the Church who take pleasure, in their moments of relaxation, in what you call improper conversation, literature or correspondence. They feel the strain of being continually pure; they realize that all strains are pernicious, and that there is no action without its reaction. They unbend. Only invertebrate folks do not unbend. They dare not, because they have no backbone. They know that if they once unbent, they could not straighten themselves out again. They make a virtue of their own organic defect. . . ."

He advises Denis,

"Taken in over-dose, all these churches and pictures and books and other products of our species are toxins for a boy like you. They falsify your cosmic values. Try to be more of an animal. Try to extract pleasure from more obvious sources. Lie fallow for a while. Forget all these things. Go out into the midday glare. Sit among rocks and by the sea. Have a look at the sun and the stars for a change. . . ."

Even though the speeches of Mr. Keith are often long, they do not provide the author with sufficient space for his reflections. Sometimes Mr. Martin was used as a mouthpiece; at another time the Count. Douglas was obviously wary of writing what a critic might call "autobiographical stuff." A convenient device was to make derogatory remarks about a character who would express the author's view. Mr. Martin "was a hirsute and impecunious young Hebrew of low tastes, with a passion for mineralogy." Yet Mr. Martin in talking with the groping Denis is obviously Douglas:

"A fellow can't live without vices. Here you are, with lots of money, stewing in a back bedroom of a second-class hotel and getting up at five o'clock because you like lying in bed late. Is that your way of mortifying the flesh? Got a soul, eh? Get rid of it. The soul! That unhappy word has been the refuge of empty minds since the world began. . . . Chastity be blowed. It's an unclean state of affairs and dangerous to the community. You can't call yourself a good citizen till you have learnt to despise it from the bottom of your heart. It's an insult to the creator and an abomination to man and beast. . . . A man who marries—well, there may be some excuse for him, though a love-match is generally a failure and a money-match always a mistake. The heroes, the saints and sages—they are those who face the world alone! A married man is half a man. . . . Ruskin. Good god! He's not a man; he's an emetic."

The Count, who is patently a Latin, may express the author's despair of the Nordic western world:

"What is the outstanding feature of modern life? The bankruptcy, the proven fatuity, of everything that is bound up under the name of Western civilization. Men are perceiving, I think, the baseness of mercantile and military ideals, the loftiness of those older ones. They will band together, the elect of every nation, in god-favored regions round the Inland Sea, there to lead serener lives."

ROMER WILSON

(Mrs. Florence Roma Muir Wilson O'Brien) has been frequently referred to as "a flash in the pan." Her big book was *The Death of Society* (1921). As we have noted previously, H. C. Harwood, a first-rate critic, rated it with *Passage to India* and *Women in Love*. "One or the other of these three books deserves to be called the best book of the 1918–1926 period," said Harwood.[21] It was awarded the Hawthornden Prize and it helped to establish the unmoral tone of postwar fiction.

The book has a subtitle: *A Novel of the Future*. Reason for this is not hard to find. A rich and aging intellectual agrees to the adultery of his wife because she sees in the deed her own fulfillment. But there is more to the novel than this. Not only are the lovers spiritually re-created, but the wife's lyrical and pantheistic utterances are against all social restraints whatever.

What Henry James called the *donée*, or situation, here borders upon the realm of fantasy. One Rane Smith, intellectual, happens upon the continental chateau of one Igman, writer, and asks for a night's lodging. The two are congenial and Igman asks Smith to stay as long as he likes. The reader suspects that an attachment will soon be formed with one of Igman's enlightened daughters. Not so. The wife, blessed with perpetual youth because of the beauty of her thoughts, reciprocates Rane Smith's affection.

Rose Igman is a woman of the future. Her perfections, even her husband admits, are unlimited. The bright fires of her spirit illumine the world which surrounds her. She desires to consummate her love for Smith, and the husband, though consumed with jealousy, cannot say that she is wrong. Says Rose Igman to Smith:

[21] "The Post-War Novel in England."

I owe nothing to either man or woman. My name? My husband's name?—those belong to Society. Is your love wicked when it springs straight from your heart—my gladness wicked which springs fresh from mine? Who shall we hurt? ... My soul belongs to nobody: I—Rose Chriastensen—am my own. My body is my soul's servant and friend, and by it I can completely know other souls as I know my own.

The two spend the night together and their love is stronger than before. At the prospect of separating "they gave themselves up to complete despair. They were astounded, horrified, aghast, and clung to one another in silence." The thought of suicide occurs but Rose Igman is quick to meet it: "But then where would our love be? Rotten in the bottom of the lake with the cold fishes." Similarly Rose rejects the idea of leaving her husband and her happy home: "If you asked me I should leave my home. You do not ask me. We love one another too much to ask each other's lives." Smith, on his part, was "filled with godliness and grace and pride. ... What he had seen could only fill his heart with joy and peace, and give the intricacies and pettinesses of everyday a finer meaning, his heart a tenderness toward the human race, his mind a greater tolerance toward blindness and stupidity."

Greenlow (1927) is a regional novel in its setting and atmosphere, but the author's insurgent and pagan spirit remains much the same. This time the unconventionalities are not isolated on a Scandinavian estate; relatives are on hand to protest. The author is obviously a protagonist of the emotional Jill who divides her love between two men. One thinks of the writings of George Egerton in the nineties, but Romer Wilson has more subtlety, more variety, the same intensity. Jill, an orphan, loves the hills and valleys of her country place, and she loves Jim, a native, who cycles over for week ends from the workshops of a neighboring city. Jill muses:

I love Jim. I understand him. His mind cannot go outside of his body. He thinks and acts with his body. His love of this valley is sensuous. He is quite right in his instincts, but the poor miserable beast cannot find the right beyond his instincts. He is lost when he has to face difficulties that his senses cannot solve. Jim is a dear beast. I love him. He is part of this valley to me. He matches the hills. But I wish he could be at peace and see how right his instincts are, and have the courage to follow them.

During Jim's absence Jill sees much of John, a writer from the city who comes to adore her. She does not love him at first, but he is persistent. Witness a scene, Jill speaking:

He kissed me and crushed me and I fought and kicked him. "You mushy toad," I cried, "you dirty dog! I hate your nasty kisses. O, God damn your horrid face." But I was not cross. We had a great fight there. I pulled his hair and kicked him, but he didn't care. At last he had enough and let me go. O, I was all out of breath with laughter.

So Jill comes to love John, but not so much as she loves Jim. However Jim loses his job and refuses her offer of the farm. Thereupon she concentrates upon John, scandalizes her relatives, and marries John after he has accepted the hospitality of her house for the night.

The early novels of Romer Wilson were not well received. They were written during the war and reflected her travels in Germany. The scene of one of them was laid in a German pension in peace times. No animus was expressed. Critics objected to her detachment and the unheroic quality of her narrative. The foreword to *If All These Young Men* reads as follows:

If all these young men were as hares upon the mountains
Then all these pretty maidens would soon follow after.

A critic who remarked that Romer Wilson's young men were not worth following perhaps made no mistake. He said nothing of her maidens.

ROSE MACAULAY

As someone remarked in the postwar years, Rose Macaulay was looked upon as a highbrow by the flappers and as a lowbrow by the intellectuals. As a matter of fact, she stood squarely between. For the flapper there was absolute clarity, an easy style, a good story, a lively presentation of family situations, and a mild flavor of pessimism pervading the conversations of a recognizable upper crust. For the highbrow there was a broad sanity and a tendency to *épater le bourgeois*, witty observations, a sympathy with pagan values, and the realistic portrayal of a lost generation of doubting and diffident young people who were discovering a world in which there was no meaning, no order, no sense.

The tone of Rose Macaulay's work is sprightly and belies the author's pessimism. But the pessimism gradually obtrudes as the reader discovers that the characters which are presented sympathetically acknowledge no values, no obligations, and the pressure of no lasting affection. Caprice and obsession but prey upon the spirit as it travels through the void. Successive books intensify the impression of nihilism even while the author with humane amusement deftly sketches the color and variety of a life that is no whit dulled by its hopelessness. Poetry often reveals in a flash what the novelist takes volumes to tell, and Rose Macaulay's poetry gives the point of many novels:

> The tent is shaken and rent ... Oh a wind
>   Drives from the wild, keen blue,
> And God, the Lord God of Anarchy,
>   Breaks through ...

* * *

> Go through the door.
> You shall find nothing that has not been before,
> Nothing so bitter it will not be once more.

* * *

> Two deathless flames burn ...
> The white flame, like a star, of beauty immortal;
> The red flame, like a sword, of unperishing hate.

* * *

> So bankrupt of hope and blind
> To faith and love, we'll find
> We, even we, joy in things small and kind.

Miss Macaulay has written some thirty novels. She had written eight before she struck fire with *Potterism* (1920), an attack upon bourgeois values and everything false, ornate, insincere, pretentious, slushy, and absurd. The attackers are college lads, eager, independent young people who are invariably good company. Says Gideon,

"Oh Lord, we are all Potterish, every profiteer, every sentimentalist, every muddler. Every artist directly he thinks of his art as something marketable, something to bring him fame; every scientist or scholar who fakes a fact in the interest of his theory; every fool who talks through his hat without knowing; ... every secondhand ignoramus who takes over a view or a prejudice wholesale, without investigating the facts that it's based on for himself. You find it everywhere, the taint; you can't get away from it. Except by keeping quiet and learning and wanting truth more than anything else."

Dangerous Ages (1921), shows Rose Macaulay at her best. Here we have bachelor girls who know psychoanalysis and birth control, and are bent upon leading their own lives; young women who go out for careers as a means of obtaining the larger freedom; elderly women whose interest in ideas increases with the years. All of them feel that they should leave an imprint upon life—something other than children. They are lighthearted, and stern only in the belief that life should afford some intense reality. And Miss Macaulay holds that, life being short, they do well to make the most of things in their none-too-rational fashions.

Potterism and *Dangerous Ages* established Miss Macaulay's reputation as the defender of youth's revolt. The pattern of her work is obvious. As in *South Wind*, people with ideas are brought together and issues are raised which afford the author the opportunity for satire. Before the war, and before *South Wind*, her novels had been topical, serious, and critical. After the war she became derisive, and in the rapid sequence of her novels she was careful never to rework a situation. *Told by an Idiot* (1923) is filled with the follies and peculiarities of successive periods—Victorian, *fin-de-siècle*, Edwardian, and

Georgian. In *Orphan Island* (1924) she plays with the development of an island community subjected to the inbreeding of Victorian ideas. *Crewe Train* (1926) shows an unconventional young pagan in the process of being domesticated. *Daisy and Daphne* (1928) is an amusing presentation of a dual personality. *Staying with Relations* (1930) is a reversion to the Douglas influence with a tropical setting, sharply contrasted characters, and a story where things really happen. *They Were Defeated* (1932)—American title *The Shadow Flies*—is a novel steeped in seventeenth-century atmosphere and concerned with Robert Herrick and his friends. *Going Abroad* (1934) shows Miss Macaulay in prankish mood demolishing the Buchmanites as she treats university folk and others assembled at a summer resort on the Spanish Basque coast. Basque bandits capture the party on a motor trip and take it to a mountain hide-out, thus providing the element of plot distinctive of the Douglas technique. *I Would Be Private* (1937)—again Norman Douglas—is a satire of fads, among which are quintuplet-idolatry and surrealism, on a Caribbean island where dissimilar individuals are collected together by fortuitous circumstances.

This tedious summary has been necessary to indicate the variety of Rose Macaulay's subjects. She has written too much and too rapidly, but her dexterity is remarkable and the "unredeemed levity" of her castigation of cranks and poses has become increasingly evident with the passage of years.

ALDOUS HUXLEY

We have every reason to expect that the novelist who writes of his own intellectual ferment will write about his own conception of the novel. With Aldous Huxley our expectations are fulfilled. Philip in *Point Counter Point* (1928) mentions what the critics say of himself (and of Huxley): "zoologist of fiction," "learnedly elfish," "a scientific Puck." And Philip indicates the cardinal principle of fiction as being based upon a new way of looking at things, which he calls "multiplicity":

> Multiplicity of eyes and multiplicity of aspects seen. For instance, one person interprets events in terms of bishops; another in terms of the price of flannel camisoles; another ... thinks of it in terms of good times. And then there's the biologist, the chemist, the physicist, the historian. Each sees, professionally, a different aspect of the event, a different layer of reality. What I want to do is to look with all those eyes at once. With religious eyes, economic eyes, homme moyen sensuel eyes...[22]

Huxley's novels are, obviously, dramatizations of this multiple view. The various characters are highly specialized types.

The indebtedness to Norman Douglas is obvious. And, like the persons in *South Wind*, Huxley's scientists and historians and writers are really learned. Sometimes, as in *Point Counter Point*, the author calls our attention to the fact that he is portraying types by pointing out their idiocrasy or "perversion away from the central norm." Thus Burlap is "a pure little Jesus pervert," Philip "an intellectual-aesthetic pervert," Spandrill "a morality-philosophy pervert," and Rampion "a Jeremiah." Obvious types in *Antic Hay* (1923) are a blasphemous scientist, a bored woman, a vociferous Bohemian, and the incarnation of the author. The author is staging a symposium of divergent views. And most of his characters are scientific intellectuals.

Let us return to Philip's views:

> Really any plot or situation would do. Because everything's implicit in anything. The whole book could be written about a walk from Picadilly Circus to Charing Cross. Or you and I sitting here on an enormous ship in the Red Sea. Really nothing could be queerer than that. When you reflect on the evolutionary process, the human patience and genius, the social organization that has made it possible for us to be here, with stokers having near apoplexy for our benefit, and steam turbines doing five thousand revolutions per minute, and the sea being blue, and the rays of light not flowing round objects, so that

[22] Huxley, *Point Counter Point* (New York, The Literary Guild of America, 1928), 294.

there's a shadow, and the sun all the time providing us with energy to live and think—when you think of all this and a million other things, you must see that nothing could well be queerer and that no picture can be queer enough to do justice to the facts.[23]

In other words, the ball can be set rolling anywhere. Even less than with Douglas, the interest is independent of event. One is reminded of Huysmans, who seems to have discovered the charm of erudition in fiction. To Huxley, whose favorite reading for some years was *The Encyclopaedia Britannica*, the love of precise information becomes an aesthetic ideal.

Since the story is anything or nothing, the views of the characters are everything. Huxley makes no distinction between the dialogue novel and the novel of ideas. I quote from Philip's notebook:

Novel of ideas. The character of each personage must be implied, as far as possible, in the ideas of which he is the mouthpiece. Insofar as theories are rationalizations of sentiments, instincts, dispositions of soul, this is feasible. The chief defect of the novel of ideas is that you must write about people who have ideas to express—which excludes all but about .01 per cent of the human race.

So unimportant is structure in Huxley's novels that events seem unarranged, and hence real. The author intersperses his narrative with diaries, notebooks, and letters; he enters at will the consciousness of all characters while he plays hop, skip, and jump with the reader's attention. The semblance of truth is more fully conveyed than by a well-ordered narrative, and in this matter the influence of Huxley over his contemporaries has been wide.

But even wider has been the effect of his philosophy. His characters have cast off Victorianism, but they are no better off than the Victorians. They have not found out how to live abundantly, and every new effort proves equally futile. They grope for fulfillment in approved fashions—by submerging themselves in great causes, by devotion to art or socialism, by experiments in passion, by losing themselves in contemplation,

[23] *Ibid.*

by faith in the activity of pure conscious intelligence, and even by absorbing themselves in fads and hobbies. But all lead to boredom or restlessness or to some bad end.

In the postwar world Huxley became known as the champion of awareness—a pathetic sort of awareness. Man is freed from illusions only to find that he needs an illusion to live for. With the prospect of failure before him, man would continue to search and learn. "The proper study of mankind is books." Not until the appearance of *Point Counter Point* in 1928 was there a break in Huxley's nihilism. But in *Point Counter Point*, Mark Rampion, who somewhat resembles Huxley at the age of thirty-four, steals the show. To be thoroughly aware one must attain the necessary harmony of spirit and flesh. Says Rampion,

> A man's a creature on a tightrope, walking delicately, equilibrated, with mind and consciousness and spirit at one end of his balancing pole and body and instinct and all that's earthy and mysterious at the other. Balanced. Which is damnably difficult. And the only absolute he can know is the absolute of perfect balance.

The world is filled with creatures who try to be more than human:

> And all perverted in the same way—by trying to be non-human. Non-humanly religious, non-humanly moral, non-humanly intellectual and scientific, non-humanly specialized and efficient, non-humanly the business man, non-humanly avaricious and property-loving, non-humanly lascivious and Don Juanesque, non-humanly the conscious individual even in love. All perverts. Perverted toward goodness or badness, toward spirit or flesh; but always away from humanity.

But except for what might have been a passing phase in Huxley's later work, it is not evident that he casts his own lot with humanity. We think of him as being primarily interested in "a little group of intelligentsia clinging together in a grossly hostile world." For the most part he stands against things; not against man but against his aims—against mechani-

zation, against any exalted conception of love, against losing
one's self in high impersonal endeavor, against relying upon
science. To stand for humanity implies a sympathy with human
hopes and fears. Huxley's own sympathies are constricted. He
is the thwarted romantic with a critical sense that demands the
castigation of hope and effort. One of the scenes in *Antic
Hay* that remains longest with us is the one in which Gumbril
and Mrs. Viveash peep in on Shearwater's scientific experiment:

> Shearwater sat on his stationary bicycle, pedalling unceasingly
> like a man in a nightmare. The pedals were geared to a little wheel
> under the saddle, and the rim of the wheel rubbed as it revolved
> against a brake, carefully adjusted to make the work of the pedaller
> hard, but not impossibly hard. From a pipe which came up through
> the floor issued a little jet of water which played on the brake and
> kept it cool. But no jet of water played on Shearwater. It was his busi-
> ness to get hot. He did get hot. . . . Shearwater was always at his post
> on the saddle of the nightmare bicycle, pedalling, pedalling. The
> water trickled over the brake. And Shearwater sweated. Great drops
> of sweat came oozing out from under his hair, ran down over his
> forehead, hung beaded on his eyebrows, ran into his eyes, down his
> nose, along his cheeks, fell like rain drops. His thick bull neck was
> wet; his arms and legs steamed and shone. The sweat poured off him
> and was caught as it rained down in a water-proof sheet, to trickle
> down its sloping folds into a large glass receptacle. . . . Shearwater had
> air enough. Another time, Lancing reflected, they'd make the box
> air-tight and see the effect of a little carbon dioxide poisoning on top
> of excessive sweating. It might be very interesting . . . he had been
> pedalling ever since lunchtime. At eleven he would go to bed on a
> shake-down in the laboratory and at nine tomorrow morning he
> would re-enter the box and start pedalling again. He would go on
> tomorrow and the day after; and after that as long as he could stand
> it. One, two, three, four. Pedal, pedal, pedal.

This is a heightened instance of futility. Huxley uses it as
the culmination of a despairing tour taken by Gumbril and
Mrs. Viveash ("tomorrow will be as awful as today"). But if
science fails, there is love. What is love, or sex, to the critical

eye of Huxley? H. C. Harwood's exposition deserves to be quoted:

> The more carefully one pursues a life of quiet wisdom, the more bitterly is one betrayed by the irrelevances of sex. It is just possible for some simple-minded people to stumble into some transitory equilibrium, to love as cattle or sheep, and attain, if not happiness, at least tranquillity, but the subtler, the more intellectual derive from their ludicrous passions nothing but pains and degradation. The man who ignores sex is contemptible for being less than man. The man who admits sex is contemptible as being less than monkey; sewn into a monkey's skin, suffering from a monkey's itch, and with all a human intelligence helplessly contemplating an animal's amours. Mr. Huxley's imagination is chained to sex as something alive might be chained to a corpse, and with loathing and fear it struggles in vain for freedom. His philosophy contemplates a male world out of which from time to time the male intelligence struggles to be free.[24]

Although Mr. Harwood does not take into consideration the possibility of Huxley's conversion to Lawrence in the latter part of *Point Counter Point*, he sees better than other writers the pathetic indignity which Huxley was at pains to apply to the procreative urge.

I have endeavored to show the main lines of Huxley's significance as it has been felt at large. In his post-1932 groping, Huxley has not taken his following with him. Even admirers of Huxley are dubious about his recent implications, and many who admired him as a cynical realist are disappointed in his pacifism. In his latest effort to recapture his public, *After Many a Summer Dies the Swan* (1940), the author seems to have abandoned his desire to lead the human race upward and onward. He writes again with his usual gusto of the imbecilities of the highly privileged. Is he dissatisfied with his groping or with his failure to convince? Probably both. No doubt we shall hear something further from him after the whole matter of mystical experience is further incubated. A brief account

---

[24] "Some Tendencies in Modern Fiction."

of Huxley's groping is necessary for an understanding of his total implication.

Huxley had early cast his lot with science. He was attracted to Lawrence because he could partly reconcile Lawrence with instinctive urges of which science must take account. But Lawrence provided no essential stimulus. Hereafter he would merely not deal with sex as naughty and "a seven-years itch." As shown in *Brave New World* (1932), he was fostering a progressive dislike for the world under scientific dispensation. Science was an instrument of the Philistines. It was making the world so bad it would soon be unbearable. In the sterile post-Ford world the man who liked Shakespeare would soon be an anachronism. Shakespeare was infinitely better. What then?

Huxley took a dive into otherworldliness, Asiatic mysticism, and wishful thinking. The *summum bonum* was the mystical experience. It could even be cultivated. Separateness, and hence anarchy and evil, was the lot of mortals under an empiric-materialistic dispensation. Charity (nonresistance and love), intelligence, and mystical awareness of what lies beyond our immediate sensual experience were proper human aims. Both spirit and flesh were sure to respond to discipline and purposeful concentration (meditation). The unpardonable sin was specialization, separateness (attachment to things):

Biological specialization may be regarded as a tendency on the part of a species to insist on its separateness; and the result of specialization ... is negatively disastrous, in the sense that it precludes the possibility of further biological progress, or positively disastrous in the sense that it leads to the extinction of the species. In the same way intra-specific competition may be regarded as the expression of a tendency on the part of related individuals to insist on their separateness and independence; the effects of intra-specific competition are ... almost wholly bad. Conversely, the qualities which have led to biological progress are the qualities which make it possible for individual beings to escape from their separateness—intelligence and the tendency to co-operate. Love and understanding are valuable even on the biological level. Hatred, unawareness, stupidity and all that makes for increase of separateness ... have led either to the extinction of the species, or to its becoming a living fossil, incapable of making further biological progress.[25]

So Huxley brings to the support of mystical conclusions the science which has failed to justify itself on a material plane.

In *After Many a Summer Dies the Swan* we gather that Mr. Propter expresses the somewhat submerged speculations of the author. Time is essentially evil; the true good is the quest for eternity, not immortality; eternity is realizable now.

WILLIAM GERHARDI

is the first person who ever dared to proclaim the Great Russian Soul a comic thing. Born in St. Petersburg, the son of a wealthy English manufacturer living there, he was educated in Russia and later at Oxford. Serving as military attaché to the British embassy at Petrograd during the revolution he became familiar with the plight of dislocated Russians, and on his two trips around the world he scraped acquaintance with cosmopolitan types. Beginning in *Futility* (1922) as the satirist of Russian naïveté and shyness he extended his range in *The Polyglots* (1925) by shifting his scene to Vladivostok, Harbin, and Japan, where he might satirize with broader perspective the uprooted specimens of a disintegrated world. Then follows extravaganza and a variety of moods—kittenish, gay, scatterbrained, mad, sometimes brilliant, sometimes wistful, as the author takes the world to task for its absurdities.

Gerhardi's reputation rests largely upon his first two novels. In *Futility* the brooding Slavic nature is personified in Nikolai, separated from his wife and supporting a household consisting of his mistress and his daughters, aged sixteen, fifteen, and

---

[25] Quoted by Helen W. Estrich in the *Sewanee Review* for January–March, 1939. Miss Estrich carefully traces the development of Huxley's thought in *Eyeless in Gaza* (1936), *The Olive Tree and Other Essays* (1936), and *Ends and Means* (1937). She proves rather conclusively the influence upon Huxley of F. M. Alexander *(Man's Supreme Inheritance, Conscious Control of the Individual, The Use of Self)*. Her article is required reading for those who would trace the involutions of Huxley's thought.

fourteen. Nikolai wants a divorce, not to marry his mistress
but a schoolgirl friend of his daughter. In a topsy-turvy world
the wife consents to the divorce but changes her mind when
her lover goes broke. So mistress and wife set up a millinery
establishment together, and the yearnings of Nikolai's brooding soul remain unsatisfied. Says Joseph Wood Krutch, "Gerhardi's book is the hearty laughter of common sense at those
vagaries which are the source of all man's absurdities and all
his sublimities."[26] *Futility* is devastating, funny, and delightful.
Gerhardi knows his Russians better than any other English
writer, and *Futility* did much to laugh the Russian novel out
of countenance in England.

In *The Polyglots* the scene shifts through various localities
of the Far East. Here the author gathers together an amazing
collection of cosmopolitan relatives who have been whirled
together by the forces of revolution and change—Russian
exiles, Belgian refugees, Czech military men, and odds and ends
of human flotsam. The characterizations are vital, even while
the author is portraying devitalized people. He has a youthful
fondness for reprehensible qualities, even ascribing them to
himself. With mellow resignation, irony, and burlesque he
sketches the panorama of a depraved and disintegrated world
where the most absurd things may happen.

Russian atmosphere is again present in *Jass and Jasper*
(1928)—American title *Eve's Apples*—in which the author's
"register" attaches himself to a family of Russian refugees and
makes love to the daughters. Wells's influence here replaces that
of Douglas. A fanatical scientist, convinced like Gerhardi that
the existing world is not worth preserving, destroys all life
other than that on a selected mountain in the Tyrol. *Pending
Heaven* (1930) is a satire on Don Juanism, showing a sophisticated young bohemian—a writer and lover—pondering the
springs of action. *The Memories of Satan* (1932)— with Brian
Lunn—is an extravaganza, a scarcely successful episodic history of mankind. *Resurrection* (1934) is good entertainment,

26 A review of *Futility*, *Nation*, May 16, 1923.

centering upon the conversations that ensue after a man has divined that after death he will continue in an astral body.

Gerhardi proved pleasing to postwar taste because of his spontaneity, his love for the ludicrous, his ability to skate on thin ice, and the contagion of his gaiety. His satire goes deep because it is sincerity rather than pretense that affords him amusement. Like Huxley he has fun with people who are both sincere and inept.

MICHAEL ARLEN

No doubt the intelligent reader of 1925 anticipated for Michael Arlen some definite minor place in literary history. According to Beverley Nichols in 1927 "Arlen had had, with *The Green Hat*, a reverberating success. It had succeeded and succeeded—and succeeded." The royalties from *The Green Hat* (1924) amounted to half a million dollars, and we are told that Arlen's small, immaculate figure alighting from his white custom-built Rolls-Royce in Paris was a sight looked upon with something akin to awe. Mr. Nichols remembers a momentous event:

I remember sitting, during this pregnant period, with Frederick Lonsdale, and hearing the telephone ring. Over the wire came Arlen's voice announcing that he had cut thousands of words out of his new novel. The news, in this tense atmosphere, seemed of vital importance.[27]

The most an indulgent critic may today affirm is that Arlen's writings were sometimes graceful even when they were ornate; that they possessed a certain technical efficiency, borrowed from Maupassant and the elliptical method of Conrad, which put the reader on his mettle; and that they are of historical importance in showing the partiality of a war-conscious generation for a manner of mild decadence, a precise and exotic discrimination, a flavor of sin.

Granted this much, it seems necessary to add that Arlen

[27] *Are They the Same at Home?* (London, Jonathan Cape, Ltd., 1937), 24.

enjoyed scant support among English critics. He was damned in America after Mencken attacked his "rented dress-suit fiction." Claude C. Washburn drove nails into his coffin when he remarked in the *Nineteenth Century*,

> The reason why the authentic manner is *baroque,* even rococo, heavily encrusted with ornament, is a melancholy reason. ("That was a gloomy reason," Mr. Arlen would say.) It is that there is a certain lack of body in sophistication. To eschew the passions—or perhaps not to eschew them, but to smile at them—to be polished, suave and unobtrusively superior, is delightful, but limits one a bit. ... And Iris, the radiant, the well-beloved, what is Iris? What but a very young man's dream of a woman—experience plus innocence, a prostitute with the soul of a virgin?[28]

John Shand in the *Adelphi* was permanently displeased with Arlen's men: "Although they are not intelligent, they are subtle, so subtle that they do nothing but the wrong thing at the wrong moment in an unexpected manner."[29]

WYNDHAM LEWIS

has been called the "best natural satirist since Hogarth." His satire is broad and vivid, but seldom acute. He is alive only when he opposes interests and attitudes contrary to his own, and there is some truth in Middleton Murry's statement, "This man hath a demon." Although Mr. Lewis is loosely allied to the English tradition of Jonson, Shirley, and Shaw, he is more savage and much more unreasonable than they.

Mr. Lewis once painted the top of the Eiffel Tower Restaurant—and made a fortune for the restaurant. It is perhaps the painter's vision, the vorticist eye, which enables him to see men as monsters or automatons, or both. There is a note of exasperation in his writing as he pictures a world devoid of dignity, sense, and generosity. Nor is he sympathetic to the world congenial to him—made up of Latin Quarter figures, bohemians

---

28 "Sophistication," October, 1925.
29 "An Explorer in Mayfair," March, 1926.

in general, homosexuals, and disciples of Apollo. *The Apes of God* is a title which applies to more than one of the author's novels, since it suggests the brutality of his vision.

Of the sophisticates, perhaps Mr. Lewis has suffered next to Michael Arlen the indignity of being *démodé*. *Tarr* was once hailed as the story of "a lonely and savage intelligence fighting ruthlessly to keep himself free from the shabby emotional compromise of his fellows."[30] Yet *Tarr* is scarcely good reading today. Tarr himself strikes us as a mouthing theorist who regales cardboard figures with an egotism sadly reminiscent of—Gissing! The hero declaims of art with no especial distinction, and he hashes up what Wordsworth and Poe said much better of science, what Nietzsche and old worn-out Carlyle said much better of democracy, what Shaw said much better of sentiment.

The Childermass (1928) is a sort of nightmare, showing the world under the disintegration of time-philosophy. The characters change their ages and they flit about in space with elaborate confusion. The object is ridicule and the castigation of shams. There are no women in the book.

In *Tarr* sex is a joke and the author's treatment of it is ribald. Elsewhere he avoids the subject, or handles it with complete coldness. In *The Wild Body* he writes, "Sex makes me yawn my head off; but if I catch sight of some stylistic anomaly that will provide me with a new pattern for my grotesque realism, my eye sparkles at once."

Tarr was an influence upon Joyce. Thereafter Mr. Lewis used many of Joyce's effects.

THEODORE F. POWYS, VILLAGE ATHEIST

T. F. Powys will doubtless go down in literary history—'way down—as a curiosity. He is important only as representing a unique phase of the experimentation of the 1920's. With him experimentation is not technical. His surrealism is one of

---

[30] *Nation,* September, 1926.

wet and slippery ideas. No people just like T. F. Powys' people ever inhabited the earth, and a *tour de force* of alarming proportions is perpetrated when these peculiar and irrational people are made simple villagers of "Wessex." The trick is an old one; it is merely a modern rendering of Ben Jonson's theory of "humours." The reader makes the proper adjustment in his values and sees that the author is employing his characters merely as symbols. The charm of fantasy is lacking, so allegory is used with moralistic intention. Yet allegory is traditionally employed for detailed exposition of simple formulas. T. F. Powys' thought is oblique and upside down even when it is not merely cockeyed. He is haunted by Evil, an attribute of God. There is little wonder that critics are most often derisive. Writes Gerald Bullett in the *Saturday Review:* "Malice, envy and all uncharitableness, spite without reason and fornication without fun: this is the stuff of rural life as Mr. Powys sees it."[31] A critic for the *Spectator* says of *Mr. Tasker's Gods:* "The whole countryside was the haunt of malice and cruelty and sottishness and every kind of vice; and if virtue ever raised its head it was sure to be poleaxed."[32] A critic for the *Bookman* was not overimpressed by *Soliloquies of a Hermit:* "No doubt one day we shall find all the mystic writers leaving their pens and their burrowings into the unutterable mystery of God's being, and instead busy themselves all day long planting cabbages."[33]

It is not necessarily pedantic to presume that a formal education may serve to give a writer balance. T. F. Powys became a farmer rather than attend a university, and in so doing he missed, at least, certain short cuts to synthesized knowledge. So the scholar must consider T. F. Powys' most philosophical book, *Mr. Weston's Good Wine* (1927) as singular in a rude sort of way, although provocative and stimulating. Death as oblivion is desirable because it is the only escape from a terrible

[31] A review of *Mockery Gap*, September 12, 1925.
[32] A review of *Mr. Tasker's Gods*, February 28, 1925.
[33] J. B. Chapman, "Theodore Francis Powys," March, 1928.

God, and from the terrible part of God that is in one's self. But the terrible God is jealous of his treasured possession, oblivion. So love and fecundity cheat God—who will punish those who copulate by forever damning them to immortality. So man may not love, except he love his mother earth—and even here he may be punished by God's jealousy for loving too much. God is Evil and may not be opposed, no more than the baser part of one's nature may be opposed. The "immortals" are therefore the base, those who are chained to life and doomed to immortality by their worldliness and greed and hardness of heart and cunning.

Other novels of T. F. Powys have less of this diabolism with a puritan bias, but they are equally incredible. In *The Left Leg* (1923) a long-short story of ninety pages, a lustful old farmer wants to possess literally everything in the village of God's Madder. *Mark Only* (1924) possesses a Hardy theme: a pitiful figure is arrayed against hostile forces, and his struggle is in vain. But in this novel the diabolical intrigues of a lame pauper give the essential Powys imprint to the story. *Mr. Tasker's Gods* (1925) is a dramatic contrast of good and evil. One group of people is possessed of calm; another group, composed of a lecherous clergyman and his lecherous sons, represents the base. Mr. Tasker's gods are pigs. He feeds his father to them, literally.

All of T. F. Powys' thoughts are not demonic. He hates hypocrisy, he hates the ugliness of cities, he has sympathy for the oppressed, he has a tenderness toward innocence, he is at times avowedly pantheistic. Yet he will be remembered for his faults; for what Gerald Bullett sweepingly stigmatized as "dismal nonsense."

TRADITIONALISTS

CLEMENCE DANE

is a writer of dramatic narrative in which tragedy, tinged with romance and social comedy, finds decorous and often vivid expression. She uses the tested ingredients of fiction, and her talent lies in making them seem new, or at least interesting. It is altogether fitting that she should have written a defense of the traditional English novel. Says Miss Dane:

> With the Waverley Novels the tradition of the English novel was established once for all. Its recognized ingredients were to be in future —a good plot, modern or historical, a family background, a love story, adventure to taste, an air of reality, a flavour of fantasy, a happy ending, social or spiritual, some humor, and now and again a beautiful bloody shock! This was the British traditive novel as the British Gentle Reader conceived it in his thirsty mind: and Sir Walter Scott, letting down his pitcher into the waters, gave him his first long drink. ...

> But the European War was another matter. It broke in two the life of the nation: and mentally it did exactly the same to the life of literature. The four years were as a gulf fixed between two states of existence. Only the young could cross it. ... Never surely did a generation of creative artists, violently active and alive, find themselves more oddly situated. The Writer was alive; but his Gentle Reader had escaped him. ... The convention of the eternal feminine has changed as much in four years as it usually changes in forty. ...

So the Gentle Reader returned to the writers of the past:

> The Gentle Reader certainly noticed very little difference, as far as literature was concerned, between the rule of Victoria and the rule of Edward—the rule of George Eliot and Trollope or the rule of Galsworthy and Bennett. Lovers of Defoe and Richardson had their Bennett, derived via Charlotte Yonge and George Eliot and Gissing. Galsworthy, derived from Fielding via Trollope and Thackeray, gave them manners and morals.

> Of all the older novelists left today, the most typical is perhaps John Galsworthy, though even he does not altogether preserve the balance between the three main elements. He all but ignores the element of fantasy, and his sense of romance is narrow in expression. He uses the traditive form greatly, but he does not surrender to it: he does not let it use him for its own purposes. There is only one writer of standing at work today who does thus surrender himself. This is Hugh Walpole. ...

Other than to Walpole, the Gentle Reader wondered where he should go for "the old-fashioned tale with the innovation in idea which modernizes it."

The Gentle Reader began to wonder if it was impossible to expect any of the younger writers to write about new ideas in an old-fashioned way. The Gentle Reader sighed in fact for the traditive novel brought up to date. . . .

A nation that is bounded by its traditions is dead: a nation that despises its traditions is damned; but a nation that uses its traditions and adds to its traditions has, in life as in literature, the future of the world in its hands.[34]

In her post-1924 novels Miss Dane wrote for the Gentle Reader. Her first novel, however, published in 1917, possessed naturalistic qualities, and the two following ones bore marks of the Jamesian technique in attempting to dramatize the point of view. *Regiment of Women*, the first novel, is a study of environmental influences and something of a tract against a girl being reared in an exclusively feminine milieu. A schoolgirl falls under the capricious domination of a teacher who subjects her to alternate moods of exultation and despair. After the girl's suicide the author continues the account to show that in the case of another student subjected to the same influences a way out is provided by love for a rather typical male. *Legend* (1919) and *Wandering Stars* (1924) suggest the Jamesian influence. *Legend*, preserving the classical unities, presents the ghoulish scene of a wake where the off-stage dying of a woman novelist affords the opportunity for her intimates to dissect her life. Only a stranger, to whom the views are presented, guesses the real truth—that the novelist was really in love with her dull husband. The eventual appearance of the ghost is a regrettable bit of stage technique. *Wandering Stars*, a play within a play, shows a modern working out of an old story: the neglected wife by evoking the memory of her husband's former ardor manages to fall in love with his incarna-

[34] *Tradition and Hugh Walpole* (New York, Doubleday, Doran & Co., 1929).

tion, while the husband, suspecting his wife of a lover, is moved to win her back.

Wandering Stars is somewhat fantastic, and there is much of the unreal in *Legend*. Katherine Mansfield, for one, was displeased with this new note in Miss Dane's work and wondered why, in *Legend*, Miss Dane had turned aside from life to concentrate her powers upon "reviving, redressing, touching up, bringing up-to-date these puppets of a bygone fashion." Yet this early work lacks much of the romantic extravagance of *The Babylons* (1927) and the spectacular showmanship of *Broome Stages* (1931). In *The Babylons* Miss Dane deals with the old theme of a family curse—not a mental taint but a family devil who preys upon a family for four generations, one woman in each generation. What she succeeds best in doing is to give lively pictures of background—furniture, dresses, manners. But the novel is primarily for those not to be offended by coincidences, gypsies and ghosts, moonlight settings, repeated violent deaths, and the glamor of aristocratic furbishments. *Broome Stages,* another chronicle affair, deals with the devotion of a family of actors to the aggrandizement of their house and the perpetuation of authentic stage traditions. The individual life histories are brimful of drama as the author records the doings of a reckless, passionate, improvident family from the middle of the eighteenth to the beginning of the twentieth century. A rich theatrical background lends atmosphere and interest to the lively narrative.

Hugh Walpole

According to J. B. Priestley, Walpole is "still one of the young enchanted, living in the jolliest of all possible worlds. He has an eager and appreciative rather than a soberly critical intelligence."[35] The uncritical enthusiasm of Walpole's spirit has resulted in dramatic narratives in a wide variety of modes and settings. Says Chavelley, "His opportunism is flagrant. He

---

[35] "Hugh Walpole," *English Journal,* September, 1928.

seems to have espoused simultaneously all the literary fashions of his day."[36] But Walpole tired of the fashions of his day and retreated into those of a bygone era. From *Portrait of a Man with Red Hair* (1925) onward his writings possessed not only the romantic coloration of his earlier novels but became filled with the stock ingredients of romantic narrative—queer folk, picturesque and fantastic environments, tender sentiments, strong emotional scenes, gypsies and scamps and villains, an atmosphere of terror, sudden turns, violence, and death.

Even in his early works, written under the tutelage of Henry James, Walpole was never a conscientious realist. *Mr. Perrin and Mr. Traill* (1911)—American edition *The Gods and Mr. Traill*—might be considered an exposé of an educational system were it not that the rivalry and jealousy of the two teachers is overdrawn for dramatic effect. The life-novel *Fortitude* (1913), labeled "a true and faithful account of the education of an explorer" (treated in Chapter XIII), is written with the glamorous zest of a treasure hunt. Old tricks are employed: a golden-haired girl met by the hero in Cornwall shows up at his London boardinghouse. *The Duchess of Wrexe* (1914) has a certain realistic pattern—the revolt of the younger generation against the domination of the old duchess—yet here as in *Fortitude* a sentimentality for things traditionally English obtrudes. Says Douglas Goldring with proletarian bias,

Like Mr. Henry James, whose influence upon his work is observable, Mr. Walpole has an instinctive fondness for that secret "enclave," now being gradually left stranded because of its reduced circumstances and its obstinacy, which contains "the best people." The core of our social life which he has chosen to explore is a trifle absurd, a trifle pathetic, but at least it is life of a sort. In ten years' time, perhaps, the "hopeless" but rather delightful people who in his pages take such a dominant part in the country's affairs, who belong to the "ruling class," may be pushed altogether out of the limelight. When that happens Mr. Walpole's novels will always be available to remind us of what they were like. ... For Mr. Walpole is charmingly old-

36 *The Modern English Novel*, 219.

fashioned enough to have a liking for duchesses: they really thrill him. And for the moment, his books appeal to those novel readers who also have a liking for duchesses. (The people who are most keenly interested in titles are not housemaids, as it is a popular fallacy to suppose, but the titled.)[37]

Following the influence of James, the strongest influence on Walpole's works was Russian. Perhaps the popularity of the Russian novel at the outbreak of the war moved him to join the Russian Red Cross, when defective eyesight kept him from enlisting in the British military forces. The venture was a fortunate one. Frank Swinnerton records that upon the publication of *The Dark Forest* (1916) Walpole took "unquestioned place as the leader of the then younger generation." Simultaneously Walpole testified to the influence of the Russian novel in England:

> The influence of the French novel, which was at its strongest between the years 1885 and 1895, was toward Realism, and the influence of the Russian novel, which has certainly been very strongly marked in England during the last years, is all toward Romantic-Realism. Such a novel as *The Brothers Karamazov*, such a play as *The Cherry Orchard* are there before us, as the best possible examples. We might say, in a word, that *Karamazov* has, in the England of 1915, taken the place that was occupied, in 1890, by *Madame Bovary*.[38]

The Russian setting provided Walpole with a background upon which he could look without sentimental attachment, and the Russian novel suggested the sounding of depths and terrors in the warfare between good and evil. In *The Dark Forest* (1916) and its sequel, *The Secret City* (1919), extreme forms of disharmony are made vivid only to be resolved into a spiritual tranquillity. Walpole is at his best here for the figures of his imagination need not be tempered by that mixture of good and evil which we are likely to observe in native character.

In the postwar world Walpole lost touch with the current of English fiction. Rebellion was not in his veins. *The Cathedral*

---

[37] *Reputations* (London, Chapman and Hall, 1920).
[38] *Joseph Conrad* (New York, Henry Holt and Co., 1916).

(1922) harks back to Trollope, with a convincing portrayal of a cathedral town and a less convincing portrayal of an archdeacon's defeat. *The Old Ladies* (1924), with a similar setting, sympathetically records the doings of the less important personages within the town. Walpole's method in this novel has been likened to that of Flaubert. Perhaps of his novels it will live the longest.

FRANCIS BRETT YOUNG

is a stylist, a lover of poetry and music, a careful craftsman, a writer delicate yet virile in his sensibilities. He is loved chiefly for his atmospheric stories of Worcestershire and the neighboring counties, but he has also written of seacoast towns, of South Africa, and, with critical bias, of industrial regions. Next to Galsworthy he has created a memorable array of native portraits. Many of his accounts are filled with sentiment and tragedy. There is often artifice in his arrangement of incidents, and once in a while he goes in for melodrama.

The most distinctive of Mr. Young's novels are thematic, and the theme which most appeals to him is Beauty's unavailing struggle. Yet the hopelessness of the struggle but serves to accentuate the importance of Beauty in a world of harsh realities. "Beauty maddens me," says Edward Wills in *The Iron Age* (1916). "I'm parched, thirsty—and it's a quivering image of sweet water. I wish I may never see anything beautiful again." The theme was announced in his first novels, *Undergrowth* (1913) and *Deep Sea* (1914). It was expressed in his critical study of Robert Bridges in 1914 and came to heightened expression in *The Dark Tower* (1915), though even here the author does not drive his conclusion full home. But from *The Dark Tower* down to *Pilgrim's Rest* (1922) his seekers for beauty witness their aspirations wrecked past recall and past consolation.

From this point on, Mr. Young gave expression to a wider variety of interests. *Pilgrim's Rest* becomes a complaint against progress. *Cold Harbour* (1924) is a tale of hypnosis in an atmosphere of nightmare terror. *Portrait of Claire* (1927)—American title *Love is Enough*—presents a charming gentlewoman, with emotions in control, who discovers that "love is the only reality in this fantastic, ironical life." *Key To Life* (1928) declares in favor of loyalty over love. *My Brother Jonathan* (1928) tells of a person, thought dead, who returns to create a tragic family situation (his brother Jonathan has married his girl). *Mr. and Mrs. Pennington* (1931) is social satire, timely, gay, and kept rolling by the presence of a villain.

In the view of the Gentle Reader, Mr. Young's reputation stands or falls with *Portrait of Claire*, which was awarded the James Tait Black Prize. Yet for those who seek in fiction the intensity of an author's reaction to life, *The Young Physician* (1919) will best serve. Written under the influence of Compton Mackenzie (to whom *The Black Diamond*, 1921, was dedicated), it is a life-novel from Edwin's fifteenth year to his disillusionment and flight to sea as a ship's doctor in early maturity. Mr. Young quotes Thomas Traherne, "so that with much ado I was corrupted and made to learn the dirty devices of the world." A more suitable quotation could hardly be found to exemplify the purposes of the book. The educational background parallels Mr. Young's own. The poetic and philosophic Edwin is bullied, shocked, and imposed upon in public school; and he is offended by the gruesome experiences in medical school and in slum surgery. What is tender in his soul remains attached to a frail and delicate mother. As the story progresses, Edwin's protective love for her becomes transferred, with no psychological difficulties, to a sensitive girl whom he would rescue from an ugly world. But Mackenzie's fascination for Beauty enmeshed by Evil comes in to spoil an otherwise good book. Edwin, after a fight with an enemy of school days, tracks him down to Rosie's bedroom. What makes the matter worse is that Edwin knows the enemy to be diseased. His idol shattered, Edwin seeks the open seas.

◄§ XVI §►

DIFFUSION, 1929–1940

THE WAR-NOVEL, 1929–1931

DURING the war there were, of course, many novels about the conflict written by civilians. The less said about these novels the better. Their function was inspirational. What is here referred to as the "war-novel" consists of more or less personal accounts written by those who possessed a close personal remembrance. Strangely enough, the war-novel was delayed for a decade following the cessation of hostilities, for so long as the painful memories of the war persisted, the novelist could not well linger over its harrowing scenes, nor could he in the victory years find a ready public for indictments of inefficiency and waste.

In its first phase the war consciousness found a refuge in sophistication and sex and science. In its second phase, the war-novel, it turned to bitter indictment. Both reactions were the result of the same revolt, the same spiritual anarchy. According to H. M. Tomlinson, who served as a war correspondent and should be informed, the young warriors on returning from France.

lost faith in their neighbors—and that loss is called, by some, a revolt against democratic institutions; they began to think that evil is stronger than the healing powers, and to see progress only as another name for change, generally for the worse. They feared that delicate truth had little chance in a world of huge and arrogant lies. They supposed, in fact, that most people worshipped a god who may be called Dagon, and that Dagon is a gleaming and highly efficient engine of overwhelming power which sets the pace for everything, and compels everybody in the direction of its predestined wheels. This engine, they saw, obliterated whatever got in its way. It went over truth and beauty, and nobody cared. So they gave up. As you know, most of the young men who were in the war and survived, they gave up. They did not believe in anything anymore except that 'might is right'—exactly the lie they thought they had destroyed.[1]

In 1929 and 1930 the war-novel and war-autobiography were the center of British interest. Thereafter, almost suddenly, interest waned. But even for the few years of its continuance, the movement was salutary; the causes of the revolt could now be faced and the revolt itself revaluated. Sophistication was definitely on the wane:

> At one time there was the danger lest all fiction should be dominated by a spirit fundamentally inconsistent with serious imaginative work—a spirit in which the universe is given a quiet snub and a knowing leer. ... Moreover a good omen is to be found in that the public can again bear to read about the war. ... To shrink from considering those years when twenty million perished by their brothers' hands indicated a frivolity in the reader reacting upon the writer, inducing in the latter an excessive introspection, or a meretricious fantasy.[2]

The war-novel brought about a return of interest in the tangible world. And in giving full leeway to the expression of revolt it effectively resolved the residue of the war trauma.

It is true that the war-novel was well started before 1929. C. E. Montague's *Disenchantment* (1922), *Fiery Particles* (1923), *Rough Justice* (1926) had been well received. But Mr. Montague was not in revolt, and a tone of restrained heroism pervaded his writing. Readers were interested in the art of his narration and the discreet idealization of English sentiment and English virtues, and they were pleased that the author was

---

[1] *War Books* (a lecture given at Manchester University, February 15, 1929; published by The Rowfant Club, Cleveland, Ohio, 1930), 10.

[2] Harwood, "Some Tendencies in Modern Fiction."

not too precise in his descriptions of pain. Ford Madox Ford, also, had written some remarkable war-novels, *Some Do Not* (1924), *No More Parades* (1925), *A Man Could Stand Up*, (1926). But Ford's series concerns the fortunes, marital as well as martial, of an amusing and lovable Mr. Tietjens, who is also shy and awkward and generous and frightfully imposed upon. Major Tietjens is at times a charming old fogy, and his determination to get his job done savors of the heroic; he would make good reading anywhere. R. H. Mottram's *Spanish Farm* (1924) contains an oblique portrayal of the war since the center of interest is a French farming woman; and his second war-novel, *Sixty-Four, Ninety-Four!* (1925), is chiefly remarkable for its description of the strange semibarbarous shantytown civilization on the Western Front. Herbert Read's *In Retreat* (1925) is only thirty pages long.

The war-novels of the years 1929–31 are distinctive for the fact that they reveal the gruesome details of the carnage. Equally distinctive is the fact that they sound a protest against inefficiency and waste—and, by implication or otherwise, against war itself as a way of solving international problems. So Edmund Blunden's *Undertones of War* (1929) gave vivid descriptions of "mangled heads and half-naked bodies" while it berated the lack of correlation, the dull stultification of routine, the stupidity, and general confusion which attended the British effort. Robert Graves's *Good-bye to All That* (1930), which the author called an autobiography, reveals his disillusionment from the days of 1914 when as a young man of nineteen he swallowed the war whole. With painful candor he strips war of its glory and romance and gives an unmistakable impression of hopelessness. Richard Aldington's *Death of a Hero* (1929) revolves about an incident of virtual madness induced by death and destruction and, like *Roads to Glory* (1930), protests against the ideal of sacrifice. Siegfried Sassoon's *Memoirs of an Infantry Officer* (1930), although softened by reticences of a fox-hunting squire, has yet a pacifist tendency in showing the defeat of youth. H. M. Tomlinson's *All Our*

Yesterdays (1930) castigates the blindness and folly of the struggle, and C. R. Benstead in *Retreat* (1930) gives an effective indictment of politicians. Other writers, many of them less well known, stress the vices and brutalities of a war of "mud, monotony, and misery," of "blood, mud, brothels, drink, and field punishment," of terror and ghastly experiences: *Patriot's Progress* (1930), by Henry Williamson; *No Man's Land* (1930), by Vernon Bartlett; *Medal Without Bar* (1930), by R. Blaker; *Brass Hat in No Man's Land* (1930), by F. P. Crozier.

If England of the Munich days was mentally unprepared for war, no doubt the bitter protest of the war-novel had something to do with the situation. What the war novelist wanted was no more war. Said Mr. Tomlinson in summing up the tendency,

> We are losing our old dreary fatalism over whatever our governors, hidden behind an indifferent and cheerful public, may prepare for us, and are protesting, with noticeable dislike, about being dragged into another obscene crime against the intelligence like the last world-war. We know that the pomp and majesty of it, the sombre and throaty calls to national honour and great traditions, in the light of later knowledge, is all as ugly and distressing as the thoroughly sincere fight for nuts in the zoological department where nuts are enjoyed.[3]

PERIODICAL COMMENT IN THE THIRTIES

After protest had spent itself in the war-novel and war-autobiography, despair itself grew mild. The outburst of undisguised revolt at the specific causes of disillusionment served to clear up the psychosis. Writers began to wonder what it was, outside revolt, that they really had to say. Readers became less restrictive in their demands and abnormally sensitive to new interests. Moreover Lawrence had died and Huxley was groping.

[3] *War Books*, 10.

A wave of tempered traditionalism swept over England. The English countryside, the details of regional variation, the pageant of successive generations received new treatment—with alarming revelations and a Dostoievski flavor, as in the case of J. C. Powys; with discreet suggestions of sentiment in such writers as Phyllis Bentley and Storm Jameson. Middle-class urban life in its less-known aspects was subjected to fresh and impersonal treatment by Louis Golding. H. M. Tomlinson mixed stream of consciousness and Conrad with his own love of the sea. Elizabeth Bowen followed Henry James in painstaking treatment of the finer sentiments. Cronin and Greenwood and Hanley showed a naturalistic concern with social problems. Priestley re-created with Dickensian gusto a picturesque and vivid humanity. Richard Aldington continued to express the war consciousness in his indictment of middle-class ideals. H. E. Bates, with some care for naturalistic logicality, reflected the influence of Hardy and Lawrence and Chekhov. O'Flaherty passionately pleaded the wrongs of Ireland. American novelists reached an all-time high in popularity, and the English detective novel began to take on the dimensions of big business.

We are too close to the thirties to discern a main line of development—if indeed there is one. What seems evident is a wide divergence, and a mingling of the techniques and conceptions of the previous decade. The thirties were essentially years of assimilation. Writers sought new interests rather than new ideas.

Sean O'Faolain, writing in 1935, expressed the hope that the future of the English novel would lie with those regionalists who wrote from a standpoint not imprisoned within tradition. But he considered as "most important of all" a group of novelists whom he classed as individualists—Lawrence, Strong, Garnett, Faulkner, Maugham, and Caldwell. Mr. O'Faolain was considerably alarmed. These writers express chaos rather than integration. A great literature demands some solid foundation. The conclusion was therefore in order: "We have unmade our souls and we have unmade the novel—there is no lack of courage or talent in all that: we shall not remake the novel until we remake our souls in the novel."[4]

Mr. O'Faolain's conclusion is worthy of emphasis. "We shall not remake the novel until we remake our souls in the novel." His statement is here quite similar to that of Storm Jameson:

> The difficulty, the intense difficulty, of the contemporary novelist is to form an adequate conception of life at this moment when everything is changing. . . . It is perhaps impossible for any contemporary novelist to draw far enough back from what is happening to see it clearly.[5]

Mrs. Jameson then stresses Lawrence's conception of civilization as being that of an "uprooted tree with its roots in the air." England of the thirties found no certainties, and therefore no power. Is this why its fiction, according to English critics, lacked depth, profundity, punch? Cyril Connolly neglected to provide the answer as he launched into an indictment with left-wing bias:

> *Thinness of material.* English life is on the whole without adventure or variety, 90 per cent. of English authors come from the mandarin class, the experiences from which both sexes can draw are limited to three or four, a peaceful childhood, a public school education, a university, a few years of London or the provinces in which to get a job, a wife, a house and some children. Material for one book, perhaps, which publishers and the need to earn one's living may drag out to three or four. A rigorous class system blankets down all attempts to enlarge these barriers. The English mandarin simply can't get at pugilists, gangsters, speakeasies, negroes, and even if he should he would find them absolutely without the force and colour of the American equivalent. . . .

> *Lack of Power.* This is hard to define, but I mean lack of both intellectual power, of any mastery of the situation, any real maturity (such as is found in all great novelists, although as different as Tolstoi and

---

[4] "Pigeon-Holing the English Novel," *London Mercury*, December, 1935.
[5] *The Novel in Contemporary Life* (Boston, The Writer, Inc., 1938), 6.

Henry James), and of narrative power, of punch, concision, dramatic sense. This is the most hopeless thing of all about the English novelist —one hardly ever finds a trace of it in the younger writers, although it almost knocks one over in, for instance, the longer stories of Maugham. I think one reason for its absence is that the English novelist never establishes a respect-worthy relationship with his reader. The American novelists, Hemingway, Hammett, Faulkner, Fitzgerald, O'Hara, for instance, write instinctively for men of their own age, men who enjoy the same things; 'look, go slow, don't miss this,' they seem to say, 'this will interest you—maybe you've been in this actual place or had the same thing happen to you.' It is an intimacy, which at its worst degenerates into a horrible dogginess, like *Razzle,* but in general brings out everything that is natural, easy, and unrepressed in the author as can only friendly communion with a contemporary. English novels seem always to be written for superiors or inferiors, older or younger people, or for the opposite sex. ... I suppose the climate is to blame, there seems something in it that gelds and arranges all English writers, substituting timidity and caution for freedom and curiosity, hence all the flatness, dullness, feebleness of the novel, and hence, also, above all, the stagnation.[6]

If there is any need for testimony of a powerful American influence, the above quotation will serve. It is directly in line with what Ford Madox Ford told me in 1937: "There are no important English novelists at the present time. The war killed the men who would have written great novels. The best novels are now written in the middle states of America." Reacting against constraint and fashionable constriction, English readers turned their attention oversea. A critic for the *English Review* (1935) saw, rather hopefully, "a gruff and northern" revival of romance:

> Mr. Hemingway is the most notable novelist of this type. ... He is outwardly rough, uncouth, a swaggerer, one who knows all about life, a he-man; but underneath he is shy, sentimental, thinks the best of everybody, is strongly emotional; if he hits a man on the jaw it is that he may not weep on his shoulder. To display his inward feelings explicitly, to define them, would be unmanly; he muffles his emotions

6 "London Diary," *New Statesman*, November 23, 1935.

in set phrases, he writes with his thumbs, so to speak, yet sensibility is palpatant in his gruffest sentences. ... With him, almost for the first time since the Icelandic sagas, romance becomes healthy. ... *A Farewell to Arms* is an important book because it deprives the superior person of any reason for despairing; it is important to the ordinary man because it shows that every man is a potential hero.

Romance that is gruff and northern runs counter to Mrs. Woolf, so the critic includes her in the general movement by saying that she is romantic in a womanly way, "and that all that wit and whimsy and waywardness is the womanly equivalent of a deeper, darker, more passionate stuff that a man asks from a romantic writer." By way of a parting shot he suggests that Mrs. Woolf is "delightful when she writes about books, scarcely so delightful when she writes them."[7]

But American fiction was not the sole cause for discontent with the local product. Writing in the following year, 1936, Elizabeth Bowen expressed the regret that English readers limited the scope of a writer's work. The novelist cannot interest the public in social movements. Class, she says, is a subject totally unpopular,

> There is little attempt to write up the class struggle palatably; probably it would be impossible to do so. Only exceptional novels show it by implication. ... There are startlingly few things that the public cares to hear about. Sex, or love, is a popular subject because self-love and the private imagination luxuriates around it. Adventure, being fantasy, is safe ground. Children, animals, and the upper class appeal to tenderness and to curiosity: it is impossible for the reader to document himself fully around them, so that the writer has full scope. ... It is not that subjects do not exist, but that writers are not empowered to tackle them. At present the greater number of novels and plays are claustrophobic—one feels, as in a dream, a ghastly, unreal constriction. Modern French and Russian novels are giving the lead toward a greater plainness and vitality: is there any reason why that should not be followed here?[8]

[7] G. S. Fraser, "The Revival of Romance," July, 1935.
[8] "What We Need in Writing," *Spectator*, November 20, 1936.

In 1937 another critic for the *Spectator* protested that a feminine view dominated English fiction:

Publishers, booksellers, and librarians tell us that women read far more novels than men. It is not merely that women have time for reading, but that, on the whole, men have given up modern novels. Stupid men find them too hard; clever men just do not read them. From my own knowledge I should say that the average man of the professional class does not finish (though he may begin) more than two or three novels a year. . . . Is it also true that most novels today are written by women for women or, at all events, that the fashion and demand are made by women, and that the men are following the lead? Has novel-writing become something like tapestry-weaving in the mind, so fine and subtle that women can deal with it more deftly than men? Consider Mrs. Virginia Woolf's novels; there is a sharpness, a sensibility about them that you will not find in the work of any living man. . . . We have lost the art of describing action, or, rather, we have left it to the persons who compose films.[9]

William Plomer attempted (1936) to answer the question "whether there have been any dominant fashions in the subject-matter of the novel?"

Clearly we cannot ignore the abdication of sex in favor of crime. This has no doubt been accounted for by the fact that in everyday life it is much easier than it used to be to get away with sexual indulgences (the erstwhile "fate worse than death" having been discovered to be a healthy pleasure), but murder, theft, and blackmail still remain rather chancy occupations.

Otherwise Mr. Plomer speaks of Priestley's "humanity, energy and liberal sympathies," and he points to the popularity of regional fiction.[10]

John Strachey in deploring the present state of fiction (1938) praised the detective story because "here are books which the authors evidently enjoyed writing and the readers unaffectedly enjoy reading." With communist bias he suggests that the detective story is a mild, innocent drug "against the fate which has overtaken us." He concludes,

[9] E. L. Woodward, "Marginal Comments," April 9, 1937.
[10] "The Contemporary Novel; Its Subject-Matter," *London Mercury*, October, 1936.

To say that the detective story is the only vigorous, thriving branch of English fiction, is the most bitter criticism of English fiction which one can make. It means that they, the English writers, and we the English readers, cannot bear anything but the most complete form of "escape literature" which can possibly be imagined.

Otherwise Mr. Strachey finds hope in a group—mostly of young proletarians—who write "straight narrative fiction as against psychological analysis." He continues,

> It may well be that it is in this beginning that hope for the future of the English novel lies. There are some young novelists—Mr. Arthur Calder-Marshall, Mr. Rex Warner, Mr. Day Lewis, Mr. Norman Collins, for instance, most, but not all, of whom have a pronounced sociological slant—whom the critics are watching with the liveliest expectations.

Of the highbrow novels Mr. Strachey says, "They are, to a certain point at any rate, true pictures of the kind of people whom they describe—and there seems not to be the slightest reason why they should have been written." He makes one exception—the novels of Elizabeth Bowen: "These are the classical descriptions of the banality and despair of the English middle classes."[11]

Was the English novel of the thirties in as bad a state as its critics testified?

No. As we have seen from the analyses of periodical comment in previous chapters, destructive criticism prevails even while many good novels are written, and it often merely foreshadows change. We are, nevertheless, concerned with the tenor of criticism in order both to evaluate past developments and to see the direction of effort at the moment war intervened.

On the whole it may be observed that no controversy raged during the thirties. There was no sharp conflict of ideas even though there was protest. The whole front was comparatively quiet except for the work of sappers, the distribution of propa-

---

[11] "The Golden Age of English Detection," *Saturday Review of Literature*, January 7, 1939.

ganda leaflets, raids, and the concentration of forces. No new operations were definitely in progress, but there were the beginnings of many new operations.

Of these a left-wing movement seems most important. It is foreshadowed in the democratic urge of Mr. Connolly, in Elizabeth Bowen's despair with an effete order of things, in Strachey's communistic derision. Novels of James Hanley and Walter Greenwood gave the movement impetus.

In a previous chapter we traced the hostile critical reaction against Virginia Woolf. In spite of this reaction, Mrs. Woolf continued to be read, and her knack for making the trivial seem momentous was admired more than the books themselves. Her influence persisted. Yet in the thirties we witness a general reaction against technical dexterity and coterie fiction. Discriminating critics join with everyone else in demanding punch and action and a vital treatment of vital interests. It is significant that at this moment a critic echoes George Moore's protest, 1885, that fiction is written for women and that men do not read novels any more. Does the criticism suggest that there will be a masculine reaction?

In all probability it does, but to the literary historian it suggests that a long and involved transition has come to a close. The urge to see "truth" and to tell it has passed through successive stages. With the naturalists Englishmen explored social problems and national institutions; in the life-novel they dissected personal problems and sought to express a philosophy of living; in the days of postwar bitterness they entered the special "worlds" of various writers in whose distortions of truth they found an atmosphere congenial to despair. With the impressionists they entered a non-world, devoid of values, and with Joyce and Mrs. Woolf and the Huxley of *Eyeless in Gaza* they became aware of the mind's infinite complexity and the separate planes of emotional experience involved in thought and action. A maudlin, behavioristic "truth" emerged which was small consolation, even to its authors. Afterwards came a catharsis. The truth all had fled from, the gruesome reality of war, was faced, and anarchism itself was confronted fairly—nay, re-experienced. Finally the conviction that reality might take myriad forms was less certain. It seemed worth while to inquire. It seemed, somehow, less certain that earth's base was built on stubble. On what base, then, was earth built? It was all right to say you didn't know. It was also all right to inquire.

Technique similarly passed through stages of involution. In the days of naturalism, plot and subplot were replaced by a theme taken from life and this, for a time, outmoded by a spiritual life history. Afterwards came the fortuitous association of conflicting temperaments, the marshaling of protagonists, the subjective altering of probability for the enunciation of a special view of the universe. Stream of consciousness followed and then, in the war-novel, a veiled or unveiled autobiography. But a new technique did not replace former techniques and, in the post–1930 years, a general fusing, a mixture of this and that, was noticeable. Anything or everything was possible, but in the late thirties we see a reversion to conventional form, refreshed by the experimentation of late years.

WRITERS OF THE THIRTIES

RICHARD ALDINGTON

wrote probably the best English novel about the war, *Death of a Hero* (1929). Captain George Winterbourne, maddened by the death and destruction of war, rushes into a stream of bullets and is killed. The prologue shows the indifferent reception of the news by father, mother, wife, and mistress. Thereafter the events of Winterbourne's life are taken up in order—his Victorian rearing, his bohemian life as a painter, his part in the war. It is a bitter novel, savage, wrongheaded, and ruthless. In it Mr. Aldington announces the ideas which were to dominate his fiction: he would regenerate the system which made war possible; he would attack middle-class ideals, chivalry, and noble gestures; he would castigate women, Victorian and modern; he would emphasize the lasting beauty of wind, sky, sea, and heath.

The Aldington novel is obviously subjective, obviously the expression of the author's indignation. Mr. Aldington, a distinguished poet, was effective through his intensity even when his technique was rather clumsy, and he continued to express in fiction the postwar bitterness long after other writers had abandoned it. When in *Women Must Work* (1934) he turned to the futility of feminism, he was scarcely successful. There is little merit in *Seven Against Reeves* (1938), a comic presentation of a submerged husband.

Roads to Glory (1931) consists of thirteen war stories based largely upon the author's experience and reactions. Primarily the stories are dominated by disgust and a sense of futility.

All Men Are Enemies (1933) likewise reveals the war psychosis. It is an attack upon class consciousness, business, "social personalities," the constraints of conventional marriage; and it dimly reveals Anthony's search for a simple, tangible happiness which is somehow linked up with an early love, Katha, with whom he lost touch during the years of war. Anthony's search is for a way of life:

"Try to understand this—my moral world, my interior life have collapsed. My present life is purely reflex, almost vegetable. . . . I don't want an ideology, I want my sensibility again, but I want it healthy and invulnerable. . . . I'm sick of death and dead bodies, sick of cold loneliness, and honour. The touch of that living woman's body gives me life. . . ." In bread and wine he tasted sunlight and rain, the hard berry of wheat and the firm pulp of the grape, the fragrant essence of clean earth.

But Mr. Aldington seems unwilling to trust Anthony's exposition of his view. In an Author's Note he explains the "finer fuller life" in words that might be written by Lawrence:

It is the life of the here and now, the life of the senses, the life of the deep instinctive forces. If we do not live in these we scarcely live at all. We have been taught so long that life must have some exterior end and justification that we have forgotten that living is itself enough, that to be alive and conscious is itself an excellent and miraculous experience. ... How easily and carelessly we abandon real life! Our sense of smell is atrophied; our ears are corrupted by urban noises, overworked by radio and telephone; we eat our bread without tasting the sunlight, the rich earth, the sweet air which created it; our sight is degraded in a thousand ways: and we are afraid of touch, which we have been taught to consider dangerous, base, and indecent.

Very Heaven (1937) continues the attack upon the spiritual bankruptcy of the world.

LIAM O'FLAHERTY

is a native of the Aran Islands, where, it is said, patriotic Irishmen go to learn their native language. Over the Norman Irish gateway in Galway, across the bay from Aran, there is an inscription: "From the Furious O'Flahertys Good Lord Deliver Us."

One of the most lurid and passionate of writers, Mr. O'Flaherty has the virtues and the vices of his native land. He is tempestuous and devoted to liberty, yet his motives are chaotic and his rage is often a matter of impulse. He has written epics of the wrongs of Ireland only to turn vengefully on individual Irishmen. Some mention of his early life is necessary in order to understand him.

In August, 1918, he was invalided out of the army. With five pounds as a start, which he raised by gambling to twenty pounds, he went to London, where he lived a roving and needy life for two years. He was successively brewery foreman, hotel porter, and clerk in a business house. At this stage of his life he showed an interest in communism, for it seemed to offer something more virile and sane than the old morality.

Disillusioned by "a sterile and inglorious war," he signed up on a boat going to South America. At Rio he abandoned the ship and remained in the port until he read the news of the founding of the Irish Republic. Thereupon he returned to Ireland, only to discover on his arrival that he had lost all interest in the affairs of the Republic. A trip to the orient was next in order. O'Flaherty worked his way on one boat and then on another. Afterwards he went from Smyrna to Gibraltar to Canada to the United States. He worked in Canada as a laborer; in New York as a porter at the Knickerbocker Hotel. Gradually he lost his sense of rebellion and became cured of the war. He decided that not the war but nature had given him his restlessness. His thoughts returned to his native shores. What place could be more desolate than this outcast land! He would make his soul dance on her rough stones. He would tune his song to the rhythm of the great sea that beat her coast, and he would emerge better fortified than if his own arms alone carried the burdens of his soul.

The author's writings reflect the chaos of his life. There is no philosophy, no integration. He has little liking for his countrymen, little faith in humanity. A typical figure emerges in many guises, "a creature more animal than human, cunning, sly, with just enough leisure and intelligence to drink himself into a mood for crime." The type is epitomized by Gypo in *The Informer* but is also found with little change in *The Assassin* and *The House of Gold*. Yet many of the novels contain more complicated types, and where these appear we have "melodramas of the conscience," which suggest Dostoievski. Father McMahon renounces Lily in favor of the priesthood and after Lily's unfortunate marriage is whirled in the vortex of self-scorn, drunkenness, hypocrisy, and histrionics (*Thy Neighbor's Wife*). Brian Crosbie, physical coward and religious mystic, achieves martyrdom in an exciting soul-struggle (*The Martyr*). A young Catholic fanatic is driven to murder a prostitute as an act of purification but, after arranging for suspicion to fall on another, realizes that he has committed common murder with jealousy as its motive (*The Puritan*).

The passion and violence of O'Flaherty is but dimly suggested in the themes of his novels. He spoke no empty words when he resolved to tune his song to the rhythm of the great sea that beat his native shores. Everywhere there is primitive physical violence, reckless impulse, greed, and cruelty; and the full force of the author's dramatic fervor is exerted by riveting our attention upon physical manifestation of the strongest emotions. Take, for example, the scene in which Red John, gone mad because of the infidelity of his wife, waits stark-naked beside the door to attack the seducer. The man on coming out

saw Red John standing naked by the wall. He stood with wide-open mouth and staring eyes. His face got cold and then turned white. His nostrils distended. He stared into Red John's eyes and Red John stared into his.... Then Red John yelled and tore his jaws open to the utmost with his two hands, as if trying to vomit his fear in the intensity of his yell. He drew up his right leg to his buttock and struck against the wall with his sole. "Go away," he screamed, "go away; you are going to kill me ..."

Although naturalistic in his view of human depravity, in his brutality, and in his insistence upon physical reactions, Mr. O'Flaherty is too forceful to be pessimistic, too violent and too melodramatic to present us with a study of humanity. His distortions are those of the expressionist. His anger at the priesthood crops out everywhere. Yet his success is due to this very intensity, to an unerring sense of dramatic fitness, and to his ability to proceed with the straightforward telling of his story.

H. M. TOMLINSON

in his tribute to Conrad suggests the influence that dominated his own writing:

Somehow, life seems justified only by some proved friends and the achievements of good men who are still with us. Once we were so assured of the opulence and spiritual vitality of mankind that the loss of a notable figure did not seem to leave us any poorer. But today, when it happens, we feel a distinct diminution of our light. That has been dimmed of late years by lusty barbarians, and we look now to the few manifestly superior minds in our midst to keep our faith in humanity sustained. The certainty that Joseph Conrad was somewhere in Kent was an assurance and a solace in years that have not been easily borne.[12]

As in the case of Conrad, something of the sea's enigmatic expanse pervades Mr. Tomlinson's spirit. Thus Katherine Mansfield expresses her view of Mr. Tomlinson:

> We feel that he is calm, not because he has renounced life, but because he lives in the memory of that solemn gesture with which the sea blesses or dismisses or destroys her own. The breath of the sea sounds in all his writings. Whether he tells us of an accident at a minehead, or the front-line trenches in Flanders, or children dancing, or books to read at midnight—if we listen it is there and we are not deceived. There is a quality of remoteness and detachment in his work, but it is never because he has turned aside from life. ... He is always that foreigner with keen wondering glance, thinking over the strangeness of it all.[13]

There is nostalgia in Mr. Tomlinson's writing, a yearning for the days of "imaginative exploration and experiment." The present offers little to him:

> Men were entangled enough with their costly and elaborate contrivances; they had made an ugly prison for themselves and locked it from the inside. What did they proudly call their muck, brought about by their ingenuity? Civilization. Away with it! They were fouling their star.[14]

A glance at the snow on Helicon and a vision of marble temples is enough to send the architect Travers from a civilized present to the ends of the earth. He has no compunction about leaving his wife in the hands of the man who shall win her, and much of his roving is without purpose. But the conclusion expresses his hatred of civilization. He allows himself to be blown up in

---

[12] "On the Death of Joseph Conrad," *New Statesman,* June 11, 1927.
[13] *Novels and Novelists* (New York, Alfred A. Knopf, Inc., 1930), 10.
[14] *The Snows of Helicon* (New York, Harper & Bros., 1933).

a temple on Colonna after technicians have decided that the site is needed for a power station. And what is *The Snows of Helicon* but a flight from folly to the vast reaches of the soul?

Gallions Reach (1927) is an earlier, less thematic work. Here the roving of Colet is the result of a tangible danger. Colet embarks on a ship because he has murdered his heedless, moneygrubbing employer for no other reason than that he heartily disapproved of him. He is wrecked in the Indian Ocean and later has terrible experiences in the Malay jungle. From these he emerges with the determination to go back to England and face the music. According to Rebecca West, the book should have ended with the jungle scenes; a great natural force "need not buffet man about to make him stagger but can do it with its silence and immobility." She concludes:

> The motive of the non-neurotic writer, as Mr. Tomlinson shows, is to reconcile by understanding and appreciation the disorder of life with the order he knows by experience as an established fact within himself. Perhaps this makes us a little envious of him.[15]

All Our Yesterdays (1930) is something more than a war-novel, since it sketches in panorama the greed and corruption of international policy from 1900 to 1914 as well as the culminating folly of the war.

The Tomlinson novel progresses, as does the Conrad novel, through glimpses of action. In the forefront is the consciousness of the chief character, the obsessions and visions of his disorientated mind. A mood is evoked but never described. It is by reason of the mood that the outlines of the characters are blurred, that their voices all sound alike, that their decisions are dim and their courses uncharted. All must fit into the loose indirection of the author's drift.

JOHN COWPER POWYS

is a disciple of the great Russians—and in particular of Dostoievski. He feels that *The Idiot, The Possessed, The*

---

[15] *The Strange Necessity* (New York, Doubleday, Doran & Co., 1928), 264.

Brothers Karamazof, as well as "King Lear," express best "the heroic grandeur possible to real human persons." Like the Russians he cares little for the perfection of "form" in the novel: "The soul of man has depths which can only be fathomed by an art that breaks every rule of the formalists and transgresses every technical law. . . . No, I am all for the moralists the prophets the preachers the logus-utterers the philosophers as against this detestable fuss about people's 'art.' . . . My writings—novels and all—are simply so much propaganda, as effective as I can make it, for my philosophy of life. It is the prophecy and poetry of an organism that feels itself in possession of certain magical secrets that it enjoys communicating. . . . I love it when a novel is thick with the solid mass of earth-life, and when its passions spring up volcano-like like glowing pits and bleeding craters of torn convulsed materials."

These selections from Powys' *Autobiography* indicate the subjective nature of his writings and suggest that his central figures are only extensions of his personality. They have the mental conflicts, the phobias, the aversions, the aesthetic delights of their author. If they hate God, it is because the atrocities of the world have made Mr. Powys hostile. If they disbelieve in Christian love, it is because Mr. Powys felt himself supported by Nietzsche and Lawrence in the view, and because he believed that "Dostoievski himself was doubtful about it." If cruelty is dramatically presented, it is because Mr. Powys felt that cruelty was unforgivable and should be punished. And if at length a character makes some order out of chaos, it is because Mr. Powys admires "a character that is a rod of iron to itself and a well-spring of tenderness and pity to others; a character that forces itself to be happy in itself, blames no one but itself, and compels itself to clear away obstacles from the path to happiness for every organism it encounters."

The J. C. Powys novel possesses several distinguishing characteristics. One is that the author has an uncanny perception of

the *genius loci*, the underlying psychic forces that are associated with the "soul" of a place. And the characters are closely
integrated with the atmosphere. They breathe its air, feed upon
its sights and sounds, and would be native to no other region.

Another quality is that J. C. Powys is fascinated and
repelled by physical passion. The author, who confesses to
"a morbid fastidiousness, a super-refined, almost *maidenly* de-
testation of the grosser aspects of normal sexuality," fills a
whole countryside with violence. When we seek the explanation, we find it in the author's confession: "my peculiar saurian
lust, so insatiable and so impersonal, was more like a mad
specialized craving, than like the natural bubbling-over of the
great amorous instinct that makes the world go round."

Ducdame (1925) deals with the influence the dead exercise
over the living. An exhausted and neurotic aristocracy hears
commands from the tomb. The intimate relationship between
Rook Ashover and Lexie Ashover recalls the affection of the
author for his brother Llewelyn. A sensitivity to the changing
moods of earth, a poetic exaltation, pervades the book.

In *Wolf Solent* (1929) Wolf is tormented by the complexities of his nature, by his conception of the God-Devil, by the
mixture of good and evil within himself, by the diverse influences of Gerda, Christie, and his mother. In his extremity
he finds that he has lost Gerda and Christie and everything
he supposed necessary to his happiness. But suddenly it occurs
to him that in the past his desires and affections but served
to bind him, and that now he is free:

In the recesses of his consciousness he was aware that a change had
taken place within him, a rearrangement, a readjustment of his ultimate vision, from which he could never again altogether recede. ...
That sense of a supernatural struggle going on in the abysses, with the
good and the evil so sharply opposed, had vanished from his mind. ...
What was left to him now was his body. Like the body of a tree or a
fish or an animal it was; and his hands and his knees were like
branches or paws or fins! And floating around his body was his
thought the "I am I" against the world. This "I am I" included his

new purpose and included his will towards his new purpose. "There is no limit to the power of my will," he thought, "as long as I use it for two uses only ... to forget and to enjoy! ... My will can do anything when I limit it to 'forget ... enjoy.'"

A Glastonbury Romance (1932) differs from the "personal" novels of J. C. Powys in that the village of Glastonbury is the subject of the story, and the author has purported to give, in one thousand pages, the whole life of the village. The central conflict is between those who want to commercialize the village and those who want to preserve its traditional quality. Yet the novel is not so simple as its theme suggests. It is colorful, mystic, and sometimes maniacal. There are miracle-workings, communist uprisings, revolutionary demonstrations, and such a combination of manias, occult influences, and sex obsessions as only J. C. Powys can conceive. "In each apparent saint is the potential sinner, in each apparently faithful wife the potential harlot."[16]

L. A. G. STRONG

is a literary descendant of Hardy and Phillpots. He has written of eastern Ireland, the western Highlands, and Dartmoor with lyrical understanding, and in his later novels he has integrated his characters with the atmosphere. The feeling of a region permeates the story. Says Mr. Strong of his typical procedure,

I see a new novel as a landscape at first, with hills and perhaps a seacoast and bays and promontories. There are one or two clouds obscuring features of the picture. Presently the clouds began to clear away, and then I have the main events, represented by the main landmarks.

Besides his tendency to saturate his pages with atmospheric description, Mr. Strong is notable for his use of dialect and quaint turns of phrase, the humor and human quality of his

[16] R. H. Ward, *The Powys Brothers* (London, John Lane The Bodley Head, Ltd., 1935), 50.

peasants, and the alternation of idyl and violence in his accounts. He has little regard for probability even though he does not, like Hardy, use an involved plot structure. He chooses rather to present a grim opposition of interests. In *Dewer Rides* (1929) an ill-starred pair of lovers are forced to a long engagement which gradually drives the man to impulsive roughness and to offenses that are fatal to the relationship. *The Brothers* (1932) contrasts two fishermen: the kindly but slow-witted giant Fergus with the wily coward Peter. As the story progresses from youth to old age, drama is furnished by a rivalry that develops with the adoption into the family of the orphan Mary. *Seven Arms* (1935) takes us back to Scotland of a hundred years ago, where only Gaelic is spoken. Jeannie, the stronger of twin sisters, dominates her rebellious sister to the verge of the grave.

J. B. PRIESTLEY

Before writing *The Good Companions* (1929), Mr. Priestley had written *Benighted*, something of a tale of terror and love-making, and he had collaborated with Hugh Walpole in *Farthing Hall*. He had written seven books of light, chatty essays; and he had published a half-dozen volumes of critical studies, handling English writers of the past in a sympathetic and conservative manner. There was plenty of buoyancy and vitality in all this writing, there was much downright competence, and there was absolutely nothing new. When Mr. Priestley was twenty-nine, six years before he wrote *The Good Companions*, he made a clean break with prevailing tendencies of the contemporary novel and affirmed his loyalty to the writers of a less critical past:

If I am reading for pleasure, I rarely take up a modern novel. The fact is, modern novels, our serious, intellectual, satirical novels, terrify me. I do not let it be known. Indeed, I have never confessed it before, but it is the solemn truth—they terrify me. ... Our novelists frighten me because they are both omniscient and uncharitable, which no one else ever was. I do not mind those who attack the industrial system or slum landlords (though I never read them) because I do not happen to be either a factory owner or a slum landlord myself, and so their onslaughts pass over my head. It is the others, those who hold up the mirror to ordinary society, who always leave me so dazed and apprehensive that I have given up reading them, at least for my pleasure. They fasten upon the smallest details of conduct in ordinary social life, and make everything appear to be so terribly significant that they make me positively afraid of going out and mixing with my fellow creatures. They seem to have access to social codes entirely unknown to me. Everyone is weighed in balances infinitely delicate, and mysteriously found wanting. . . . They serve up everyone with that bitter sauce of theirs; their wives (or husbands), their parents, children, friends, neighbors, landladies, shopkeepers and all . . . they will curse you for a clumsy swindler if you are in business, politics, or a profession, and set you down as a neurotic weakling if you are an artist. . . . They cannot hope to entertain us with their poor, halting tales, so they have given up trying, and prefer to frighten us so thoroughly that we shall not even dare to stop reading them.[17]

And so, convinced that "our contemporaries enjoy nobody in their books," Mr. Priestley expressed the desire to "escape into the clean open air of a genuine tale." He plainly preferred the novelists of even a distant past: "Our older novelists, whom I read with increasing pleasure, dealt with normal people simply as normal people, and presented their humorous, odd and eccentric personages as such, and enjoyed them, and consequently make us enjoy them to this day."[18]

The welcome given to *The Good Companions* testified to the fact that a very large number of Englishmen were interested in good-fellowship, pathos, invention, and lucidity. The popular reaction was well expressed by St. John Adcock,

I am so tired of reading, in the way of business, such a lot of this pretentious stuff which can scarcely pass for novel with any but precocious and unwholesome schoolboys, that no doubt I was ready for a change, and I had not read far into *The Good Companions* of Mr.

[17] *I for One* (London, John Lane The Bodley Head, Ltd., 1930), 119–23.
[18] *Ibid*.

J. B. Priestley before I began to feel that I had escaped out of the conventional unconventionality and stuffy atmosphere of that half-world into the varied, vigorous life of love and toil, of humor and sadness, goodness, badness, cruelty, kindness, misery and happiness that makes the whole world such an infinitely miscellaneous, troublesome, interesting and more decent place to live in.[19]

The Good Companions, a semipicaresque novel, concerns the fortunes of three sharply contrasted people who rescue a stranded group of players from insolvency and, in spite of vicissitudes, lead the company to success; thereafter disaster falls upon the troupe, which turns out all to the best for most of the members. This hearty tale, optimistic on the whole, evidently won for Mr. Priestley the kind of acclaim that he did not favor. He became positively angry when people hailed him as a Good Companion. Later he found it necessary to declaim against the virtues credited to both his characters and himself:

> The people in question were not idyllically good-natured and self-sacrificing. (Except by comparison with some of the monsters that pass as characters now in fiction.) ... They were an ordinary set of fairly decent mummers. Sometimes they were jealous of one another, let one down, bickered and quarreled and got drunk, were silly and stupid. There was nothing astonishingly noble about them. ... My countenance does not radiate faith and optimism. Nobody rushes to me for comfort and cheer. My outlook tends to be pessimistic.[20]

Surprising is Mr. Priestley's disavowal of any Dickens influence: "I have, like any sensible reader, the heartiest admiration for his [Dickens'] great comic and grotesque passages. But I have never been inspired to write a line by Dickens."[21]

In *Angel Pavement* (1932) Mr. Priestley continues to give panoramic effects with the gusto of a good showman as he pictures a magnificently competent mountebank succeeding in getting control of a somnolent business and directing it to

---

[19] A review of *The Good Companions, Bookman,* September, 1929.
[20] "The Good Companions," *Literary Digest,* January 2, 1932.
[21] *Ibid.*

glowing success, only to skip out with all the cash at the proper moment. The delineation of old-fashioned, stodgy elements of London dealing with the medley of enterprise is effective. This time Mr. Priestley leaves his characters, except the villain, on the very brink of despair, but the comic mood prevailing throughout the story prohibits the reader from considering it very important.

Subsequent novels by Mr. Priestley have shown a search for variety and a trend toward fantasy. Perhaps the author's objections to imputations of optimism are responsible for *Faraway* (1932), a treasure-hunting story, in which the skeptical hero is of the opinion that nothing turns out right and that everything beautiful dissolves on closer view. In the play, *Time and the Conways* (1937), and *I Have Been Here Before* (1937) the author introduces situations in which a psychic knowledge of the future colors the present.

Louis Golding

The novels of Louis Golding are distinguished by the fact that they are normal and uninhibited. The spirit of the author is untouched by war and the postwar bitterness. Mr. Golding, very much like Israel Zangwill, writes stories of Jewish people that are moving, humorous, pathetic, and sometimes tragic. He is not much concerned with social problems, experimentation, "time-sequence," and the superimposing of levels of consciousness. Yet his technique is modern in its omissions, its lack of explanation and retrospect. There is, moreover, a finesse, a dexterous lightness, and a buoyancy that often reminds us of Bennett. Mr. Golding is not at all times a conscientious realist. In *Day of Atonement* things happen as a result of sudden death, a pogrom, a street accident; in *Miracle Boy* the author tells a romantic and tragic story; in *Store of Ladies* he uses a well tried device: the fortuitous grouping of sharply contrasted characters. His range is wide and he strikes for the best-seller market. Often he writes novels about non-Jews.

In his best novel, *Magnolia Street* (1932), Mr. Golding makes us interested primarily in people; he tells all kinds of odd facts about all the different people who inhabit the Jewish side of Magnolia Street and the Gentile side. The treatment is thus gossipy, intimate, and panoramic. Once the personalities and interrelationships are established, the author shows the heartaches, affections, passions, aversions, and sympathies which separate and unite Jew and Gentile during the twenty years following 1910. Mr. Golding knows his people well. He once stated, "I will say finally that till I went up to Oxford as a young man, I lived in Sycamore Street, and that Jews lived on one side of the street and Gentiles on the other."[22]

Day of Atonement (1925) is essentially tragic. A combination of causes had made Leah suffer terribly for Judaism. Now married to Eli, her great trial comes when Eli is converted to Christianity. Leah's consciousness of Eli's sin is accentuated by the persecutions which the Jews heap upon him. When she can stand the strain no longer, Leah murders Eli to atone for his great wrong.

Store of Ladies (1927) is light in tone and vastly amusing. This story is entirely about Gentiles. It is social satire with very much of a naturalistic vision. A rich middle-class widow begins to taste life with some bohemian associates. She becomes enamored of Jimmy, a Cockney lightweight boxer, whom she inveigles to live under her roof by appointing him athletic tutor of her puny youngster. As complications develop, she moves the ménage to Italy, but Jimmy continues to be interested in everything else but his benefactress. He even becomes the rage among her feminine acquaintances; and she, to rescue him from his devotion to the one woman who will not have him, feels obliged to import his Cockney sweetheart, Emma. Mr. Golding seems to have picked up bodily both Jimmy and Emma from the slums of Morrison and Whiteing. The benefactress is portrayed with much subtle regard for subconscious motives.

[22] "I Revisit Magnolia Street," *Menorah Journal*, Winter, 1936.

A. J. CRONIN

is frequently spoken of as the man who has restored the English novel to sanity. He has proscribed experimentation and has returned to the methods of the naturalists. In fact, he is a naturalist, using modern issues, values, and themes. Like Zola he is a critic of contemporary civilization and something of a propagandist. If, like Zola, he sometimes employs melodrama, it serves the direct purpose of focusing attention upon matters of social significance. Mr. Cronin does not shrink from stark tragedy and the indictment of social forces responsible for social ills. And yet his naturalism is lightened by minor chords of sentiment, by occasional little triumphs for the deserving, and by the presence of dogged honesty and unobtrusive courage among at least a portion of the island's inhabitants. Evil has the upper hand. But tomorrow . . .

Hatter's Castle (1931) was welcomed as a meaty book, rich in humanity; a book which restored the English novel to the sense of physical fact and the logic of events. Like the books of Priestley it created a sensation because it was sensible and by no means hard reading. But no one could call Mr. Cronin buoyant and boyish. *Hatter's Castle* was harsh. Indorsement of it showed that people who couldn't stand Mrs. Woolf could stand tragedy. The book itself, a long novel, told the story of James Brodie, a hatter of strong, dominating character, trying to grasp what was beyond his reach. His cruelty to his family was followed by the disintegration of his character. Here was Nemesis mixed with normality, and Englishmen as well as Americans liked it.

Three Loves (1932) is equally intense, more thematic. Lucy Moore loses her three loves—her husband, her son, and her God —because her love is possessive.

The Stars Look Down (1935) is, like *Hatter's Castle*, the story of ambition. Here Joe Gowlan, a lowly-born miner and opportunist, starts his career by purchasing a medical certificate to keep him out of the army. He triumphs over his upright associates and progresses to Parliament and the control of several mines. This time there is no Nemesis. The author knows well the life of the Northumberland miners, and the mine itself is the scene of gripping drama. The scenes of "Tynecastle" and the vicinity are largely taken from Newcastle-upon-Tyne.

The Citadel (1937) ends as propaganda for socialized medicine, but the novel is more than this. It is, like Lewis' *Arrowsmith*, the struggle of a keen young scientist to maintain his integrity and to do a fair job for humanity. As company doctor in a mining community he fights sloth and ignorance among the populace as well as the depraved inaction of health authorities. Upon falling into the Slough of Despond he is given the opportunity of fashionable practice in London. But here the incompetence and trickery stir him to revolt against "useless guinea-chasing treatments, the unnecessary operations, the crowds of worthless pseudo-scientific proprietary preparations we use."

There is vigor and fire in Mr. Cronin, moving incidents, well-etched characters. One hundred and fifty-four thousand copies of *The Citadel* were sold in England in eight months; 267,000 copies in America during eleven months.

H. E. BATES

In a day when probability is slighted, or prized in strange guises, H. E. Bates has written several novels distinguished by a logical relation of character and circumstance, by severity, and by a high artistic purpose that belies his prosaic name. He has read widely, and a variety of influences are suggested in his work. He is like Hardy in his disposition to treat of farmers and of life's little ironies; but he interposes a variation on Hardy themes by suggesting that individuals defeat themselves, or are beaten by what they think of themselves. He is like D. H. Lawrence in responding to the elements and to the spirits of forest and river, in his love for the earth and his attention to atmospheric conditions, and in his attention to the physical concern of men and women. He is like Chekhov in his care for muted chords and in the lack of completion which character-izes his fifteen volumes of short stories. And he is sometimes naturalistic in the logic of events which is relentlessly presented and in his deliberate facing of human nature in its mean and ugly aspects. Bates is still young, thirty-five in 1940, and much may be expected from him.

In view of Mr. Bates's later realistic bent it is perhaps re-markable that he first published, at twenty-one, an improbable atmospheric tale of the bittersweet disturbances of youth (*Two Sisters*, 1926). After several volumes of stories he next wrote *Catherine Foster* (1929), which placed him in the Maupas-sant camp. This work follows Maupassant's precept that the novelist should merely pick up his characters at one stage of their lives and conduct them to a succeeding stage. *Catherine Foster* is the simple story of a woman who loves her worthless brother-in-law. The flame illuminates and then dies down as Catherine, deserted by her lover, decides to make the best of her conjugal relationship.

There is little similarity between the novels of Mr. Bates which follow, and the sequence does not reveal a central direc-tion to his effort. *Charlotte's Row* (1931) and *Spella Ho* (1938) have an industrial background, but they are separated by the excellent rural novels *Fallow Land* (1932) and *The Poacher* (1935). Even the industrial novels are widely dissimilar. *Char-lotte's Row* concerns the domestic affairs of indigent people who inhabit a narrow cul-de-sac surrounded by factories, while *Spella Ho* describes the dramatic rise of Bruno Shadbolt, a man obsessed with the idea that women and money are alone important.

The themes of the rural novels suggest the author's natural-istic leanings. *Fallow Land* describes the fruitless struggles of a woman to improve bad land when both the husband and the sole remaining son hated it. *The Poacher* describes the life of a man raised up in poaching, his hard struggle in becoming an independent farmer, and the lure of petty poaching that results in his downfall. *A House of Women* shows the progressive love of the land felt by a girl reared to be a barmaid; a marriage took her to the farm where, at first, she regretted a change in the pattern of her life.

Critics have been unstinting in their praise of Mr. Bates's descriptions. They note his obvious failure in dialogue.

WALTER GREENWOOD

Two of Mr. Greenwood's best novels carry a quoted foreword, "The time for change is rotten ripe; so let change come." Both novels are terrible, naturalistic revelations of English slum life. They definitely recall Arthur Morrison's *Tales of Mean Streets* and *A Child of the Jago*. But Mr. Greenwood's slums are not, like those of Morrison, the habitations of thieves and the indigent poor. The strength of Mr. Greenwood's indictment lies in the fact that his slums are the residential localities of skilled labor. The picture he draws is black and grim, even in good times. It is chronically tragic with the advent of unemployment and the dole. It approaches despair when the Means Test is introduced to tighten the conditions of unemployment relief.

Mr. Greenwood's novels are naturalistic. And yet there is no relentless hounding of an unhappy victim to his inevitable grave. Mr. Greenwood's creatures struggle, and they have rare gifts of homely, idiomatic utterance. Situations, particularly in *Love on the Dole* (1934), are desperately intense, and the background of oppression and misery is enlivened by sufficient nightmare horrors to entrap the most slothful of readers.

Love on the Dole is the story of Harry Hardcastle from boyhood to maturity, but it is also the story of his family's progressive decay. When Harry is forced to marry and to take his bride straight to the workhouse, it would seem that the story has reached its end. But his sister Sally provides the spark that gives the story its ironical conclusion. Bereft of her lover through the forces of oppression and beaten down by the effort to provide for her father and mother, she is yet undaunted. Deliberately she sells herself to a lecherous old politician and brings the whole family to employment, and therefore happiness.

The story is told with ingenuity and effectiveness. The purposes of a Greek chorus are served by a tippling group of old crones who comment on passing events with a worldly wisdom induced by decades of poverty-fostered shiftiness. The action of the novel is confined to crowded interiors, uncleansed by running water. Only occasionally does the author startle us with a vista:

> From its brow, if you sit with your back to the setting sun, the huge stricken area of the Two Cities sprawls away east, north, and south. Like a beleaguered city from which plundering incendiaries have recently withdrawn, a vast curtain of smoke arises as from smouldering ruins. And the tall chimneys standing in clusters like giant ninepins, spouting forth black billowing streamers, write their capricious signatures on the smudgy skies.

His Worship the Mayor (1935)—American title *The Time Is Ripe*—describes two different aspects of the same city. On its satirical side the story concerns a small tradesman with political ambitions who rises in an improvident political atmosphere to the dignity of Lord Mayor. In ironical juxtaposition is the naturalistic account of hard times for the Shuttleworth family, culminating in the father's insanity and death. The author's introductory panorama suggests the social purpose of his exposé:

> ... the whole world was the Two Cities' market; the world paid tribute for its cheap goods.
> What remains?
> A couple of surly profligates brooding on a century of prosperity; a couple of sprawling old drabs dreaming on a misspent youth that is irrevocable. And like ragged skirts the dreary acres of dilapidated slumdom spread out in all directions, a mocking, derisive and damning indictment of the practical application of that economic theory to which Manchester gave its name.

This time the setting shifts back and forth from the plate-glass fronts of tradesmen's establishments to the slum quarters scarcely a block distant, and takes in political clubs, hospitals, and charity bazaars. In this novel the author takes liberties with the naturalistic method, for his subject is complex. He would show that native worth is of small account in political prefer-ment and that philanthropy is used to trick the poor out of a wise use of the ballot. The chief departure from the naturalistic scheme of things is that the events of the story hinge upon a bequest. Edgar Hargraves, the shopkeeper, is first revealed to us as poor and timorous and incompetent and henpecked. After the bequest he is the tool of crafty politicians who advance his interests as well as their own. The crowning folly is the pros-pect of knighthood; price, including the office of Lord Mayor, £5,000. As if to be sure that the proper stigma is attached to knighthood, Mr. Greenwood sees to it that the community pawnbroker is elevated to this dignity.

Mr. Greenwood is described by his publishers as "an Eng-lish workman, when he can find work." He has no specific solutions for the abuses he reveals; he would suggest a general and revolutionary solution. What good is it, he would say, to protest against automatic machines when the industry is mak-ing no money? And if the industry is making no money, why protest that apprentices at seventeen shillings a week are used to run the automatic machines until they are graduated as skilled mechanics and thus made eligible for retirement on the dole? His sympathies are obviously with the socialist who dies in a prison hospital after being fired from his job. To this socialist, commodities should be made available to all and freely swapped for labor.

PHYLLIS BENTLEY

Her favorite subject is the chronicle of one or more families associated with the textile industry of West Riding in York-shire. Her best novel, *Inheritance* (1932), covers the longest period of time—from the early nineteenth century to 1931—and gains much of its interest from the dramatic presentation of a struggle between capital and labor for a hundred years. Up until modern time when the cloth industry collapses and the Oldroyd blood runs thin, the author succeeds in giving a vivid presentation of the Luddite Rising, the Chartists, and the foundation of the unions. Other novels by Miss Bentley rework the textile background. *Carr* (1933) deals with the development of the industry during Victorian days and the family histories of the Carrs and the Ainleys. *Sleep in Peace* concerns the interrelations between two textile families during the years 1910–30—one family being aristocratic in its tastes and religious tendencies, the other more bourgeois in its ideals, and of dissenting faith. *Modern Tragedy* (1934) concerns the depression years. An honest young man, because of his wish to marry, closes his eyes to the dishonesty of his partner in the management of a textile mill. The tragedy which results involves many people.

Miss Bentley is sufficiently well informed about the textile background of her stories. She is not always subtle in her expression, employing broad terms where others might prefer acute descriptions of psychological states. She employs coincidences, and her altruistic hopes are shaded with Victorianism.

In her early novels Miss Bentley was not indulgent to Victorian failings. *The Partnership* (1928) suggests that love is for the strong and the daring. Lydia the intellectual has a husband and children and an affair on the side, while her maid experiences only a lukewarm relationship. *Spinner of the Years* (1928) reveals the disastrous effects of a marriage for convenience.

Storm Jameson

(Mrs. Guy Chapman) is easily placed as the latest exponent of the English family chronicle and the person who has probably brought that particular mode of narration to its highest perfection. In a series of five books she has delineated the affairs of a shipbuilding family and has maintained through successive generations the traditions of English pride, shyness, obstinacy, consideration, and general intrinsic worth. In many respects she is a modernized Galsworthy. Her people are truly complicated individuals, the tangles of sentiment are intricate, and the modern scene is described with some sympathy for its changed codes.

Mrs. Jameson's faults are closely linked with the exigencies of chronicle-writing. Since family traits and the opposition of temperaments are the essential elements, the novelist must "heighten our interest in the characters of his story, so that we care intensely what happens to them. He must introduce delays, surprises, bewilderments."[23] What Mrs. Jameson says of one of Bennett's novels is applicable to her own characters:

> These men and women, so calmly and faithfully going about their little daily tasks, are the battle-grounds of terrific forces. Love, jealousy, passion, hatred, courage, daring—all the monstrous emotions of a Webster play are here at work.[24]

It is obvious that for such dramatic effects as Mrs. Jameson desires, the psychology is likely to be synthetic, the pictures picturesque. And yet in her effort to catch the flavor of successive generations Mrs. Jameson is successful. Ford Madox Ford has guided her in understanding the period of the war and the postwar days. She states that in his four Tietjens novels (concluding with *The Last Post*, 1928) he has

> succeeded in creating a picture of the years between 1912 and 1926 which wipes out (as a flame from a furnace would wipe out the light of a candle) such a picture as that drawn by Mr. Galsworthy in *The White Monkey* and *The Silver Spoon*. No other work . . . has so imprisoned the restless and violent spirit of those years when the ground moved under our feet.[25]

---

[23] Storm Jameson, *The Georgian Novel and Mr. Robinson* (New York, William Morrow & Co., 1929), 12.
[24] *Ibid.*, 16.
[25] *Ibid.*, 34.

In her own delineations of postwar attitudes Mrs. Jameson is generally unsentimental and aware, though by no means bold. Like Ford she gives an intimation that integrity and the finer English qualities are their own justification. To make life "clear and meaningful," she holds, is as little as you can do for the average reader. He must be given "something to take away into his own private corner. Some word to live by. Some spark at which to warm himself."[26]

Mrs. Jameson's first trilogy was centered about the life of Mary Hervey. In *The Lovely Ship* (1927) her life is carried through the trials of two marriages and the birth of three children. In *The Voyage Home* (1930) she is, at forty-five, the owner and director of great shipbuilding yards, which she was left by Mark Henry Garton. Finally, in *A Richer Dust* (1931), she is an old woman, inflexible in will but frustrated in her desire to have a grandson carry on the business and unwilling to effect a reconciliation with her daughter, Sylvia Russell. The greater part of this volume is concerned with the unhappy marriage of Mary's grandson, Nicholas Roxby, and his disorientated postwar years. The trilogy was republished, 1932, in a single volume, *The Triumph of Time*.

The second trilogy concerns the fortunes of Mary's granddaughter, Hervey Russell, daughter of the unreconciled Sylvia. In *That Was Yesterday* (1932), *Company Parade* (1934), and *Love in Winter* (1935), Hervey's unhappy married life is traced. At the age of thirty she goes to live with Nicholas Roxby. The last two volumes give a vivid picture of demoralized postwar London.

In 1936 Mrs. Jameson wrote something of a thriller in portraying England under native fascist rule. Liberalism is gone and gentlemen beggars walk the streets. An enthusiastic dictator, Hillier, supplies the catchwords that inspire the young with ideals of sacrifice and national purity. Only the mutterings of submerged but unconquered Communists suggest that the seeds of a subsequent revolt are already present. *In the*

[26] *Ibid.*, 45.

Second Year has been unfavorably compared with Sinclair Lewis' *It Can't Happen Here* (1935). The Lewis influence is obvious.

As a critic of the novel Mrs. Jameson is distinguished by a broad sanity and not a little acumen. She is particularly conscious of the fact that a novelist of the later thirties can have no stable vision: "The future has shrunk to a narrow personal fear. Tomorrow I may be out of work. Tomorrow there may be war." D. H. Lawrence foresaw the chaos that we now experience. He saw

> that our material and mechanical civilization has reached its limits, that it is going to be destroyed by force that it has repressed, that we are at last being presented with the bill for our past cruelty, greed, folly, for the ugliness we have wilfully created. 'We have no future; neither for our hopes nor our aims nor our art,' he says. 'Vitally the human race is dying. It is like a great uprooted tree, with its roots in the air. We must plant ourselves again in the universe.' Lawrence died just in time, before his certainty—it was a personal certainty—of the continuity of human experience could be changed by what is happening in 1937. It is one thing to foresee chaos. It is another to live in it.

So, says Mrs. Jameson, Virginia Woolf epitomizes the current instability:

> Whenever, in her books, Mrs. Woolf has been able to convey, sharply and immediately, the impressions received by her senses, the truthfulness and value of her work are beyond question. She has the most exquisite sensibility to sensuous impressions. Once she ventures outside the range of this sensibility she seems to have no feeling for reality at all. ... These people give back a hollow tone when Mrs. Woolf touches them, because they are hollow. They are finished. They are Lawrence's 'uprooted tree,' with its roots in the air.[27]

Elizabeth Bowen

(Mrs. Alan Cameron) possesses the very great virtues and few of the faults of her literary antecedent, Henry James. She

---

[27] *The Novel in Contemporary Life* (Boston, The Writer, 1938), 6 ff.

is unwaveringly scrupulous in her art, and her conclusions are roughly tinged with the universal. She manages to create excitement, half intellectual and half emotional, in dealing with sharp disturbances created in quiet lives. Like Henry James in his later period, she withholds much from the reader, tantalizing him with dark possibilities and startling him with brilliant analysis. As Graham Greene says,

> It is an exquisite slight of hand: the egg was in the hat, now it is being removed from the tip of a robust woman's nose. ... To the author remains the task of making the characters understand each other without our losing the sense of mystery: they must be able to tell all from a gesture, a whisper, a written sentence.[28]

Mrs. Bowen is a naturalist of souls who scorns the fortuitous and the accidental. In following the prescriptions of the Master, she has taken her art seriously. Consequently she scorns writers of low aims who will not discipline themselves to treat new and difficult problems, writers who are not properly concerned with showing the underlying meaning and relevance of happenings:

> Most novels, most plays now kick up what appears to be significant dust: they leave the plain man or woman agreeably flustered but not at all vitally discomposed. ... Objectiveness is impossible for the imperfectly free. Also freedom from self-interest, from obsession, from nostalgia, from arbitrary loyalties is necessary if life is to be examined and the result shown. Our writers fail now in flexibility, in the coldness Flaubert desired, and in perception. There are too many imperfect artists: the imperfect artist cannot grip a subject that has to be followed, that does not offer itself or whose acceptability is not guaranteed—hence the present hedging timidity, the re-translation of clichés. ... Middle-class repugnance to an essential subject must exercise the strongest possible censorship over the artist while he remains the pensioner of middle-class taste.[29]

It may be said in Mrs. Bowen's honor that she has not permitted herself to be influenced in the slightest by middle-class

[28] "The Dark Backward: A Footnote," *London Mercury*, October, 1935.
[29] "What We Need in Writing," *Spectator*, November 20, 1936.

repugnance. Her themes are often delicate, and sometimes she gyrates when the reader thinks she should progress. Moreover her conclusions are generally not solutions. The characters must continue on with their problems. All this is in accordance with what James learned from the naturalists. And, like the naturalists, Mrs. Bowen is by no means a conservative. In a critical comment she indicates that the novelist must lead the public rather than be content to write for a ready market:

We want, if novels and plays are to do more than to merely detain us, a more natural approach to life on the part of their authors, and at the same time a more unflagging devotion to art. We want more emotion implied (not merely written up), more relevant facts stated, more vital relations shown. We want pain disabused of sentiment, fun of facetiousness. We cannot have this, or we can only have it rarely, until the public go half-way to meet the writer, and go to meet him with a more active mind, with sensibilities open, with prejudices pocketed. Expecting more from him, we are likely to get more—or, at least, to be clear about what we have not got, and so end this unfocused discontent.[30]

It is difficult to suggest the contents of Mrs. Bowen's various novels, since the author is bent upon showing subtle relationships between complex characters. The characters themselves are sharply defined and not easily forgotten, but the events, baldly stated, are remarkable for their simplicity. Only the first two novels are thematic: The friendship between a handsome widow and a moody young girl creates so much excitement in a Riviera hotel that the young girl's engagement to one of the guests is prevented (*The Hotel*, 1927). English and Irish people of good family living in Ireland during the Revolution try to avoid reference to the conflict, but it creeps into the heart of each (*The Last September*, 1929). Later novels, like the later novels of Henry James, gave less attention to background and more to purely personal relationship. In *Friends and Relations* (1931) the mutual affection between the wife of one person and the husband of another is inferentially

[30] *Ibid.*

shown. *To the North* (1932) is the story of two pairs of lovers, with special attention given to a sensitive soul ensnared by a brutal one. *The House in Paris* (1936) shows a developing romance and its effect upon others. *The Death of the Heart* (1939) reveals the deterioration of a girl of sixteen, partly caused by the fact that her sister-in-law read her diary, partly because her sweetheart, twenty-three, was unwilling to commit himself so early in life.

Obviously Mrs. Bowen does not possess a broad social consciousness and an interest in the broader phases of human endeavor. Often there is sensibility for sensibility's sake as she proceeds to dramatize fine shades of sentiment. Fidelity to sentiment, to personal integrity, has often a prominent place in the drama. Mrs. Bowen, in spite of her objectivity, seems to be expressing a personal conviction when she writes in *The Death of the Heart:*

One's sentiments—call them that—one's fidelities are so instinctive that one hardly knows that they exist: only when they are betrayed or, worse still, when one betrays them does one realize their power. That betrayal is the end of an inner life, without which the everyday becomes threatening or meaningless. At the back of the spirit a mysterious landscape, whose perspective used to be infinite, suddenly perishes: this is like being cut off from the country for ever, not even meeting its breath down the city street.

In technique Mrs. Bowen is influenced by Virginia Woolf as by Henry James. For one thing, she uses the "time-sequence": some people begin to talk, and the reader while wondering what on earth they are talking about picks up threads of the narrative. Stream of consciousness is employed here and there, while elsewhere the author like George Eliot, intersperses personal comments on life and living. Characteristically modern is the use of simile and metaphor: "The whole scene was varnished with spring light." "Warmth stood up the shaft of the staircase." "Portia saw her partners with no faces: whoever she danced with, it would always be Eddie." "Their oblivious stillness made them look like lovers—actually their elbows were some inches apart: they were riveted not to each other but to what she said."

PHYLLIS BOTTOME

From themes of romantic tragedy which distinguished her early work, Miss Bottome turned in 1934 to write vivid accounts of the hard-pressed world. *Private Worlds* (1934) concerns the deeply emotional life of both sane and insane. The story reveals the mixture of love, lust, and friendship in the lives of psychiatrists, male and female, in a hospital for the insane. *The Mortal Storm* (1938) is a highly dramatic presentation of persecutions during the Nazi rise to power. Miss Bottome employs violent contrasts in showing the vigor and harshness of a world dominated by a nationalistic ideology.

The author is distinguished by her moving and sensational narratives, which are often idealistic but never sentimental. She shows no great care for probability, but her settings are effective and vitally integrated with the characters and action. Except in *The Mortal Storm*, her touch is light.

Social and political institutions have no part in the earlier novels. *Devil's Due* (1931) is a story of high tragedy involving a countess and the exiled Max von Ulm in the Tyrol. *Advances of Harriet* (1933) tells of the heedless loves of a girl of seventeen, who by her lack of finesse does not get the young Frenchman she is after.

OTHERS

To select certain writers for special treatment necessitates others of exceptional abilities being neglected. There is, for example, R. C. Hutchinson, who has shown an exceptionally wide range in handling such widely different subjects as the return to London of an aged woman, a missionary, after a life spent in Africa (*Answering Glory*, 1933); the tragedy of a

318

young German of mixed blood in the strife-torn Germany of postwar days (*Unforgotten Prisoner*, 1933); the affair of a chaste don of forty (*One Light Burning*, 1935); a comedy of a family skeleton (*Shining Scabbard*, 1936). In addition he has written *Testament*, a book which Phyllis Bentley has acclaimed as "undoubtedly the outstanding English novel of 1938." *Testament* describes the ordeals of two Russian officers and of Russia herself in the years 1917–18.

Several novelists have continued the study of war consciousness. John Brophy in successive novels has revealed his hatred of war and all that war brings (*Bitter End*, 1928; *Peter Lavelle*, 1929; *The World Went Mad*, 1935). Frank Tilsey in *The Plebeian's Progress* (1933), like Mr. Brophy's *Lavelle*, deals with the difficulties faced by the generation which came to maturity after the war. In *I'd Do It Again* (1936) he describes, with possibly war-induced cynicism, the peculations of a clerk. Instead of the jail the clerk gets promotion.

A number of writers have expressed current social stirrings. In his short stories James Hanley has indicted the structure of industrialism (*Men in Darkness*, 1931, etc.) and in two unrelenting volumes he has shown the rash acts and discords pervading an Irish family on the road to enslavement by a Jewish moneylender (*The Furys*, 1935; *Secret Journey*, 1936). Winifred Holtby in *Mandoa, Mandoa!* (1933) and *The Astonishing Island* (1933) shows signs of having followed Whiteing in *The Island* and *No. 5 John Street*, for both authors give a satirical indictment of English civilization by showing, first, simple children of nature naïvely acquiring English culture and, secondly, the exploration of English civilization made by one who is a stranger to its varied levels. *South Riding* (1933) is the dramatic presentation of a man on the way to acquiring liberal and humanitarian views. Lettice Cooper, after having tried her hand at Edwardian themes, wrote *National Provincial* (1938) to show the strife between capital and labor, aristocrats and intellectual communists, in a clothing factory of, say, 1935. And the proletarian novel swung into full action in the work of Alec Brown, John Sommerfield, and Lewis Grassic Gibbon.[31]

Certain successful novels are seemingly offsprings of the sophistication of the twenties. *Vile Bodies* (1930), by Evelyn Waugh, tells of eccentric oldsters and the incredible, semi-bohemian doings of the bored younger representatives of the *haut monde* of London and the vicinity. *The Thinking Reed* (1936), by Rebecca West, and *House of All Nations* (1938), by Christina Stead, are Parisian extravaganzas concerning the interests and foibles of the immensely wealthy, and those hoping to be immensely wealthy. E. C. Large in *Sugar from the Air* (1937) writes in the Huxley tradition.

Graham Greene, a fervent admirer of Ford Madox Ford, uses the James-Ford-Conrad technique in writing fashionable melodrama.

CONCLUSION

If we list the novelists who most obviously influenced the writers discussed in this chapter, we have something like the following:

Lawrence	(Aldington)	Maupassant)		
Zola)		Hardy)	(Bates)	
Conrad)	(O'Flaherty)	Lawrence)		
Conrad	(Tomlinson)	Morrison)	(Greenwood)	
Dostoievski	(J. C. Powys)	Whiteing)		
Hardy	(L.A.G. Strong)	Galsworthy	(Bentley)	
Dickens	(Priestley)	Galsworthy)	(Jameson)	
Zangwill	(Golding)	Ford)		
Zola	(Cronin)	James	(Bowen)	

[31] For full treatment in a sympathetic vein see *The Novel Today*, by Philip Henderson, 258–87. Writing in the *New Statesman and Nation* for April 24, 1937, John Strachey called attention to the progress in establishing clubs where for 2*s.* 6*d.* books could be bought that would ordinarily have cost 10*s.* 6*d.* He records that there had been

The list probably suggests a decline in the influence of the big names of the years 1919–29—Huxley, Lawrence, Woolf—although reflections of their work are present. It suggests a return for at least a starting point to the recent past. But the writers of the thirties were not emulators. They took root and flourished, each in his own way.

Certain novelists of the thirties carried over from the twenties the yearning for light amid the general darkness. With these writers the intensity again approached that of the years 1910–15, but they hoped for less and were more resigned to failure. Perhaps the resignation to failure caused the hesitance to pose escapes. A recent writer has indicated the quandary: "The mind is the dark center from which we may see coming the darkness outside us. The late W. B. Yeats had for it a beautiful phrase, 'the mad abstract dark,' and we are all in it altogether."[32] Perhaps this conception is responsible in a way for the light tone of much fiction in the thirties, for one might be at least amused if he cannot be enlightened. It is doubtless responsible for the artistic detachment of Bates and Golding and Elizabeth Bowen, who said their say in muted chords. It accounts for the preoccupation of Cronin and Greenwood with social injustice, for they, like the Benthamites, deduced that in the absence of metaphysical values the primary concern is to lessen human disorder. Yet the search for the ideal was not lacking. Tomlinson founded a faith on personal integrity and had glimpses of perfections in the distant past. J. C. Powys in the mazes of a tangled personal philosophy found tangible happiness in the individualistic will to enjoy. Huxley burrowed into Asiatic mysticism and unearthed what no Aryan could enjoy. And Aldington in the midst of groping placed reliance in "the life of the senses, the life of the deep instinctive forces."

---

established "89 new Left Book Club discussion circles in the past month, making a total of almost 500 in under a year. . . . Our members have found in our club an association which will have succeeded by the time of its first anniversary in distributing between 400,000 and half-a-million books designed to equip their readers for the struggle against Fascism and war."

[32] Allen Tate, Preface to *Reason in Madness* (New York, G. P. Putnam's Sons, 1941).

"I don't want an ideology," he protested, "I want my sensibility again, but I want it healthy and invulnerable." In this sentence he epitomized the yearning of the thirties. Sensibility would take myriad forms. Never before was the novel less the product of a school; never before were the purposes so divergent.

If we look for an emergence of themes neglected in the previous decade, we find that social and national problems have once again come to the fore, and that there is a rising tide of dissatisfaction with the order of life in England. The private "worlds" of the postwar writers have been replaced (except in the cases of J. C. Powys, Richard Aldington, and a few others) by an interest in the outside world: in stories of crime and stories of action; in studies of personal relationship, generally involving unhappy marriage *and* some social difficulty that is entailed; in concern with industry, capital and labor, and social abuses. What seems distinctive of the years immediately preceding 1939 is the critical investigation of the social order in England, following the gradual socialization of the Scandinavian countries and the United States, the success of communism in Russia, and the effectiveness of totalitarian governments in Italy, Germany, and Spain. England was remaining comparatively unmoved, unchanged, with the Conservatives in power.

INDEX

Index

Index

Index

Roderick Hudson, 108–109
Rolland, Romain, 77, 132, 134, 141, 173, 203, 235; *Jean Christophe*, 190–92
Romain Rolland, 192n
Roman expérimental, Le, 16, 18, 32n, 111, 121
Roman naturaliste, Le, 12n
Roman scientifique d'Emile Zola, Le, 32n
Romantic, The, 225
Room with a View, A, 171
Rough Justice, 280
Round the Corner, 173
Rousseau, Jean Jacques, 39, 40
Russian influence, 135–40

Sackville-West, V., 146, 222, 248
Saintsbury, George, 6, 48
Sand, George, 44, 77
Sassoon, Siegfried, 281
Schopenhauer, Arthur, 80, 117, 148n
Scott, Sir Walter, 272
Scrutinies, 165n
Seccombe, Thomas, 3, 10
Second Blooming, The, 179
Secret City, The, 276
Secret Journey, 319
Sentimental Sex, The, 121
Sentimental Studies, 50
Seven Against Reeves, 291
Seven Arms, 300
Shadow Flies, The, 258
Shand, John, 243n, 268
Shanks, Edward, 140–41, 219n
Shaw, G. B., 117, 178, 268, 269
Shelley, Percy B., 61, 62
Sherard, Robert H., 120
Sherman, Stuart P., 68, 73, 131, 154, 188, 233
Shining Scabbard, 319
Shirley, James, 268
Sichel, Walter, 126, 127n
Silver Spoon, The, 312
Sinclair, May, viii, 134, 148, 178, 224, 225; as novelist, 158–61
Sinister Street, 134, 207
Sister Teresa, 61, 82, 84
Sixty-Four, Ninety-Four!, 281
Smoke, 167n
Smollett, Tobias, 11

Snows of Helicon, The, 295n, 296
Soeur Philomène, 59
Soissons, Count S. C. de, 137n
Soliloquies of a Hermit, 270
Some Do Not, 281
Some Modern Novelists, 152n
Some Unoffending Prisoners, 121
Sommerfield, John, 320
Sons and Lovers, 134, 210, 225, 231
Sophistication, x, 237–69
South Riding, 319
South Wind, 249–53, 257, 259
Spella Ho, 307
Spinner of the Years, 311
"Spiritualistic naturalism," 75–84
Spoils of Poynton, The, 215
Spring Days, 38, 65, 70–71
Spring Floods, 247n
Stars Look Down, The, 305–306
Staying with Relations, 258
Stead, Christina, 320
Stendhal (Henri Beyle), 134
Stevenson, Robert Louis, 15, 117, 118
St. Mawr, 232
Store of Ladies, 303, 304
Strachey, John, 287–88, 289, 320n
Strange Necessity, The, 296n
Stratton-Porter, Gene, 211
Street, G. S., 50, 51, 57
Strike at Arlingford, The, 81
Strindberg, Johan August, 71
Strong, L. A. G., 283, 320; as novelist, 299–300
Sugar from the Air, 320
Superseded, 160
Swinnerton, Frank, viii, 103, 106, 165, 214, 215, 223, 234, 239, 244, 249, 276
Sylvia and Michael, 208
Symons, Arthur, 33

Taine, Hippolyte Adolphe, 20
Tales of Mean Streets, 50, 58, 88, 89–92, 308
Tarr, 269
Tate, Allen, 321n
Technique of Thomas Hardy, The, 13n
Tennyson, Alfred, 118
Testament, 319
Thackeray, William Makepeace, 4, 118, 127, 131, 272

Index

The Printer to the Reader

Inherent in the writing of literary history and criticism is the necessity of quoting numerous selections, often at some length. Implicit in the practice of typography is responsibility for differentiating between the critical framework and the inset quotations. The traditional method employs different sizes of the same type face for this purpose, the quoted material usually being smaller and therefore less easy to read.

In this volume that convention has been disregarded by using two types, Janson for the text and Granjon for the selections. The two elements are thereby contrasted without sacrifice of legibility. It is true that the Granjon is slightly smaller than the Janson, though both are eleven point, but the difference is more in design than in size.

Purists may question the presence of Dutch and French types in a book on English literature, but they are reminded that William Caslon, the eighteenth-century pioneer in English type design, copied the Dutch faces currently in use in his country, and that those letter forms had, in turn, been modeled upon the types of Robert Granjon and other French designers

THE UNIVERSITY OF OKLAHOMA PRESS

NORMAN

Flaubert - Madame Bovary
Whiteing, Richard
Crackenthorpe
George Egerton
Ella D'Arcy
Morrison - Tales of Mean Streets (Mod. Lib.